Intergovernmental Management

SUNY Series in Public Administration
Peter Colby, Editor

ROBERT AGRANOFF,
with the assistance of
VALERIE LINDSAY RINKLE

Intergovernmental Management

HUMAN SERVICES PROBLEM-SOLVING
IN SIX METROPOLITAN AREAS

State University of New York Press

To my uncles, Louis Agranoff and Ben Stern

Published by
State University of New York Press Albany

© 1986 State University of New York

For information, address State University of New York Press, State University Plaza, Albany, N.Y., 12246.

Library of Congress Cataloging in Publication Data

Argranoff, Robert.
    Intergovernmental management.

    (SUNY series in public administration)
    Includes index.
    1. Social work administration—United States—Case studies. 2. Federal government—United States—Management—Case studies. I. Rinkle, Valerie Lindsay. II. Title. III. Series.

HV91.A55   1985   350.84'0973   85-30358
ISBN 0-88706-089-7
ISBN 0-88706-090 0 (pbk.)

10   9   8   7   6   5   4   3   2   1

Chapte 1 only

Contents

Preface

Thousands of government officials practice intergovernmental management everyday, yet formal attention to the process is relatively new. As a result, it appears essential to translate the experiences of those who have successfully dealt with the issues for the benefit of those who are currently facing them. In determining the focus of this study, emphasis was placed on the way officials solve problems in making programs work within six given locales. The laboratory selected is the local level because in a federal system that is where federal and state programs ultimately have to work. Emphasis is on the routine transaction because it is as fundamental as the dramatic in defining how the federal system works.

This study deals with management within a highly fragmented system: it does not address reform. Politicians and academics have criticized the federal system as being too intergovernmentalized or congested. The Advisory Commission on Intergovernmental Relations' *Federal Role in the Federal System* and David Walker's *Toward a Functioning Federalism*, call for basic changes, such as the sorting out of the functional roles of levels of government, consolidation of federal grants, simplification and standardization of requirements, and review and reform of regulatory requirements. While these issues are important, they are also beyond the scope of this study, which emphasizes how to live with the existing intergovernmental system. No matter what changes occur in the coming decades, the United States will continue to have a mixed intergovernmental system that is continually being redefined, requiring adjustments that are similar in process, if not in form, to the instruments herein. As a result, continued research must focus on the operations of intergovernmental management.

An earlier and different version of this study appeared as a report, *Intergovernmental Problem Solving: The Local Perspective,* for the Project SHARE Information Clearing House series. The research was funded through SHARE by its sponsor, the Office of the Assistant Secretary for Planning and Evaluation, U.S. Department of Health and Human Services. Valerie Lindsay Rinkle served as coauthor of that report, and a substantial amount of her work is contained in this book.

Timeliness is always a problem with a research publication, particularly when the period from field research to final production spans four years. Constant updating of information has somewhat reduced this problem. When federal programs have been changed, such as in the cases of Title XX Social Services and the Comprehensive Employment and Training Act, short references to those changes are made. Minor changes to the local problem-solving structures are also noted. However, the cases in this study have been written in the present tense, since the primary purpose of the book is to explain an ongoing process, not to chronicle the development of intergovernmental bodies. This presents some difficulty, particularly in light of the demise of the Baltimore Blueprint. Nevertheless, it was felt appropriate to document all intergovernmental procedures as if they continue.

The authors wish to thank over 80 persons from the six sites who were kind enough to share their time and information with us. We especially thank the principal contacts in each of the sites who were extraordinary helpful in setting up appointments and directions, providing documents, and a "home base" in the field: Kathleen Emery in Dayton, Frank Price in Indianapolis, Barry Mastrine in Columbus, Manuel Esquibel in Pueblo, Tom Coyle and Jean Boone in Baltimore, and Bernadette Corde and Ed Singler in Seattle. The School of Public and Environmental Affairs at Indiana University was kind enough to provide support beyond that covered by Project SHARE and for that we sincerely thank Dean Charles Bonser and many staff members. Particular thanks go to Rosemary Gerty, who gave valuable advice and assistance in editing the case studies. Zola Agranoff, Sharon Harmon and Marietta Swango typed the drafts of the manuscript. Many persons have read versions of the report and monograph: Eileen Wolff, Delores Delahanty, Robert Raymond, G. Gregory Buntz, Alex Pattakos read the original report. Peter Colby provided valuable perspectives and suggestions as he reviewed this manuscript, and Michelle Martin, editor at the SUNY Press, Nancy Sharlet, Production Editor was invaluable in production of the manuscript.

CHAPTER ONE

The Problem-Solving Dimension
of Intergovernnmental Management

In the last ten years a steady demand for governmental services in health, education, housing, income maintenance, employment and training, and personal social services has forced governments at all levels to become more interdependent. Many social issues facing communities proved to be beyond the responsibility and capability of a single level or type of government, or of the private sector. Governmental and private-sector agents found they had to work together to manage difficult problems.

This book explains how agents representing governments work out problems. It explores intergovernmental management, an emerging concept in the study of affairs between governments, reflecting the increase in public officials who work at the margins between their governments. The context for the study is human services problem-solving in six metropolitan areas, with particular focus on the structure and process of formal bodies created for the resolution of those problems.

The problems these intergovernmental managers were able to solve were primarily adjustments to the operation of federal and state human services programs within their communities. In no way did they lead to fundamental changes in the social structure or resolve complex problems within their metropolitan areas. Successful efforts led to results such as the following: a county-wide services decentralization strategy, a systematic block grant allocation process, a joint-agency transportation program, a general revenue-sharing allocation process, a joint-agency human services information system, a model plan for increasing client access to services, a change in the welfare-intake process, a program for reducing waiting time in local service agencies administering federal-state programs, an interagency program for dealing with adolescent pregnancy, a multiagency contract monitoring system, a study of de-

1

institutionalization of ex-mental patients that led to a group home-zoning ordinance, coordinated delivery systems by human services subsectors or target areas, a common data base for planning, a multiagency computerized information and referral service, and emergency housing services for the homeless. These are not the type of fundamental solutions that eliminate major social problems nor do they lead to any substantial realignment in the federal system. These issues are representative of "getting things done" in a day-to-day, operational fashion.

Emphasis on routine managerial activity is a neglected area in the examination of intergovernmental affairs. Most of the assumptions and conclusions about the workings of the system have been built on an analytical framework that maps major service, regulatory, and financial patterns. This was necessary, given the need to describe rapid and substantial changes in governmental interactions occurring during 1950-1980. New programs authorized by legislative bodies, regulations and guidelines promulgated by bureaucrats, grant applications and reports generated by grantees, and the actions of public officials attempting to make it all work for their respective interests contributed to the essential analysis. Analysts and practitioners needed to describe broad structural changes in order to understand and operate within a changing system.

As patterns of intergovernmental behavior and operations became clearer, evidence indicated that interactional exchanges involved complexes of transactions among actors playing roles representing their governments. Concern about intergovernmental relations emphasized dramatic events that shaped managerial responses: regulatory and deregulatory initiatives, intergovernmental policy positions of elected officials' organizations, key court decisions defining essential relationships between governments, new federal government initiatives for handling grants operations, newly established quasi-governmental mechanisms designed to implement policy, adjustments to the stringency or flexibility of programs, and major struggles between agents representing the grantor or grantee, the regulator or the regulated. Focus on these events flowed predictably from concern over the need to operate within a rapidly expanding system whose boundaries were ambiguous.

More recently, attention to questions of operation within the system has included the daily routines and adjustments that take place within the parameters of more dramatic events. As politicians and managers seek to make grant and regulatory programs work, they find they need to make specific contextual applications. Most important for this study, actors at the community level find the need to mesh directives and specifications from federal and state programs with a local jurisdiction's operations and to use these programs to meet local priorities and needs. These actions, while more difficult to document and pattern, also contribute to the definition of a working intergovernmental system. Examination must also focus on nondramatic, but equally essential, definitional operations.

The managerial focus on seeking solutions, like those achieved in the six metropolitan areas, is at the core of intergovernmental management. As the system of grants and regulatory activity between governments and government agents grew, so did the need for interaction. Federal and state programming expanded considerably between 1950 and 1980. Consequently, the number of transactions needed to work out key issues and make programs fit both funder intent and recipient concerns increased. Problems in the six communities are symptomatic of those in other areas; they are generated by federal and state programs, with local impact, where the locals find a need to adjust the system in order to make the system work.

The concern of this book is a central aspect of intergovernmental management, its problem-solving orientation. Uncovering the key dimensions of this issue should benefit both scholars and practitioners. The more that is understood about the practice of intergovernmental management, the more realistic and useful will be academic discourse. By the same token, a more accurate and coherent conceptual approach should enable practitioners to better understand situations before acting on them.

INTERGOVERNMENTAL RELATIONS AND MANAGEMENT:

A CONCEPTUAL FRAMEWORK

The growth in public systems has created hundreds of new relationships between the federal government and the states, between the federal government and local governments, between the states and local governments, between local governments, and between governments and the private sector. The dynamics of these interactions tend to involve the transfer of money through categorical grants and, in some cases, over more flexible block grants. Intergovernmental fiscal transfers and program designs have altered formal theories of American federalism, which stresses the independence and divided functions of each level, to an intergovernmental relations where the cutting edge lies in the relationships between levels of government as those actors share in the performance of expanding functions.[1] Thus, intergovernmental relations (IGR) has emerged as the result of a complex and interdependent system, involving an increase in governmental units, in the number and variety of public officials, in the intensity and regularity of contacts among these officials, in the importance of these officials' attitudes and actions, and in the preoccupation with financial policy issues.[2]

Diel Wright has identified intergovernmental relations as having five distinctive features. First, unlike federalism, which tends to emphasize national-state and interstate relationships, IGR also recognizes national-local and interlocal relations. It encompasses all the permutations and combinations of relations among units of government.

Second, IGR has a human dimension, inasmuch as the actions and attitudes of public officials are at the core. William Anderson once asserted that:

> It is human beings clothed with office who are the real determiners of what the relations between units of government will be. Consequently, the concept of intergovernmental relations necessarily has to be formulated largely in terms of human relations and human behavior.[3]

Third, IGR includes officials' continuous, day-to-day patterns of contact and exchanges of information and views. The participants are primarily concerned with "getting things done" through relatively informal, practical, goal-oriented arrangements that can be realized within the officials' formal, legal, and institutional context.

Fourth, public officials—legislative, executive, and judicial—at all levels of government participate in reaching intergovernmental solutions. Increasingly, they undertake these roles as administrative officials.

Fifth, IGR has a policy component generated by the intentions, actions, or inactions of public officials, including administrative officials. As economic and political complexity increased, the ability of legislatures and courts to deal with continuous pressure for policy change has been reduced, relatively speaking. That puts greater pressure on administrators to formulate policy, including that which must emanate from intergovernmental interactions.[4]

While there is not complete agreement about the nature of intergovernmental management (IGM), it is considered to involve daily transactional relationships for some purpose between component governments in a system of governments. The IGM component of intergovernmental relations, then, places emphasis on the goal achievement relationships identified by Wright, since management is a process by which cooperating officials direct action toward some goal.[5] All of the features mentioned by Wright are also operative in IGM, particularly policy development/implementation behavior, but the primary emphasis is on the process by which specified objectives are met.

While IGM behavior is by no means new, the term is. Wright suggests that IGM may well be the newest phase in intergovernmental relationships, representing a sharp and distinct departure from previous eras in federalism and IGR. He identifies IGM with three special qualities:[6] (1) a problem-solving focus, i.e., "an action oriented process that allows administrators at all levels the wherewithall to do something constructive";[7] (2) a means of understanding and coping with the system as it is, including perspectives on how and why interjurisdictional changes occur, guidance on how to cope with the system; and (3) emphasis on contacts and communication networks.

Transactional arrangements in the solving of problems between governments are as old as jurisdictional interactions themselves. It is their accelerated pace and complexity that has brought attention to IGM. Expansion of grant and regulatory activity has led to large-scale mutual dependence, which in turn has led to a need to systematically process these relationships. Wright attributes the increased focus on IGM to three causes. First, there is increased calculation activity. Governments, for example, try to determine who benefits by the formula distribution of funds, to weigh the costs and benefits of grants, and to assess the risk of noncompliance with requirements versus the cost of compliance. Second, there is concern over the fungibility issue, or the ability to shift or exchange resources received for one purpose to accomplish another. Third, there is the need to deal with overload, which leads to excessive cost, ineffectiveness and overregulation. These conditions, explains Wright, have highlighted the role of public managers. Increasing complexity, interdependence, uncertainty, and risk have enhanced the status of actors with experience, expertise, and knowledge—attributes characteristic of appointed managers.[8]

As a result of this concentration on the process of managing intergovernmental affairs, a new administrative lexicon reflecting IGM activity has emerged. Terms such as requests for proposals, assurances, preapplications, crosscutting requirements, program-specific requirements, program guidelines, reimbursement procedures, site visits, preaudits, cooperative agreements, subcontracts, and waivers have meaning for those who work with them on a regular basis. Also a result of IGM processes, but perhaps less visible are management approaches and techniques that deal with calculation, overload, and exchange. These approaches include: (1) management initiatives such as new allocation modes, planning adaptations, structural redesigns, fund transfers, new reporting systems, and governmental capacity development; (2) policy development, such as new means of planning and allocating grant funds, consolidated planning, new policy initiatives, and pass-throughs of grant planning from federal to state governments and from state to local governments; and (3) changes in the management of service delivery such as the use of federal funding opportunities to combine or coordinate client services, the development of new systems of client management, modes of training and development, use of volunteer efforts, collaborating with the private sector, or taking initiatives with other governments in meeting emergencies.[9] These approaches are representative of IGM actions taken by officials in this study.

The activities under analysis here involve a focused look at problem-solving activity in IGM. Field investigation indicates that the broad concept identified by Wright is operative. Through the process of solving problems important to them, governmental officials necessarily have to understand and cope with the system as it is and network for communications. But it is the *process* of seeking solutions to problems that appears to be the key to unlocking the nature of IGM; thus, the analytical focus on problem solving.

The heart of the analysis of the structures and process in the six metropolitan areas centers on the reasons why these officials were successful in solving problems. Although they varied in their degrees of success, all six communities were relatively successful compared to previously reported efforts at intergovernmental cooperation and coordination. Because previous literature has reported extreme difficulties in achieving cooperation/coordination, this process was considered central to the study. The problems normally cited for preventing mutual adjustments by independent organizations include: lack of legal or statutory authority; problems of agency autonomy or turf protection; lack of high level administrative support for, or incentives to, coordinate; lack of perceived agency interdependence or feeling of resource dependency; lack of general understanding; and difficulties in standardizing procedures.[10] Therefore, major analytical concern focused on the factors responsible for overcoming problems of coordination and, thereby, responsible for success in IGM. The framework proved to be based on four major concerns.

First, a constitutional-legal-structural context needs to be recognized and confronted. Governments and organizations must be treated as legal, independent, and equal entities. Legally defined roles and relationships are foremost concerns in problem solving within multijurisdictional settings. That jurisdictions are independent—based on certain constitutional authority, legal delegation or perhaps taxing and operating authority, as well as in modes of operations—appears as a first principle of IGM. As David Walker once suggested, IGM is more than merely planning, organizing, and delivering services within a single administrative system. The essential issue is jurisdictional—meaning separate political, personnel and bureaucratic systems—giving IGM its "distinctive, nonhierarchic, nonsystematic, non-superior-subordinate character."[11] To view the maze of relationships as a unified system is misleading, Walker suggests; but to treat the process as a series of disciplined servicing endeavors within a number of separate governmental jurisdictions is to ignore the "ever-increasing inter-jurisdictional character of contemporary management."[12] The jurisdictional question proved to be a significant component of determining responsibility and action, but was also a factor in nearly every transaction. On the other hand, Grosenick has suggested that while autonomy is a critical issue, some means of cooperation and communication is necessary for effectiveness.[13] Thus, while concern for respecting differences between jurisdictions is real, so are attempts to seek adjustments between them.

Second, the political dimension of IGM closely follows the legal-jurisdictional. Governmental actors appeared to be successful when they recognized the political nature of their task. In the process of working out solutions to problems, politics—both partisan politics and interorganizational politics—must be explicitly acknowledged. Getting jurisdictions to agree on a solution means involving elected political leaders and top administrative officials, which guarantees that both types of politics will be played out. As Seidman has indicated, the lack of authority in the federal system guarantees that "power is nowhere concentrated; it is rather deliberately and of set policy scattered amongst many small chiefs."[14] This fact is recognized by the actors when they put politics "up front," in order to find out what the interests and stakes of the relevant parties are, and then attempt to force solutions by making accommodations where they can.

Third, there is a technical dimension to every problem approached. Since the structures studied are dealing with human services problems, the technical questions tended to focus on issues relating to organization, planning, and services delivery. Typical are concerns, such as using census data, conducting needs and systems assessments, devising day-care standards, licensing and operating group homes, developing approaches to treating substance abusers, developing information and referral systems, and doing contingency planning. These issues bring specialists—planners, data specialists, clinical directors, agency directors, and program heads—into the picture, as well as politicians and executives.

Fourth, successful IGM requires a joint task orientation. Somehow the jurisdictional issues, political pressures and technical questions have to be forged into a working solution. Ordinarily, this is done by bringing them out into the open and seeking adjustments toward the goal of attacking a specific problem. The two most important ingredients for success seem to be: (1) maintaining a consistent focus on the problem at hand, and (2) making adjustments to resolve that particular problem. Focus on the specific task (e.g., finding housing for the mentally ill, increasing access to services, or developing a comprehensive child-care system) may seem obvious, but many unsuccessful attempts to coordinate have been hollow attempts to "get together," "work together," "reduce duplication," or what Pressman calls the "pseudo-arenas" for intergovernmental affairs, such as joint boards, joint task forces, or requirements for coordination plans or for comprehensive plans.[15]

From this perspective, success is based on joint efforts toward agreed-upon issues. Seeking adjustments in the system in order to accomplish specific tasks is based on time-honored modes of operation, bargaining and adjustment. Ingram's study of federal grants concludes that, since both grantor and recipient possess important resources, rather than buying compliance, grants merely create an opportunity for bargaining.[16] Problem solving in the six communities created the opportunity to leverage grants with federal and state officials, adjusting them to local needs and priorities. Glendenning and Reeves understand the need to seek such adjustments when they conclude that, "The most dominant pattern emerging from intergovernmental change is that of pragmatic intergovernmental relations within the federal system — a constantly evolving, problem-solving attempt to work out solutions to major problems on an issue-by-issue basis, resulting in modifications of the federal and intergovernmental systems."[17]

Problem-solving success in IGM depends, therefore, on forging jurisdictional, political, technical and task concerns into a focused, issue-based problem solution.

BACKGROUND: PROBLEM SOLVING AND THE IGM PROCESS

Problem solving (PS) is neither a new approach nor is it used exclusively in IGM. PS is loosely used as a "catch-all" label to identify a variety of managerial tasks (and is sometimes regarded as the essence of management). It is used here as a technique that managers can select from a number of other working processes. PS is a systematic process that can be used both inter- and intraorganizationally. Because this is an IGM study, the focus is exclusively *between* organizations. For the purpose of this study, PS is treated as a formal process, although it is obviously undertaken more frequently on an informal or ad hoc basis.

Formal interorganizational PS involves a systematic and pragmatic search for solutions in situations where organizational representatives mutually recognize a discrepancy between a current state and desired end, openly and creatively explore options, and reach a solution that is beneficial to more than a single interest.[18] As Brown suggests, "Problem solving involves clarifying common interests and differences, developing trust and communicating accurate information between parties, flexibly exploring alternatives and the potential for mutual benefit, and choosing alternatives that maximize gains for both parties."[19]

The Roots of Problem Solving

The development of PS as a process applicable to IGM derives from two managerial traditions: (1) creative leadership and decision making, and (2) conflict resolution. Evidence of the use of PS in IGM can be indirectly traced to selected public policy implementation studies.

Problem solving was initially identified in various works on creative leadership and decision making. Nearly two decades ago, Kepner and

Tregoe defined problem solving in *The Rational Manager* as a process that "begins with identifying the problem, continues with analysis to find the cause and concludes with decision-making."[20] They go on to describe a series of concrete steps that aid in problem analysis and decision making that have become widely recognized and used in executive development.[21] PS also gained recognition and popularity in books and manuals that stress creative thinking in management, the most popular being Edward DeBono's work on the development of lateral thinking modes[22] and Koberg and Bagnall's *The Universal Traveler*, a guide to "creativity, problem-solving and the process of reaching goals." Similarly, administrative theorists such as Herbert Simon, in *The New Science of Management Decision*, identify PS as one important type of decision making, in which rational choices that take account of various aspects of the situation lead to greater effectiveness. Simon defines such decision making as comprising four principal phases: (1) finding occasions for making a decision (intelligence activity), (2) finding possible courses of action (design activity), (3) choosing among courses of action (choice activity), and (4) evaluating past choices (review activity). In other words, problem solving allows the manager to combine actual experiences with information, options and choices; a lengthy process of alerting, exploring, and analyzing that precedes that final moment, and the process of evaluating that succeeds it.[25] He concludes: "Problem-solving may be viewed as a means of reaching non-programmed (*non-routine*) decisions by reducing them to a series of programmed (*routine*) decisions."[25]

PS, as a means of conflict management, received initial attention from two sources. First, in a standard work on labor-management relations, *A Behavioral Theory of Labor Negotiations*, Walton and McKersie built on concepts identified by Mary Parker Follet[26] and Harold Lasswell.[27] Both had identified the idea of "integrative" solutions to conflicts, as an alternative to compromise. Unlike compromise, where no new ideas are generated, an integrative solution gives rise to something that is new or previously did not exist. Walton and McKersie use this idea to demonstrate that when labor and management were able to engage a process that transcended the narrow bargaining issues, new solutions were created for the good of both parties. These integrative solutions either offered both parties a gain in absolute terms over their respective positions (thus, neither party experienced a loss) or involved only token sacrifices and thus little change in the status quo.[28]

Second, studies of managerial approaches to reducing intraorganizational conflict identified PS as one important means of resolution. In Lawrence and Lorsch's landmark study, *Organization and Environment*, they found that "confrontation" or problem solving (as opposed to smoothing over differences or forcing solutions) proved to be the most prevalent and productive means of handling interdepartmental conflicts.[29]

This mode of dealing with conflict was described as managers openly exchanging information about the facts, and then working through their differences. Similarly, studies by Blake and Mouton,[30] Grenier,[31], Guest,[32] and Pondy[33] all found that open processes between superiors and subordinates leading to mutual discussion and an exploration of problems were important means of reducing friction. This conflict reduction approach is said to increase the chances that a solution optimal for the whole organization is reached.[34]

L. David Brown has identified PS and bargaining as productive conflict management interventions. He concludes that too much conflict in a situation (either within or between organizations) leads to escalation and too little to suppression or withdrawal; whereas productive conflict can be managed by the two approaches.[35] In an interorganizational context he distinguishes between the two:

> Interorganizational bargaining involves the representatives' recognition of both conflicting and common interests, but focuses on issues in which one organization's gain is perceived to be tied to another's loss. Representatives recognize their differences, communicate information in guarded and selected terms, and act to control each other's options without escalating past shared limits.[36]

> Interorganizational problem-solving, in contrast, brings together organizational representatives in circumstances dominated by issues of which common interests are perceived as more important than conflicting interests. Problem-solving involves perceptions of similarities of common concern, relatively open exchange of information, and search for alternatives that benefit both parties.[37]

Combining creative leadership and decision making with conflict management, PS involves open and shared conflict management through some means of creative diagnosis and decision making where two or more parties benefit from the solution.

Studies of public policy implementation suggest that PS-like processes are often used to make intergovernmental programs work. Bardach refers to "fixing" as a type of PS in his study of California's state-county mental health programs, particularly when actors take "means adjusting certain elements of the system of games."[38] This type of fixing involved, "lending a helping hand," "imposing a new set of priorities," "setting political forces in motion," and "trying to rewrite local zoning ordinances."[39] Meltsner and Bellavita's study of an educational proficiency "policy organization," that is, an interorganizational network of activists involved in making a program work, avoided routine decision rules and operating procedures[40] by anticipating the future, encouraging participation, and helping people responsible for the programs do their work.[41] Radin and associates' evaluation of a federal experiment allowing twelve states to consolidate their state plans revealed that many of the changes desired by state officials did not necessarily require seeking formal waivers (approval to disregard an administrative requirement), as had been anticipated, nor the need to bargain out differences. Numerous issues were resolved by development of mutually satisfactory solutions, or through joint administrative action or merely federal administrative interpretation that a desired practice could be followed.[42] Similarly, Williams' block grant study concluded that in many cases bargaining between federal and local officials was simply not enough to make programs work; there is a need to develop additional capacity to make program repairs and adjustments along the line.[43] The need for this type of capacity emanates from a policy implementation process that, as Elmore has suggested, relies on a number of different organizations, with variegated loci of authority, expertise, skill, and proximity to the task. He concludes that, "formal authority, in the form of policy statements, is heavily dependent on specialized problem-solving capabilities farther down the chain of authority."[44]

In order to understand and generalize about the complex process of adjustments necessary to solve problems, this inquiry focused on the flow of activities that lead to successful resolution. The order of PS activities was investigated according to a sequence of events formulated from the management literature and from two previous intergovernmental studies that initially identified state and federal officials' use of this approach.[45] Interestingly, there is convergence among persons who have described the process.[46] Simon is one of many who see the process as sequential:

> Problem-solving proceeds by erecting goals, detecting differences between present situation and goal, finding in memory or by search some tools or processes that are relevant to reducing differences of these particular kinds, and applying these tools or processes. Each problem generates subproblems until we find a subproblem we can solve—for which we already have a program stored in memory. We proceed until, by successive solution of such subproblems, we eventually achieve our overall goal—or give up.[47]

Walton and McKersie, who examined interorganizational joint problem-solving, depicted the following sequence: problem recognition and definition, search for alternatives, search for consequences of alternatives, evaluate the alternatives against criteria, reach a mutually satisfactory solution, accept the best solution possible. Their process also suggests that parties continually redefine problems, alter criteria and search for better solutions.[48]

Since the study also involves the process of bringing together intergovernmental parties and postdecision activities requiring independent parties to act, the IGM sequence was modified to incorporate these steps. The PS sequence investigated included: convening of decision-makers, identifying the problem, developing a course of action, implementing the decision, and monitoring the decision. This, then, became the process sequence that was investigated when specific problems were solved. Although the exact sequences may vary by site and problem because of differences in structural development and procedure, the investigation was designed to examine approximate flows of activity.

Problem solving in IGM was therefore examined from a similar perspective, in both definition and sequence, following previous works on management and intergovernmental policy. This framework allows for a comparison with intergovernmental relationships in other policy areas and managerial settings.

SIGNIFICANCE OF THE STUDY

Human services is a particularly important lens through which to examine intergovernmental management. Nearly one-fifth of the gross national product is devoted to human services programs. Nearly two-thirds of the growth in federal and state intergovernmental programming is in the program areas identified as human services. Human services is an enormous enterprise, involving most of the 80,000 governmental units in the United States as well as a wide range of nonprofit and for-profit actors in the private sector. Its very size, coupled with recent social and economic tensions, has shifted attention from growth to management, including management between governmental units and sectors.

IGM in human services is an important strategy because most programs involve the transfer of funds and imposition of program requirements between levels and types of governments. At the local level, it means that complexity has accompanied growth. Categorical grants have led to federal and state funding and a patchwork of providers in both governmental and nongovernmental sectors. Federal grants brought local governments into the picture and then extended beyond general purpose government (GPG) to a host of nonprofit, quasi-governmental and private providers, as well as to special purpose governments.

Human service programs exist within the geographic boundaries of a local government jurisdiction operating under one or more of the following auspices:

1. Several units of local general purpose governments, e.g., cities, counties, towns, townships

2. Special purpose local governments, e.g., school districts, mental health districts, transportation districts, special education districts, sanitary districts, and water districts

3. Direct federal program operations, e.g., Social Security Administration offices and Veterans Administration offices

4. Direct state program operations, e.g., substate units of state public assistance, rehabilitation, employment security, mental health, and other agencies

5. Regional units of state umbrella or consolidated human service departments where substate functions are combined

6. Regional, quasi-government, special purpose planning program agencies, e.g., area agencies on aging, health systems agencies, CETA prime sponsors, (formerly) law enforcement assistance agencies, regional housing authorities, community action agencies

7. Regional agencies representing general purpose governments, e.g., councils of governments, regional planning agencies, and regional development districts

8. Voluntary service delivery agencies, e.g., settlement houses, family service associations, Salvation Army, Catholic charities, mental health associations, homes for the aged, institutional programs, senior centers

9. Proprietary agencies, e.g., nursing homes, home health care agencies, group, and sheltered homes

10. Solo practitioners or group practices, e.g., medical, nursing, social work, and psychology.[49]

These complex, and often confusing, organizational arrangements mean that local GPGs do not automatically play the same role at the local level that states do at the state level. Indeed, local GPGs are often bypassed in categorical programming, through direct national contact with the states, special purpose local governments, quasi-governmental units, or private agencies. A local unit attempting to get human services delivered to a client or to solve a nettlesome problem often finds that the services and programs available to mount a response are outside their jurisdiction's control. This, of course, crystalizes and compounds the human service task at the local level, suggesting a need for an emergent type of management.

A series of post-growth-era problems has accelerated that need. The first problem facing local governments is overall reduction in the level of financial support for human services programs.[50] In the late 1970s it was popular to speak of a leveling off in the growth of resource support. By the ealry 1980s it became clear that serious reductions were in order.

These reductions first occurred at the federal level when Reagan became president. Federal assistance to state and local governments was reduced for the first time since World War II. The seven block grants enacted in 1981 were unique in that they represented "new" programs enacted with reduced levels of funding. A number of discretionary programs were proposed for elimination. In addition, important corollary programs to core human services programs—such as CDBG, GRS, and urban development action grants—were either reduced or under consideration for elimination. Also, new and serious attempts were made to curtail costs in such entitlement programs as AFDC, Medicaid, Medicare, and Food Stamps through eligibility cutbacks and increased federal restrictions. Finally, serious attempts were made to examine the solvency problems in programs that depend on contribution-based trust funds, such as Social Security and Medicaid.

Since the bulk of these programs are federal, they have direct or indirect spin-off effects on state and local governments. Entire programs and service units are faced with elimination, consolidation for the purpose of absorbing reductions, spin-off to the nongovernmental sector, or some other form of cutback. The result is fewer public dollars for human services for the first time in half a century.

Furthermore, short-term and long-term trends suggest that the demand for human services will increase or at least remain constant. Even if unemployment decreases, there are certain to be increasing numbers of older Americans. Moreover, there is a growing recognition that other human problems—such as those of the handicapped, abused, neglected, or chronically ill—deserve public support. Once these problems are recognized in public policy, the demand for them is unlikely to decrease, even in light of funding reductions.

A second problem is a changing federalism, or devolution, of public human service responsibility to state and local governments. Much of the previous human services programming was initiated by the federal government. That posture is beginning to change. Presidents Nixon and Ford each proposed a "new federalism" through consolidation of categorical grants into block grants, revenue sharing, and reduction of federal requirements. Initiatives carried forth by the Reagan administration include new block grants, opening up categorical grants by giving state and local governments and private sector deliverers more flexibility, attempting to transfer cost responsibility to federal recipient governments, and increasing federal pressures for efficiency through greater penalties on state and local governments for eligibility errors or cost overruns. Proposals made in 1982 also offered complete "swaps" of intergovernmental programs between state and federal governments, in which one level would exclusively operate a program. This suggests that devolution also means complete transfer of federal program responsibility to state (and perhaps local) governments. Many of these changes in the federal system were previously proposed by the U.S. Advisory Commission on Intergovernmental Relations (ACIR).[51] Changing federalism therefore implies greater responsibility, as well as program authority, for state and local governments.

Reduction in the body of regulations that have been developed over the years is a third problem area. In human services, the most vociferous regulatory objections have come over administrative rules. State and local governments, for example, have alleged for years that most federal programs impose a great burden of time, cost, and paperwork. One estimate by ACIR placed the burden at about sixty regulations for each grant application.[52] Recently, attempts have been made to reduce this regulatory burden. A number of requirements have been dropped from federal grants, and new federal regulations are more carefully and centrally reviewed by the Office of Management and Budget. The enactment of block grants also reduces the burden. In addition, a number of federal agencies that have regulatory enforcement responsibilities have been reduced in scope, initially through personnel reductions, with promises of statutory mandate changes in the future. In the long run it remains to be seen whether the Congress, acting as the ultimate decision-maker on regulations, will continue to accept the entire deregulation agenda, or whether a period of adjustment and balance will begin.

A fourth and final challenge appears to be the public sector's increased recognition that it must operate interdependently with the private sector. Privatization is taking important forms. Public funding reductions have led to increased pressure on private funding bodies, such as the United Way and foundations, to increase their levels of support. Reductions have meant recognizing and finding cooperative ways to work with private service delivery agencies and to make them full partners in the local system. They have also meant recognizing and encouraging business and industry to make contributions to solving human problems, not only through increasing their financial support, but by working with governmental leaders to help solve the real service problems of communities. The latter is really encouraging the private sector to invest in and develop the "human capital" of a locale, much as it often does with local "physical capital." In terms of service delivery, privatization means increased recognition that nonpublic entities—such as families, neighborhoods, voluntary associations, and religious institutions, as well as employers—provide significant underpinnings to the formal human services system. Concern for the many facets of privatization emanates from the loss of private sector recognition and impact due to past public growth.

Many of these challenges to human services are IGM concerns. Political, economic, and social changes lead to changes in policy direction and the shape of the federal system. These changes, in turn, affect the everyday transactions between governments in the achievement of policy aims. Managing human service programs is a central government activity, in that programs are aimed at solving important social and economic problems. In this process, managers have to do many things: design programs, allocate resources, monitor progress and make programs work. The latter activity is the focus of this book, since IGM involves the need to develop new and workable means of seeking adjustments in the intergovernmental system when addressing problems that cut across jurisdictional boundaries.

PLAN OF THE BOOK

This book examines problem resolution in IGM in six exemplary cases. In the next chapter, the background for the study, the study settings, and the study approach are explained. Then chapters 3 through 8 constitute case study accounts of the structure and process of IGM problem solving in the six metropolitan areas. The case studies follow a similar format. An overview of the PS structure and its development and operations is first explained. An intensive examination of how each group solved its problems by making legal-jurisdictional, political, technical and task accommodations follows, with focus on two or three project efforts. Each case study concludes with an assessment of the group's IGM problem-solving strategy—its strengths and weaknesses. The assessment will also identify important findings and principles of IGM from the cases. Chapter 9 compares the cases and offers conclusions about IGM. Finally, a concluding chapter provides a framework for PS and the IGM process, as well as suggestions and implications for future research.

Notes to Chapter One

1. Michael D. Reagan, *The New Federalism* (New York: Oxford Univ. Press, 1972), 4, 11.

2. Deil Wright, *Understanding Intergovernmental Relations* (North Scituate, Mass.: Duxbury, 1978), 8.

3. William Anderson, *Intergovernmental Relations in Review* (Minneapolis: Univ. of Minnesota Press, 1960), 4.

4. Wright, *Understanding Intergovernmental Relations*, 8-13.

5. Joseph L. Massie, *Essentials of Management* 4th ed. (Englewood Cliffs, N.J.: Prentice-Hall, 1974), 4.

6. Deil Wright, "Managing the Intergovernmental Scene: The Changing Dramas of Federalism," in *The Handbook of Organization and Management*, ed. William B. Eddy (New York: Marcel Dekker, 1983), 431.

7. M. Mandell, "Intergovernmental Management," *Public Administration Times* 15 December 1979, 2, 6.

8. Wright, "Managing the Intergovernmental Scene," 430.

9. Robert Agranoff and Alex N. Pattakos, "Intergovernmental Management: Federal Changes and State Responses," *PUBLILUS: The Journal of Federalism* 14 (Spring 1984), 49-84.

10. Robert Agranoff and Alex N. Pattakos, Dimensions of Services Integration (Rockville, Md.: Project SHARE, 1979), Chapter 3; Robert Agranoff and Julianne Mahler, "Mental Health Systems and the Coordination of Services," in *A Community Mental Health Sourcebook for Board and Professional Action*, Wade Silverman, ed. (New York: Praeger, 1981), 295-300; J. Benson "The Interorganizational Network as a Political Economy," *Administrative Science Quarterly*, 20 (Summer 1975), 229-249; Eugene Litwak and Lidya Hilton, "Interorganizational Analysis: A Hypothesis on Coordinating Agencies," *Administrative Science Quarterly*, 6 (Fall 1962), 395-420.

11. David B. Walker, "How Fares Federalism in the Mid-Seventies," *Intergovernmental Relations in America Today, Annals of the American Academy of Political and Social Science*, 416 (November 1974), 30.

12. *Ibid.*

13. Leigh E. Grosenick, "Institutional Change to Improve State and Local Competencies," *The Administration of the New Federalism*, L. Grosenick, ed. (Washington, D.C.: American Society for Public Administration, 1973), 93.

14. Harold Seidman, *Politics, Position, and Power: The Dynamics of Federal Organization*, 3d ed. (New York: Oxford Univ. Press, 1980), 177.

15. Jeffrey Pressman, *Federal Programs and City Politics* (Berkeley: Univ. of California Press, 1975), 37.

16. Helen Ingram, "Policy Implementation through Bargaining: The Case of Federal Grants-in-Aid," *Public Policy*, 25 (Fall 1977), 524.

17. Parris N. Glendenning and Mavis Mann Reeves, *Pragmatic Federalism* (Pacific Palisades, Calif.: Palisades Publishers, 1977), 21.

18. Ralph Brody, *Problem Solving: Concepts and Methods for Community Organizations* (New York: Human Sciences Press, 1982), 17; William B. Eddy, *Public Organization Behavior and Development* (Cambridge, Mass.: Winthrop, 1981), 64; Charles H. Kepner and Benjamin B. Tregoe, *The Rational Manager: A Systematic Approach to Problem Solving and Decision-Making* (New York: McGraw-Hill, 1965); Richard E. Walton and Robert B. McKersie, *A Behavioral Theory of Labor Negotiations* (New York: McGraw-Hill, 1965), 128.

19. L. David Brown, *Managing Conflict at Organizational Interfaces* (Reading, Mass.: Addison-Wesley, 1983), 51.

20. Kepner and Tregoe, *The Rational Manager*, 18.

21. *Ibid.*, 44-50.

22. Cf., Edward DeBono, "Information Processing and New Ideas—Lateral and Vertical Thinking," in *Guide to Creative Action*, eds. Sidney J. Parnes, *et al.*, (New York: Scribner's, 1977), 195-200.

23. Don Koberg and Jim Bagnall, *The Universal Traveler* 6th ed. (Los Altos, Calif.: William Kaufman, 1981).

24. Herbert Simon, *The New Science of Management Decision* (Englewood Cliffs, NJ: Prentice-Hall, 1977), 40-41.

25. *Ibid.*, 70.

26. Mary Parker Follett, *Dynamic Administration: The Collected Papers of*

Mary Parker Follett, ed. H.C. Metcalf and L. Urwick, (New York: Harper and Row, 1942), 34-35.

27. H.D. Laswell, "Compromise," *Encyclopedia of the Social Sciences* 4 (New York: MacMillan, 1937), 147-49.

28. Walton and McKersie, *A Behavioral Theory,* 128-29.

29. Paul R. Lawrence and Jay W. Lorsch, *Organization and Environment* (Boston: Graduate School of Business Administration, Harvard, 1967), 77.

30. Robert R. Blake and Jane S. Mouton, *The Managerial Grid* (Houston: Gulf, 1964), 165.

31. Larry E. Greiner, "Patterns of Organizational Change," *Harvard Business Review,* 45, 3 (May/June, 1967), 121.

32. Robert H. Guest, *Organizational Change: The Effect of Successful Leadership* (Homewood, IL: Dorsey, 1962), 50-58.

33. Louis R. Pondy, "Organizational Conflict: Concepts and Models," *Administrative Science Quarterly,* 12, 2 (Spring 1967), 313.

34. Lawrence and Lorsch, *Organization and Environment,* 73-74.

35. Brown, *Managing Conflict,* 52-53.

36. *Ibid.,* 223.

37. *Ibid.,* 224.

38. Eugene Bardach, *The Implementation Game: What Happens After a Bill Becomes a Law* (Cambridge: MIT Press, 1977), 274.

39. *Ibid.*

40. Arnold J. Meltsner and Christopher Bellavita, *The Policy Organization* (Beverly Hills, Calif.: SAGE, 1983), 213.

41. *Ibid.,* 188.

42. Beryl A. Radin, Robert Agranoff, C. Gregory Buntz and Edward Baumheier, *Planning Reform Demonstration Project Evaluation,* (A Report prepared for the Office of the Assistant Secretary for Planning and Evaluation, U.S. Department of Health and Human Services, October, 1981), Chapter 7.

43. Walter Williams, *Government by Agency: Lessons from the Grants-In-Aid Experience* (New York: Academic Press, 1980), 235-237.

44. Richard F. Elmore, "Backward Mapping: Implementation Research and Policy Decisions," in *Studying Implementation: Methodological and Administrative Issues,* Walter Williams, *et al.,* (Chatham, N.J.: Chatham House, 1982), 23.

45. Robert Agranoff, Edward Baumheier, Julianne Mahler and Ellen Slaughter, *Models for Coordination of Health and Human Services* (A report prepared for the Health Resources Administration, U.S. Department of Health and Human Services, October, 1979), Radin *et al.*

46. Brody, *Problem Solving,* 198; *Ibid,* Chapter 7; Eddy, *Public Organization Behavior,* 65; Kepner and Tregoe, *The Rational Manager,* 54-55; Koberg and Bagnall, *The Universal Traveler,* 20; Lawrence and Lorsch, *Organization and Environment,* 205; Walton and McKersie, *A Behavioral Theory,* 137-38.

47. Simon, *The New Science,* 70.

48. Walton and McKersie, *A Behavioral Theory,* 138-39.

49. Robert Agranoff, "The Public Sector and Governmental Structures," *1981 White House Conference on Aging: Technical Background Paper* (Washington, D.C.: Government Printing Office, 1981), 31-32.

50. This section is adapted from: Robert Agranoff, "Meeting the Challenges

and Changes in Human Services Administration: Devolution, Deregulation, Reduction, and Privatization," *Journal of Health and Human Resources Administration*, 4 (Spring 1982), 384-85.

51. Wayne F. Anderson, "Foreward" in Raymond A. Shapek, "Managing Federalism: Evolution and Development of the Grant-in-Aid System," (Charlottesville, VA: Community Collaborators, 1981).

52. U.S. Advisory Commission on Intergovernmental Relations, *The Future of Federalism in the 1980s*, M-126 (Washington, D.C.: ACIR, 1981), 30.

CHAPTER TWO

Study Background, Settings and Approach

To understand the reasons why local governments and the private sector need to form bodies to solve intergovernmental problems, some information on the development and operation of human services programs is necessary. This chapter therefore begins with a brief overview of federal, state, and private sector impacts on human services. Then a brief account is provided of attempts to change the intergovernmental human services system toward a more manageable, coordinated system. Particular emphasis is placed on the most visible strategy—services integration—which was then replaced by more focused, problem-related efforts. Emergence of the local intergovernmental problem-solving approach as an alternative to other strategies is then identified. Next, the six PS case study settings are introduced. Finally, the research questions and the study methodology are described.

PROBLEM BACKGROUND: PUBLIC AND PRIVATE IMPACTS

Federal Impacts

The major federal impact on human services has developed in the last fifty years, stimulating growth throughout the entire public and private sectors. The impact has both service and regulatory dimensions.

The service impact story is perhaps the best known. Beginning with the New Deal of the 1930s, the federal government established nationwide programs by offering states incentives to participate and by requiring statewide (no local option) program coverage. Thus, the Social Security Act and several other pieces of legislation brought on the beginning of an intergovernmental partnership,[1] establishing an early and predominant pattern of an increasingly national agenda in human services,[2] but with direct linkages to the states as the predominant implementors. This pattern continues today, with the major human service programs filtering through the states by way of grant and contractual relationships. The "state plan," a blueprint for the program and contractual relationship between the partners, has become the primary document of grants-based federalism.

Local governments joined the expanding national agenda during the 1960s and 1970s. In addition to any historical responsibilities they had in public health, welfare, and child welfare, local governments began to participate in national human services programs through the Economic Opportunity Act (OEO), Model Cities, the Comprehensive Employment and Training Act (CETA), General Revenue Sharing, and numerous small federal programs. A sample survey of county roles in the *County Year Book* for 1975 identified approximately 80 percent of all counties with some welfare responsibilities, 75 percent that administer public health and medical assistance, 60 percent administering mental health programs, and 9 percent with individual or consortium CETA prime sponsors.[3]

Larger cities in particular have adopted multiple human service roles since the 1960s. A 1977 U.S. Conference of Mayors survey revealed that cities with populations over 50,000 are most likely to have some involvement in thirteen general service areas: aging, consumer protection, counseling, day care, drug and alcohol abuse, health, income maintenance, information and referral/outreach, income services, manpower, nutrition, recreation, and youth.[4] Thus, the predominant federal-state funding mode masks a notable growth of local government involvement in federal programs, either through the state or by direct grant relationship to the federal government.

A related development in intergovernmentalization is the movement from general programs—e.g., cash assistance and institutional care—to increasingly specific programs. The federal vehicle for such programs has been special-purpose legislation: targeting populations and services in laws, regulations, planning requirements, and program guidelines. The major vehicle is categorical grants-in-aid. Categorical grants identify problems and set priorities on a national basis and allocate resources on a targeted basis. They often carry restrictions on (1) the program's use of money; (2) the administering agencies; (3) jurisdictions that are eligible to receive the grants; and matching, planning, accounting, reporting, and personnel requirements. Problems of classification prevent an exact count of the number of human service programs (the enactment of block grants in 1981 reduced the number somewhat), but it is estimated they account for about 240 of the 465 federal assistance programs.[5]

The regulatory impact of the federal government on human services is just as real but perhaps less well known. Regulation at the federal level began in the economic sector and moved progressively to health and safety and finally to issues of social equality. The Advisory Commission on Intergovernmental Relations (ACIR) reports that forty-one major federal regulatory agencies have been created since 1863. Six of the fourteen agencies created in the 1960s and 1970s, were concerned with health and safety, seven with social equality.[6] In addition to these specific regulatory activities, the federal government's regulatory role expanded either as a result of conditions placed on grant programs, by separate pieces of legislation, or as a result of court decisions. Regulatory programs with the greatest impact on human services programs include P.L. 94-142, which mandates equal education for the handicapped; equal employment opportunity; various court-ordered school desegregation decisions; and regulations governing the rights of the handicapped to equal access to public facilities. Each of these, and hundreds of similar regulations, share some type of national government origin, and are usually required as a condition of additional funds. They do not, however, provide service or implementation money for local agents to carry out these requirements. As is the case with most regulatory policies, the means and resources of carrying out a decision are left entirely with the regulated. Regulatory provisions imposed by one government on another almost always require a great deal of interactive cooperation over a wide range of issues, from interpretation to measure of the extent of compliance by the regulated.

State Impacts

There are three ways the state may impact on local areas: it can serve as an intermediary administrator of federal programs, as an administrator of state-operated programs, and as the funding agent of state-local programs. Historically, states have played a central role under their reserved powers and, in some cases, by further delegation of power to local governments. Despite increasing national growth in human services, the states remain pivotal, tying the system together through cooperative relationships with other levels of government.[7]

A number of federal-state programs place the states in critical positions in the delivery of human services: among them are Aid to Families with Dependent Children (AFDC), Medicaid, Food Stamps, unemployment compensation, vocational rehabilitation, education programs for the disadvantaged and low-income, and nine block grants in health, education and social services enacted in 1981. Although in a few states—particularly those with county-administered welfare programs, strong county government, or both—some programs are state-local in design and administration, they are essentially state programs. State government agencies are not only intermediary agencies with the federal government, they also operate most of these programs directly. States may impose operating or services requirements in addition to federal requirements. At the local level, the federal-state program tends to operate as a unit of the state government. What this means for local jurisdictions is that a great deal of their federal program relations, either on a policy or client service basis, involve state government transactions, inasmuch as the state is the key operating intermediary.

State programs present local actors with similar intergovernmental situations. Despite the presence of small federal grant programs to stimulate activity or improve services in mental health, developmental disabilities, substance abuse, child welfare, family services, youth services, public health services, corrections, probation, and parole, states remain the primary actors. In most states these services and substate or local service units tend to be part of state operations. A third type of state impact program is state-local in nature and can include community mental health programs, local health departments, alcoholism and drug treatment centers, educational service programs operated through local school districts, and numerous small grant programs in health and rehabilitative services to local governments and private agencies. In these programs, the primary delivery agents are local government or private organizations, but the funding source is the state government. In states like Ohio, the state government has authorized counties to create taxing districts and authorities for social functions like mental health and retardation and children's services. This means that another special purpose governmental authority operates at the local level. Funding for these programs is usually a combination of state and local funds and the special authorities are state supervised. Thus, in both the state programs and state-local programs, the state becomes an essential intergovernmental actor for local agents over such issues as policy, program changes, and client services.

The Private Sector

Nearly a century ago, private human service agencies provided as many charitable and counseling services at the local level as did the public sector. With the growth of public sector programs, private agencies suffered diminished status and attention. They remain, however, integral components of the local service delivery system. Most have become "extenders" of the public sector through government grant and contract relations. It has been suggested that with the rise of "creative federalism" in the 1960s, private agencies were brought into the intergovernmental system. President Lyndon Johnson's practical application of that phrase redefined the federal partnership principle to include direct funding of cities, counties, school districts, and nonprofit organizations, as well as of states. A wide range of new conditional grant programs both expanded the role of the public sector and brought the private sector into a closer working relationship with the public sector.[8] Thus, to speak of intergovernmental relations in contemporary human services, is to include nongovernmental actors tied to the public sector. Moreover, with contemporary funding cutbacks or nonexpanding budgets in public human service programs, many observers feel that private charitable sources, such as foundations and private delivery agencies, will receive increasing attention to compensate for shortfalls in public monies.

Private agencies, as used herein, ordinarily are those nongovernmental services delivery units that enjoy tax-exempt status under Internal Revenue Service Regulation 501(c)3. This entitles the agency to receive tax deductible contributions and absolves the agency from paying income taxes. Usually, these agencies are governed by voluntary boards of directors made up of community representatives, and which function as autonomous, self-perpetrating bodies. Private agencies are many and varied, including settlement houses, community hospitals, Boy Scouts, Girl Scouts, religious-based charities, and Salvation Army, Big Brothers-Big Sisters, Planned Parenthood, home health agencies, the Urban Leagues, workshops for the handicapped, residential treatment houses for boys and girls, adoption agencies, family counseling agencies, emergency relief organizations, hot-lines, job counseling services, family crisis centers, and community action agencies. In addition, businesses and labor unions operate some service and training programs. Private agencies usually are selective and focused in terms of the type of service they offer and the target group to whom the service is rendered. They have the capability to meet new service challenges rapidly with less concern for rules and procedures than the public sector. Finally, private agencies often find themselves "filling the gaps" by providing services where public agencies do not operate or fund.[9]

Private service agencies must be recognized as important components of the human service framework. They serve as the delivery point for many publicly funded services for which there is no real public operation. Because they are numerous, varied, locally based, and tied to the public sector through funding, they are an integral component of viable interagency and intergovernmental problem solving.

Perhaps a more significant aspect of this study is the role played by private funding bodies, particularly the United Ways and foundations. United Way agencies were primarily established to reduce duplication in fund drives, centralize funding, establish program priorities, and distribute funds from a central source on the basis of priorities. Over the years, United Way agencies have become an important source of funds for private agencies. Aggregated on a national scale, in 1981 close to $2 billion was raised nationally by local units.

As a part of the process of determining needs and making allocations, many United Way agencies have supported the development of local health and welfare planning councils to do their planning work and, in some cases, make allocation recommendations. As government programs expanded in the 1960s, many of the private agencies funded by United Way were also funded by government programs, to an extent that in many cases public funding overshadowed private funding. Since public funding needs and allocations are determined in the state capitals and in Washington, the name of the game for private agencies became grantsmanship. Subsequently, local health and welfare councils diminished in importance and many have faded away.

United Way and similarly funded agencies remain strong, independent sources of private funds and, with the growth of public programs, have begun to develop means of cooperation with the public sector, particularly on the local level. Private foundations in many communities also fund local agencies, but to a much lesser degree than United Way. The foundations have also seen the need to engage in cooperation with the public sector. Public/private funder cooperation, has become increasingly important as the demand for funds increases but available resources level off. Clearly, changes in federalism and in support levels for human services will lead to greater interdependence of the public and private sectors, leading to cooperative endeavors and solutions.

SERVICES INTEGRATION AND RELATED ATTEMPTS AT CHANGE

Local initiatives in intergovernmental problem solving are not the first attempts to confront important problems of coordination and adjustment. Indeed, a number of earlier attempts have come at the instigation of the federal government, which has fostered numerous strategies designed to ease the impact of grants. There have been numerous attempts to improve the management of the federal system in general,[10] so only those strategies which directly relate to local human service problem solving will be identified. Five notable strategies during the 1970s were either considered or pursued:

1. Services Integration Targets of Opportunity (SITO, 1971-75) was designed by the Department of Health, Education and Welfare (HEW) to seek demonstration results on components and to find techniques deemed critical to the delivery of integrated services and comprehensive approaches.[11]

2. The Partnership Grants Program (1974-79) was designed by HEW to develop methods of strengthening the capacity of state and local general purpose government chief elected and administrative officials in planning and managing the delivery of human services. The program was aimed at a number of specific objectives, including assessment of

needs; planning and priority-setting; technical assistance; and managing, defining, and rationalizing the roles of general purpose governments in human service delivery.[12]

3. Allied services legislation was introduced annually in Congress from 1971 to 1974, but never passed the hearing stage. Basically the "allied services" concept was to support grants to the states, and through states to localities, for the development of "allied services plans" thereby providing for coordinated delivery of human services. Also included were various means of strengthening the role of chief elected officials and encouraging consolidated management.[13]

4. Consolidation of federal grant programs into more flexible block grant programs, which allow for greater recipient discretion in identifying problems; designing programs to deal with them; and flexible allocation of resources was sought. Ideally block grants minimize federal reporting, planning, and other requirements; distribute funds on a formula basis; and attempt to enhance the role of general purpose governments as recipients and elected officials and administrative generalists as decision-makers.[14] During the 1960s and 1970s, experiences with such programs have included Partnership for Health (314d), Safe Streets (LEAA) Title XX Social Services, CETA, and Community Development Block Grants (CDBG). While some of these have been phased out or have lost their flexible postures, the policy debate of the 1980s includes the increasing number of block grants. In 1981, seven new block grant programs were authorized in various health and human services areas: preventive health services; alcohol, drug abuse, and mental health; primary care; maternal and child health; community services; social services; and low income energy assistance.

5. Several attempts were made to streamline or consolidate requirements for categorical grant programs. The measures would reduce the planning burden by allowing recipients to submit consolidated plans in certain areas or to simplify planning by reducing requirements. These efforts include the Alcohol, Drug Abuse, and Mental Health Administration Joint Plan, the Public Health Service Consolidated Plan, the Department of Health and Human Services Planning Requirements Reform Demonstration Project and the Office of Human Development Services Simplified Plan.[15] Again, the policy debate of the 1980s includes consolidation or reduction in requirements. Numerous changes during the Reagan administration have made the categorical system more flexible.

There are many other general strategies that attempted to facilitate intergovernmental processes and reduce confusion, such as: local functional review and coordination of federal programs; A-95, state and substate review and coordination of federal projects; attempts to create coordination within federal agencies; development of cross-cutting management capabilities; and, general management improvement.[16]

Perhaps the best-known comprehensive strategy for dealing with the complexity facing human service problem-solvers is services integration. Services integration is a multifaceted strategy encompassing numerous approaches, ranging from policy to services delivery. Robert Agranoff and Alex Pattakos examined a broad range of services integration approaches and concluded that they fall along four dimensions:

> Service delivery evolved out of a "new consciousness" of service providers. It involves a redefinition of the basic service approach to every health and social service by giving it a "human services" dimension. The dimension's focus is on the way providers approach the client, as a complex individual with multiple needs, ensuring that those needs are met. In such a human services approach the focus is multi-disciplinary, and there is a willingness on the part of the service provider to engage in many different helping strategies. The service of other agencies may also be invoked through such means as information and referral, case management, and follow-along.

> Program linkages is commonly called program coordination. In its ideal form it involves blending all of the individual services with "human services" approach into a multiagency services delivery system designed to meet the needs of clients whose problems go beyond a single agency or program. This dimension's focus is on linking needs identification, a governance mechanism, targeted outcomes, established working procedures between components, and an evaluation component. The linkage dimension includes many arrangements and mechanisms ranging from the voluntary, informal "network" between agencies and programs to structured, involuntary systems. Examples of the more formal include such mechanisms as interagency staffings and working agreements; shared services agreements; case teams from two or more agencies; interagency task forces, councils, and consortia, colocated agencies and multiservice centers; and other linkage mechanisms.

> Policy management relates to the efforts by general purpose governments (in some cases combined with other governmental units and voluntary agency planning bodies) to pull together the strands of various programs within the intergovernmental system in order to be coherent and responsive in human services. It involves a jurisdictional, public sector policy development/policy management capability across independent programs and categories of human services. This would include the meshing of the various public, quasi-

public, and nonpublic units to develop a comprehensive approach to problems. This dimension includes assessing needs, setting priorities, making allocative judgments, fostering a particular course of action, and monitoring outcomes at a "supra level" (beyond independent, categorical programs) to deal with problems rather than with service programs.

Organizational structure actually serves the goals involved in one or more of the other dimensions. Ordinarily it involves the creation of government organizational structures to support a policy management capability or a linked service delivery system, or both. This dimension includes the coordination of independent organizations, consolidation of previously existing programs, and the creation of entirely new human service organizations. In its broad, visible form this dimension represents the movement to create human service coordinators' functions in executive office(s) of cities, counties and states: develop umbrella human service departments by consolidating planning, evaluation, and management support services of previously independent service planning, evaluation, operations control, administrative support, and services delivery into a single human service department. Actually these new structures are very different, displaying a wide variety of integrating techniques and mechanisms.[17]

This report documents hundreds of efforts to solve human service problems through the various approaches to integration. Although every governmental program and locale did not actively engage in services integration, it was an active strategy during the 1970s. Federal and state officials, as well as a number of local officials, fostered elements of integration as the logical way to make a complex system work.

Many persons have suggested that by the 1980s services integration was dead as an intergovernmental strategy. There is no doubt that services integration is less likely to be suggested as a comprehensive thrust. However, it has so many components that it is difficult to ascribe its viability to any single approach. *Integrating activities*—ranging from federal government efforts in grant simplification, grant consolidation, as well as local attempts to solve problems—remain and suggest interdependent approaches. Indeed, this study attempts to point out that among the real integrating activities of the present, there are locally based, noncomprehensive attempts to selectively wrestle with the most nettlesome problems: those the community faces but for which a solution requires the participation of many parties in the intergovernmental system.

The Emergence of Local Intergovernmental Problem Solving

In its most basic form, the need for local intergovernmental problem solving emerges from the overlapping and confusing situation described in chapter 1 in which local decisionmakers find themselves. In addition, some new decision roles for local governments in human services have thrust issues on the local agenda. These roles were to a certain extent brought on by new categorical programs, but for the most part local roles—under such block grant/flexible funds programs as Title XX, CETA, CDBG, LEAA, ACTION, and Community Services Administration Programs—gave local governments increased options to meet problems they did not have under categorical programming. General revenue sharing also triggered a decision role, engendering new local human service constituencies, which made demands either to use local monies as a match for other programs or to meet local needs that were not otherwise funded.[18] Meanwhile, the local private sector became increasingly dependent on public money (which became available through various new titles in the 1960s and 1970s) while being increasingly called upon to fill in gaps where the large, but restrictive, public sector could not enter. All of these forces led to a situation in which there were several local decisionmakers. Moreover, it prompted some communities to decide that a means had to be devised to convene various actors and solve general problems of mutual interest.

Conversely, some communities got involved over specific issues; they were initially called upon to face one or more particularly nettlesome problems. While issues such as deinstitutionalization, refugee resettlement, emergency food and housing, educating the handicapped, and so on, may have been generated by other levels of government, their impact has traditionally been local. The technical aspects of program operation and compliance must be coupled with local politics. They are issues that must be faced locally, for even though the target population may not be a legally designated local responsibility, the local level is closest to the problem and thus it becomes a politically salient responsibility. Moreover, the affected citizens reside within the jurisdictions, even though possible solutions may not fit neat organizational and governmental lines.

Whether the issues that bring parties together are of a general planning or specific problem nature, they become high priority issues, thrust on human service program administrators by top political and administrative leadership. Indeed, they may well be the most important policy concerns faced by local leadership. The most important intergovernmental problem issues are typically placed on the local agenda because local officials call for a general need to do coordinated planning and policymaking, to reduce duplication or overlap, and to sift out competing claims for scarce resources. Or they wish to have specific issues dealt with that are politically sensitive, politically difficult, or potentially volatile and embarrassing.

Generally speaking, solving the type of cross-cutting local problems identified requires the cooperative efforts of a number of independent agencies and categorical programs within several local government jurisdictions, with other levels of government, and with nongovernmental entities. Problem solving of this type requires mustering of relevant political and managerial actors, and the solutions require both political and technical skills and knowledge. What is needed is a combination of coordinated planning and management, and the capability to develop comprehensive courses of action. These processes must occur at both decision and implementation levels, presenting a new challenge to governmental agencies.

The cases investigated indeed suggest attempts to blend jurisdictional, legal, political, technical and task considerations into a problem-solving mode. Some of the structures examined herein set out to engage in comprehensive interjurisdictional policy development, whereas others set their targets in a more limited fashion. All six cases evolved into problem-solving structures. As the cases document, situational factors determined this outcome. This does not necessarily suggest that a problem-solving mode is the only course of action, or that comprehensive approaches are doomed to failure. Different situational factors could lead to the opposite results. Indeed, one emergent situational factor in a number of sites suggested by the research was that success in solving particular problems gave a structure greater credibility and proof of ability to take on more ambitious comprehensive projects; facing federal funding cuts has provided such an opportunity.

THE CASE STUDY SETTINGS: INTERGOVERNMENTAL BODIES (IGB)

To illustrate how contemporary intergovernmental problem solving in human services can work, six cases were selected from around the nation. They represent varying structural configurations and problem selections. All share, however, the experience of locally initiated attempts to solve human service problems. This monograph represents a snapshot in time of the six cases in mid-1981, when the primary field work was conducted. Follow-up analysis was concluded in 1982 and 1983.

In each of the six metropolitan areas, an intergovernmental body (IGB) or mechanism, was established by mutual agreement of the member governments and private funders, who refer to themselves as partners, to identify selected issues for focus and development of a course of action. The IGBs were chosen to illustrate the mix of actors and jurisdictions, variety of problems and issues, and most importantly, how problem-solving can work. The six structures include: (1) the Dayton-Montgomery County (Ohio) Human Services Partnership, (2) the Metropolitan Human Services Commission of Columbus/Franklin County (Ohio), (3) the Coalition for Human Services Planning Indianapolis/Marion County (Indiana), (4) the Baltimore (Maryland) Blueprint, (5) the Pueblo (Colorado) Human Resources Commission, and (6) the Human Resources Coalition of Seattle/King County (Washington). Table II.1 identifies the partner membership of each IGB, as well as their general objectives and major working components.

As this summary sketch in Table II.1 indicates, each IGB involved the local general purpose government or governments as linchpin partners, as well as special districts, such as school districts and mental health authorities, and private sector actors such as United Way and local foundations. Each developed a somewhat different set of working components, although all developed some distinct means for making basic decisions and for doing the actual work on problems. While the IGBs appear to have different objectives, all share the common characteristic of attention to planning, management and coordination related to human services delivery.

These IGBs are intermediate level intergovernmental efforts. They are formal structures that stand somewhere between *more* complete structural adaptations, such as special districts and authorities, consolidations of governments, federations of government, and *less* structured intergovernmental efforts, such as *ad hoc* cooperation, mutual forums, or voluntary associations of governments.[19] As representatives of some midpoint on the continuum of intergovernmental structures, IGBs provide excellent laboratories for understanding IGM patterns.

FEDERAL SUPPORT AND THE IGBS

What is the role of federal government support in making the IGBs successful intergovernmental problem-solvers? Since the federal government has been the most interested and most willing to support integration of services as a means of dealing with growing intergovernmental confusion, an examination of its role in stimulating change appears appropriate.

A clear assessment of this issue is difficult because federal initiatives affecting the IGBs were so vastly different. The Dayton and Columbus projects received small Partnership grants when they were forming, the former for community-wide planning and the latter to accompany a foundation grant for general operations. Pueblo received its first real federal grant eight years after it was formed. It was for the development of a comprehensive planning model, out of research and development funds from an operating branch of the Department of Health and Human Services. The Indianapolis IGB has not really received any federal grants, but its formation followed on the heels of a rather large and significant SITO grant to the city and county that helped develop the local delivery system that the group operates within. The Seattle IGB has also not directly received any federal grants, but dollars have been channeled to

Table 2.1

IGB Name	Partners	Working Components	Self-Described Objectives
Dayton-Montgomery County Human Services Partnership (HSP)	City of Dayton, Montgomery County, United Way, Miami Valley Regional Planning Council (MVRPC), Mental Health Board	Policy Council Director's Group Core Planning Group Hired Staff	Enhance analytical capability of planning and managing human services through IGM
Metropolitan Human Services Commission of Columbus/ Franklin County (MHSC)	City of Columbus, Franklin County, Mental Health Board, Mental Retardation Board, United Way, Community Action Organization, Chamber of Commerce, organized labor, two foundations, at-large representatives	Board of Trustees Cabinet of Executives Hired Staff Working Committees of shared staff	Provide a bridge between the various sectors to deal with planning, financing, and service delivery
Coalition for Human Services Planning in Indianapolis/ Marion County (CHSP)	Mayor's Office, Governor's Office, City-County Council, religious community, two foundations, United Way, Indianapolis Public Schools	Steering Committee Screening Committee Staff support donated by Community Service Council	Voluntary effort of the public and private sectors to cooperate on funding coordination, information sharing, and joint planning of specifically identified needs
Baltimore Blueprint (Blueprint)	City, State, U.S. DHHS, Southwest Merchants Association, Greater Baltimore Committee, MD Department of Social Services MD Department of Mental Health	Board of Directors 5 Policy Teams Hired Staff	Cooperative effort between the three governments, the community, and service providers to reform delivery of human services in a target neighborhood of 40,000 people
Pueblo Area Council of Governments (PACOG) Human Resources Commission (HRC)	City of Pueblo, County of Pueblo, two school districts, water district	PACOG Elected Officials Citizen's Group (HRC) Hired Staff	Intergovernmental planning and coordination of funding and program activities
Human Resources Coalition Seattle/King County (HRC)	County, City, State, Region 4 Department of Social and Health Services, Region X DHHS, Pacific Northwest Grant-makers Forum, Region X Community Services Administration	Policy Body Task Forces	Address selected general problems of joint interest for planning and information purposes

projects through a number of flexible federal programs. Baltimore proved to be quite the opposite. The Blueprint was designed as a large-scale service delivery/policy reform experiment, in which the largest share of direct and indirect funds were federally supplied. Moreover, for most of its life the project was directed by a federal official. Thus, while affected and supported by federal concern for making programs work, IGBs were not part of a single federal program that can easily be evaluated.

Despite these apparent differences the nature and quality of federal encouragement of local problem-solving and service-integrating efforts can generally be assessed. Each of these local bodies was in some way affected by federal research and development efforts to better understand and operate within the complex intergovernmental system, and thus that federal role can be documented. These conclusions will be reported in Chapter 10.

RESEARCH QUESTIONS

Since the major focus of this study is on the IGM process and its problem-solving characteristics, research emphasis is placed on these and related issues. The following research questions guided the study:

1. What factors lead officials representing governments and the private sector to successfully work together?

2. Why do officials who work in close proximity to each other need to regularize their patterns of activity into formal structures?

3. How are problem-solving structures, i.e., IGBs, different from more traditional government structures?

4. What lessons in overcoming the common barriers to governmental coordination can be learned from the successes of the IGBs?

5. What factors or conditions are essential for solving intergovernmental problems?

6. What IGM sequence or process, if any, appears essential for the resolution of problems by IGBs?

7. What new avenues of inquiry in IGM are suggested by this exploratory examination of problem solving?

These research questions became the basic framework of inquiry for casting the case studies.

STUDY APPROACH

This study employed a comparative case study methodology, examining the experiences of six communities in intergovernmental problem-solving. The research approach was taken to develop six cases that explored common experiences, as well as the degree to which a common pattern and sequence of problem solving existed. As this section will demonstrate, the case study methodology is not always idiosyncratic, but can be a systematic approach to gathering data that is otherwise difficult or impossible to obtain through survey research or numerical forms. If a set of cases is developed according to a common conceptual framework, information gathered in a consistent fashion, and analysis carried forth by tracing through elements of evidence from concepts to conclusions, a case analysis can be as rigorous and explanatory as other types of studies. This study was conducted with such methodological norms.

The case studies were prepared by employing a field study, combining examination of documents and reports, conducting field interviews and observation. As the following paragraphs demonstrate, cases were carefully constructed, beginning with the contextual literature, a common conceptual framework, construction of a common field information guide, consistent gathering of information, inside-case assessments, and cross-case analysis. Adhering to such an approach helps ensure that the analysis is systematic.

The methodological sequence followed ten steps. First, major concepts and research questions were decided upon. This study grew from an earlier interest in services integration as an intergovernmental strategy and the growing concern for how to manage within the complex of grants, regulations and levels and layers of government and private sector entities. While comprehensive integration policies were submerged, significant integrating activities appeared to be continuing around focused issues and target populations. One very visible manifestation of the phenomenon was the growing number of local problem-solving structures. These bodies, whose representatives were beginning to give "show-and-tell" presentations at human services and public administration meetings, were wrestling with similar IGM issues. As representatives of their communities, responsible at the tail-end of intergovernmental chains, these bodies were attempting to cope with increasing complexity, multiple demands, and scarce resources. Their work represented horizontal relationships (between local governments) as well as vertical relationships (between levels of government). As a result, the study focused on understanding the development and operation of these bodies, as well as how they manage intergovernmentally. Since they were primarily involved in problem solving in the intergovernmental arena, these issues were explored in the literature.

The literature examination, as well as some IGB produced reports, was analyzed into a set of research questions. In such areas as the problem-solving process, there was sufficient literature to easily understand a common process and adapt it to the particular study. Also, a problem-solving sequence was a matter of general agreement in the literature and was adjusted to intergovernmental concerns. Other areas, particularly the elements of intergovernmental management, necessitated plowing new ground. Thus, research questions were necessarily more open-ended and exploratory. At the end of this stage, the concepts and issues that would be applied in the field were developed.

Second, was the selection of sites to be investigated. From a "universe" of about 25 known structures, six were selected which reflected the widest variety of circumstances. Among the most important concerns was variety of partner membership; bases of financial support; types of involvement of federal, state, and local officials; project undertakings; and, decision frameworks. Although there was concern for common denominators, there was corresponding interest in whether the IGBs could "get there" through different routes. All six first choices readily agreed to be part of the study.

Third, formating of the sources of information to be gathered followed site selection. This stage began with the development of a preliminary outline of the case studies and a very rough outline of subsequent cross-case analysis. It allowed the researchers to see what types of information was needed and where it would fit in. Specific types of information for each case study was then listed and compared with the outlines. As a result of this process it was decided that focus would be placed on structural development, current operations, key actors and decision-making, identification and elaboration of representative problem solving efforts, and local participant assessment of the process. Also, the type of previously prepared IGB documents to be requested, as well as the type of respondents who should be interviewed were listed.

Fourth, a discussion guide that would generate respondent information was developed in draft form. Unlike survey research, in which the same question is asked of each respondent (often randomly drawn) in an identical way, a discussion guide steers a conversation with preselected key actors according to a common format. The purpose is not to get highly structured information that fits into preconceived and precise numerical or categorical units but to get respondents to elaborate on and offer insights on an issue. Yet, the discussion guide is systematic because the conversations are steered to the same issues for each discussant. The guide for this study was pretested for understanding and meaning with a set of IGB actors who were not part of the study.

Fifth, site visit dates were established and documents were requested. A preliminary telephone orientation was provided by one or two key contacts in the field. In most cases, visits were scheduled so that some direct observation could be made at meetings of the IGB policy body, its working committees, staff meetings, or a combination. Presite visit documents gathered included charters, structural descriptions, meeting minutes, annual reports, and major project reports. By examining these documents before going into the field, researchers became more knowledgeable about the IGB, making the discussion with each respondent more informed.

Sixth, the discussion guide was put into final form. The pretest, the document examination, and extended telephone discussions with key persons in the field provided sufficient information to anticipate most problems and make appropriate revisions. This process also allowed for the addition of probes or examples to facilitate clarification. Since we were asking discussants to reconstruct events from as much as ten years earlier, the added probes proved valuable.

Seventh, the site visits were executed. Using the discussion guide, conversations were held with officers and staff of the IGBs, representatives of special districts, human services agency staff and board members, local politicians and private sector leaders, and state and federal officials. During the course of the conversations an attempt was made to identify and get agreement on a set of key projects that best represented the way the IGB worked. After two or three projects had been identified in the field, intensive follow-up investigations of the case followed, involving document analysis and step-by-step descriptions by key staff and IGB actors. Thus, a mini-case analysis of each project was developed, but within the context of the structure and operation of each IGB. Sandwiched between these two major activities were the meeting observations, which enriched the more systematic information gathering.

Eighth, immediately upon the conclusion of each site visit a set of postsite visit impressions was recorded. These first impressions were primarily generalizations and preliminary conclusions that might prove valuable in drawing conclusions. Some of them held up, whereas others did not, when the discussion guides were carefully examined. But they were recorded while fresh so they would not be lost in the weeks of analysis after researchers left the field.

Ninth, each case was individually written on the basis of the outline and according to a common format. Following the conceptual framework and research questions generated earlier, each case report was written by formatting the information from the field research according to the case outline. Physically, this meant that completed discussion guides were photocopied and sorted by topic, analyzed, and a pooled set of notes was generated. Documentation prepared by the IGBs and observational notes were added to the relevant sections. Then the combined information provided the basis of interpretation on each issue, and conflicting information was resolved. In a few cases where information was missing or uninterpretable, follow-up telephone calls were made to key actors. Next, actual drafting of the cases began. Throughout the data formation and drafting stages particular attention was paid to developing evidence supporting the following interpretive information: the distinctive competence or central descriptive characteristic of each IGB;

accounting and analysis of the reasons behind IGB formation; structural development processes; operations, key actors and decision processes; project accomplishment details; respondents' interpretations of the meaning and contribution of the structure; concerns that each IGB had to address when it proceeded to solve its problems; and, how these particular problem-solving processes enhanced our understanding of IGM. This interpretive approach not only ensured consistent treatment, but contributed to subsequent general analysis of the research questions.

Tenth, a cross-case analysis was performed after the cases were constructed. By going from the specific to the general, isolated data and meaningful events from the cases were recited to support relevant principles. The steps previously described were, in effect, reversed. Using the cases as a new data base, the outline, the research questions and the conceptual framework were analyzed using case information as the key links in the chain of evidence. As the research questions and other conceptual issues were considered, major concern was again placed on: (1) accurate rendition of the facts in the study, (2) some consideration of alternate explanations of the information, and (3) conclusions that were most congruent with the facts.[20] Admittedly, such selection and interpretation is more subjective than with most numerical studies (for which selection and interpretation also occurs), but it is a rigorous and consistent mode of examining and comparing information, and then drawing conclusions. Combined, the ten steps allowed for a reliable methodology that yielded useful explanation and followed accepted canons of social science research.

Use of this qualitative, but systematic, methodology proved advantageous for this study. First, since the research was largely exploring new territory, premature closure of issues and concerns was deemed inappropriate. That problem solving is one means of dealing with everyday issues was commonly known; it was not known how officials went about the process or what key adjustments need to be made in order to make programs work. Discovering the relevant dimensions reported here proved to be possible only through a detailed elaboration of how officials proceed. Had preconceived questions been asked, the risk of missing important issues would have been exceedingly high.

Second, some issues are extremely difficult to tap through more closed-ended methods of gathering information. Two concerns central to this study are politics and adjustments to federal programs. When any program involves politicians and top executives, there are bound to be political concerns, but to get key actors to reflect on intricate political moves requires considerable interviewer-respondent rapport and depth of discussion. Only after a politician or administrator has accepted the researcher as a trusted information gatherer (who will protect specifics like identifying names and positions) will he or she talk about moves, and federal officials make program adjustments they are interpreting and applying laws and regulations. They want to be able to tell you more than that they approved or disapproved a move; their reasoning in making such an adjustment, as well as any tradeoffs, needs to be explained in detail. They want the researcher to understand, for example, that upon careful legal investigation, a statutory provision prevented them from acting or that after extended discussion, reasonable program intent allowed them to act. Government officials are often unwilling to open up on certain issues unless they have an opportunity to explain their position in detail.

Third, and related, open-ended discussions have proved to be the best way to interview certain types of "elites." Although survey research is sometimes used on top officials, it is generally designed to tap the opinions of the general population. Elected officials, government administrators, not-for-profit and private sector leaders are, all in a sense, elites who are generally considered better respondents if they are allowed more freedom to react to verbal stimuli, ask for clarification and meaning, and be able to qualify their answers. Indeed, the structured discussion method has become standard practice for use with elites.[21]

Fourth, it would have been impossible to study the routines of intergovernmental management without some degree of detailed elaboration by the actors. This methodological issue is somewhat unique to this study. Although it was known that routines occurred, the structure and process of such routines was completely unknown. People who manage intergovernmental affairs communicate in terms of the results they have achieved. An IGB official will say, "We dealt with the problem of lack of access by establishing outposts." They do not speak in terms of how lack of access was decided upon as the problem or what moves were made to get the outposts. The key to the IGM process is precisely the how and the what, and such detail can only be gathered by the patient and careful means of information gathering already described.

The case study method has proved to be an appropriate means of exploring and identifying patterns in a complex federal process like IGM. As Wayne Kimmel has suggested, U.S. federalism provides opportunities for trial and error, for cumulating experience, and for generating learning from such case experiences.[22] Also, case explication and analysis can provide both analytical and descriptive perspectives on the intergovernmental system. Richard Nathan and his associates have used a similar approach—the field network evaluation study—to assess intergovernmental programs. This group has employed a series of in-field associates to describe patterns of implementation and to assess policy-relevant effects by developing case studies and comparing them.[23] Most recently, Nathan has used this approach to examine the nature and effects of federal grant-in-aid reductions on a diversity of state and local jurisdictions.[24] This methodology became familiar to the author, who participated in a field network study of planning changes and effects in twelve states, an evaluation of the U.S. Department of Health and Human Services Planning Requirements Reform Demonstration Project.[25] Moreover, use of the case study allows for development of intergovernmental concepts with a depth and breadth that narrower ranged studies do not provide for. As Robert Yin has explained, "As a research strategy, the distinguishing characteristic of the case study is that it attempts to examine: (a) a contemporary phenomenon in its real-life context, especially when (b) the boundaries between phenomenon and context are not clearly evident; and (c) in which multiple sources of evidence are used."[26] Experiments differ, Yin explains, in that they deliberately divorce a phenomenon from its context, whereas histories differ in that they are limited to phenomena of the past.[27] As the cases that follow reveal, it would be difficult to portray the dynamics of political, jurisdictional-legal, technical and task adjustments as a problem-solving process without linking these phenomena to their contexts.

The comparative case study method employed is therefore more than an enumeration of similarities and differences among cases. It is a method capable of identifying both basic patterns and exceptional conditions, as well as testing hypotheses in a preliminary manner through the careful structuring of data collection and individual case study reports. This structuring must be done prior to data collection and should be based on an analytical framework that addresses the research questions.[28] Its major advantage to the single case study technique is that idiosyncratic findings are not mistakenly accepted as representative. Its advantage, compared to large-scale surveys, is that time can be taken to probe beneath facile responses to questions and to review documents not specifically prepared for the purposes of the study.

Notes to Chapter Two

1. June Axinn and Herman Levin, *Social Welfare: A History of the American Response to Need* (New York: Dodd, Mead, 1975), 39.

2. See, e.g., Martha Derthick. *The Influence of Federal Grants* (Cambridge: Harvard Univ. Press, 1970); Harold Seidman, *Politics, Position and Power: The Dynamics of Federal Organization* (New York:Oxford Univ. Press, 1980); James L. Sundquist, *Making Federalism Work* (Washington, D.C.: Brookings Institute, 1969).

3. International City Management Association, *County Year Book, 1979* (Washington, D.C.: ICMA, 1975), 108.

4. U.S. Conference of Mayors, *Human Services in City Governments* (Washington, D.C.: USCM, 1977).

5. Deil Wright, *Understanding Intergovernmental Relations* (North Scituate, Mass.: Duxbury, 1978), 137.

6. Advisory Commission on Intergovernmental Relations, *The Federal Role in the Federal System: The Dynamics of Growth*, A-77 (Washington, D.C.: ACIR, 1980), 74.

7. Daniel J. Elazar, *American Federalism: A View from the States* (New York: Thomas Y. Crowell, 1966), 1-2.

8. David B. Walker, *Toward a Functioning Federalism* (Cambridge, Mass.: Winthrop, 1981), 102-108.

9. Paul Akana, "Coordination with Private Agencies," in *Managing Human Services*, ed. Wayne F. Anderson, Bernard J. Friedan, and Michael J. Murphy (Washington, D.C.: International City Management Association, 1977), 245-246.

10. Advisory Commission on Intergovernmental Relations, *Improving Federal Grants Management*, A-53 (Washington, D.C.: ACIR, 1977); Raymond A. Shapek, *Managing Federalism* (Charlottesville, Va.: Community Collaborators, 1981); David B. Walker, *Toward a Functioning Federalism*; Walter Williams, *Government by Agency* (New York: Academic Press, 1980).

11. DeWitt John, *Managing the Human Service 'System': What Have We Learned from Service Integration* (Rockville, Md.: Project SHARE Monograph Series, 1977.)

12. Rj. Associates/SRI International, *Assessing the HEW Partnership Grants Program: A Study of State and Local Capacity Building* (Arlington, Va.: Rj. Associates, 1978).

13. Office of the White House. "The Allied Services Act." 18 May 1972.

14. Carl W. Steinberg and David B. Walker, "The Block Grant: Lessons from Two Early Experiments," *Publius* (Spring 1977), 31-60.

15. Cf., Beryl Radin, Robert Agranoff, Edward Baumheier and C. Gregory Buntz, *Evaluation of the Planning Requirements Reform Demonstration Project of the U.S. Department of Health and Human Services.* (Report prepared for the Office of the Assistant Secretary for Planning and Evaluation. U.S. DHHS, October, 1981).

16. Robert Agranoff, "Services Integration" in *Managing Human Services*, ed. Anderson, Friedan, and Murphy, 536-38.

17. Robert Agranoff and Alex Pattakos, *Dimensions of Services Integration* (Rockville, Md.: Project SHARE Monograph Series, 1979), 9-10.

18. Robert Agranoff, "The Local Government Role in Human Services: Understanding and Management." *Proceedings of the National Network Building Conference*, (Denver, June, 1980,) 16-18.

19. Bruce B. Talley, "Intergovernmental Cooperation," in *Productivity Improvement Handbook for State and Local Government*, ed. George J. Washnis (New York: Wiley, 1980), 452-60.

20. Robert K. Yin, "The Case Study Crisis: Some Answers," *Administrative Science Quarterly*, 26 (March 1981), 63.

21. Herbert F. Weisberg and Bruce D. Bowen, *Survey Research and Data Analysis* (San Francisco: W.H. Freeman, 1977), 62.

22. Wayne A. Kimmel, *Putting Program Evaluation in Perspective for State and Local Government*, (Rockville, MD.: Project SHARE Monograph Series, 1981), 41.

23. Richard P. Nathan, "The Methodology for Field Network Evaluation Studies," in *Studying Implementation* Walter Williams, et al. (Chatham, N.J.: Chatham House, 1982), 76.

24. Richard P. Nathan, Fred C. Doolittle, and Associates, *The Consequences of the Cuts* (Princeton, N.J.: Princeton Univ. Press, 1983), 9-11.

25. Radin, et al. *Evaluation* Chapter V.

26. Robert K. Yin, *Case Study Research: Design and Methods* (Beverly Hills: SAGE, 1984), 23.

27. Yin, "The Case Study Crisis", 59.

28. *Ibid.*, 60-61.

CHAPTER THREE

Building Local Capacity: The Dayton-Montgomery County Partnership

The development of a government's capacity to manage its own affairs is considered an essential ingredient in IGM. While an elusive concept, it has been defined as government's ability to anticipate and influence changes; make informed and intelligent policy decisions; develop programs and implement policy; attract, absorb and manage resources; and evaluate current activities to guide future action.[1] Presumably, if governments possess these abilities in great measure, they will be better able to deal with the intergovernmental system and solve problems.

In Dayton-Montgomery County, Ohio, an experiment in capacity development began over a decade ago with the help of a small federal grant, and the partnership continues to enhance its area governments' abilities to manage human services programs through research, planning and problem-solving. The IGB, the Dayton-Montgomery County Human Services Partnership, stands as testimony that some federal grant initiatives do succeed and last. Success is based on local actors' ability to pursue their own changing intergovernmental agendas in a pragmatic fashion.

The partnership began in 1974 as a research-oriented project, funded by the Partnership Grants program of the U.S. Department of Health, Education and Welfare (now Health and Human Services). The partners are the city of Dayton, Montgomery County, United Way of the Dayton Area, Montgomery County Board of Mental Health, and the Miami Valley Regional Planning Commission (MVRPC). The partnership has retained its original research orientation, but is now also involved in coordinated human service planning and development. The Partnership's three-level structure—consisting of a policy council, an administrators' subgroup, and a planning group—has worked well and produced some major types of planning and decision-making information for the community.

Dayton, a city of 200,000, is the center of a four-county metropolitan area of 800,000 in west-central Ohio. Montgomery County, which includes Dayton, comprises about 600,000 of that population. Dayton received national recognition for its attempts to deal with urban problems, such as its Citywide Development Corporation and a regional Fair Share Housing Plan known as the "Dayton Plan." The Dayton area houses a major national foundation—the Kettering Foundation—which in part is devoted to solving urban problems such as effective government, intergovernmental negotiation, and neighborhood improvement. The urban affairs section of the Kettering Foundation is led by the former city manager of Dayton. Dayton has had the city manager form of government since 1913. Montgomery County is governed by three elected commissioners and a county administrator.

Public human services are predominantly county-delivered with a welfare department (which is also Title XX Social Services) and a separate health district. They also include a human service department responsible for oversight and coordination of the other two departments, which operates the CETA program and a few small programs. By stated policy, the city of Dayton does not become involved in service delivery, although it does operate CETA within the city and has been involved in financing and establishing several service delivery sites through the CDBG program. The city believes it should be responsible for seeing that others deliver effective services for its residents, making its role one of oversight, evaluation and advocacy. Areawide comprehensive planning primarily occurs in a regional planning agency, the Miami Valley Regional Planning Commission (MVRPC), which has a number of physical and social planning functions. Regional plans in some areas (e.g., health and aging) are conducted in separate agencies. Responsibility for mental health services is vested in a county-wide mental health board, a special purpose government that allocates public funds and contracts for services with private agencies. The other major sources of funding for human services are the United Way, and public programs in mental retardation, public health, welfare, and employment and training. Other human services are delivered through a private agency delivery system largely funded by the United Way, Title XX Social Services, and the Mental Health Board.

The partnership has survived within this setting because it is flexible and informal, has respect for local politics and the legitimate interests of the partners, and has produced technically sound results. Its efforts began with an intensive two-year study of the publicly funded human service system, which has supported the policy council's basic decision making and has proved useful for the planning of several other agencies. As a result, the partnership became an established entity. It has survived several trials. The institutionalized structure and previous experiences made it a natural body to help manage the cuts in federal and state funds. The partnership moved to the next step when it began to work with public and private community interests, tackling such issues as emergency food and shelter, youth employment and general community mobilization to solve problems.

DEVELOPMENT AND OPERATION

IGB Formation

The partnership evolved from earlier efforts with Model Cities and Planned Variations (an experiment to extend the focused area planning concept of Model Cities citywide) that identified key people from among the partners, who recognized the functional and political benefits of improving human services. The partnership thus began as a research effort to examine the human services system prompted by a series of interjurisdictional problems.

MVRPC was chosen as the partnership grantee because it was perceived as neutral. Research staff were hired with grant funds and housed at MVRPC. Each partner assigned professional staff to the project and appointed three representatives to the partnership's initial policy group. Together, they identified the partnership's basic goals and objectives:

1. Rationalizing the current intergovernmental structure as it relates to the delivery of social service programs

2. Enhancing the analytical capacity of decision makers at the city, county, and regional levels to define and delineate roles as they relate to human services

3. Defining the scope and function of city and county governments, the regional agency, and other entities within the existing human service system

4. Defining the role of local elected officials in the human service delivery system

5. Defining the role of the consumer in the planning, delivery, or evaluation of human service programs

6. Developing a strategy to improve and coordinate local social service planning and evaluation efforts and

7. Investigating alternative strategies for services delivery and assessing their applicability for improving and rationalizing the existing human service delivery system.[2]

By the time the IGB was ready to begin its third year, these original objectives were expanded to include the development and operation of a joint planning effort involving the major partners that would extend beyond the life of the federal funding effort.[3]

The partnership developed over a three-year period. The activities involved in the initial research effort guided the IGB's formation. The first year was spent analyzing the data, identifying problem areas, and developing a strategy to address the most critical problems. In the third year, a core planning group made up of planners from each of the partners was formed in response to the research finding of weak local planning systems. The group worked through a joint planning process that led the partnership into its final development stage by transforming the Project Task Force into the Partnership Policy Council. These four stages demonstrate how the partnership slowly integrated work products with the development of a viable structure that came about over the issue of joint planning.

IGB Structure

The partnership has retained the structure it adopted in 1977, which provides for a policy council, core planning group, and partnership staff. The policy council is composed of two representatives of each of the partners, one key decision-maker representing the partner, and one high-level executive staff person. The policy council provides guidance and direction to the activities of the core planning group and the partnership staff.[4] Recently administrators on the policy council formed a subgroup to provide ongoing direction to the partnership staff during times when the policy council was not needed for policy decisions. The director's group, as it is called, can meet more readily than the policy council because the administrators' schedules are not as difficult to coordinate as are those of the key decision-makers on the council.

The core planning group consists of one or more partner staff persons who are currently working in human service planning and delivery. Each member is responsible for informing his or her respective partner policy council representative of the group's activities. The core planning group is responsible for carrying out the partnership work plan. The group can ask other agencies to work with them and help provide the necessary information and expertise for developing a plan for resolution of a particular problem or issue. The group is led by the partnership coordinator, who is MVRPC's core planning group member. The partnership staff provides research and clerical support to the core planning group. The staff is housed at MVRPC and supervised by the partnership coordinator. Table III.1 depicts the partnership's structure.

The partnership is financed entirely out of local sources. Since the federal grant expired in 1979, each of the partners has contributed to the operation of the IGB through dedication of grant funds, in-kind contributions or actual dollar contributions. In addition, each partner contributes considerable in-kind staff time to problem-solving projects.

Table 3.1   Dayton-Montgomery County Partnership

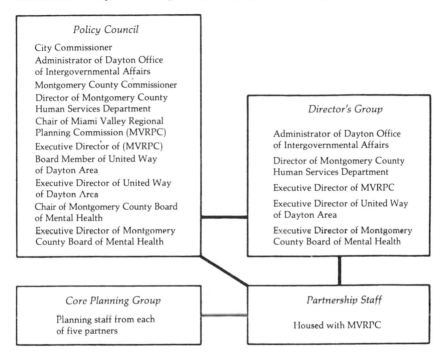

Policy Council

City Commissioner
Administrator of Dayton Office
of Intergovernmental Affairs
Montgomery County Commissioner
Director of Montgomery County
Human Services Department
Chair of Miami Valley Regional
Planning Commission (MVRPC)
Executive Director of (MVRPC)
Board Member of United Way
of Dayton Area
Executive Director of United Way
of Dayton Area
Chair of Montgomery County Board
of Mental Health
Executive Director of Montgomery
County Board of Mental Health

Director's Group

Administrator of Dayton Office
of Intergovernmental Affairs

Director of Montgomery County
Human Services Department

Executive Director of MVRPC

Executive Director of United Way
of Dayton Area

Executive Director of Montgomery
County Board of Mental Health

Core Planning Group

Planning staff from each
of five partners

Partnership Staff

Housed with MVRPC

Decision Framework and Role of Key Actors

When an issue is presented to the policy council, it decides whether the partnership will address and study that issue. If approved, the policy council directs the core planning group and the partnership staff to conduct the appropriate plan or final report. The core planning group and the partnership staff work very closely on every partnership project. The group divides the work activities into categories: the members divide into task groups according to the categories. On some projects the group divides into subgroups and might ask other community agencies to work with them on particular activities or tasks. Many times the work will become more than either the group or staff can handle. During such times of intensive work, each partner contributes part of its own staff's time to the project. The partnership staff then becomes the central coordinator, aggregating and organizing the data supplied to them by the other staffs and the core group, and producing the final reports.

The involvement of elected policy council officials with partnership staff varies with their level of commitment to human services and with the issues at hand. Even when the elected council officials support human services and the partnership, the amount of time they can devote to such matters is limited. Elected officials, particularly from the county, have been known to become intimately involved in a project when it has potential advantages for their jurisdiction. The city, which did not contribute financial support to the partnership until 1982, is not seen as having the same level of commitment to the partnership as the other actors. The city is still considered a vital member of the partnership, however, particularly since many of the target populations for the community's human services reside within the city proper. The top administrative members of the policy council have more consistent involvement with the partnership since the formation of the director's group. The members of the core planning group have a considerable amount invested in the partnership because they do the majority of work involved in the projects.

Agenda and Development

The partnership deals with issues of community human services planning and service delivery which are of mutual concern. Agenda items can be suggested by any member of the partnership's three operating components. Issues are introduced as they arise in the community, especially those that are timely and need immediate attention. Issues brought to the council are discussed and decisions are made on an informal basis. The council does not vote until it is clear that a consensus has been reached among the partners. Much of the consensus building is done prior to the meeting when the vote is made. Sometimes a "one-on-one" solicitation is performed between partners of the same sector to achieve consensus. This method of consensus building has become an informal problem-solving technique for both the policy council and the core planning group.

Partnership projects have been instrumental in shaping and refining the partnership's operating procedures. Many agencies look at the partnership for data assistance and support for problems that are unique to them; thus, the partnership included this function in its 1980 work plan. When the community was faced with the prospect of major federal funding reductions and the recession of 1981-83, the partnership responded with new involvements in research, services creation and the development of new linkages to the business community.

PROJECTS

Three projects demonstrate the core functions of the Dayton-Montgomery County Partnership as a capacity-building IGB. All three — decentralization of services, Title XX allocations, and the funding reduction impact study — indicate how joint-planning processes can enhance the ability of individual agencies to meet their needs while solving problems. These processes also demonstrate how intergovernmental managers must confront program regulations and jurisdictional responsibilities, make political accommodations, and concern themselves with the technical details of the project while attempting to resolve the issue at hand.

Decentralization Project

The decentralization strategy was one of the earlier projects undertaken. The initiative for decentralization grew out of the Model Cities-Planned Variations effort in which one area, East Dayton, built the Sunrise (multiservice) Center. This center opened in 1975 and was considered a successful effort. The policy group wanted to get involved in the multiservice issue because it felt that it was a positive project for the community and the partnership. In late 1977, the core planning group began to explore the feasibility of establishing another center in West Dayton, which was later expanded at the request of the welfare department to include the study of decentralizing all department services, using the multiservice center model.

As the process developed, the core planning group provided options and information for policy group negotiations. The latter group took on very important legal and political roles. First, those representing governments that were slated to make program commitments needed to make sure they were able to make such commitments. For example, the city had to request approval for including new building commitments in its CDBG plan. Meanwhile, county representatives had to make sure there was a political willingness and legal authority to add the additional expense of moving welfare workers out of the central office. This process involved discussions and negotiations with other county commissioners, the county attorney, and the state welfare department. Inquiries and discussions were conducted with private agencies, which were expected to place their personnel in the new centers. The lead was taken by their funders, the United Way and the mental health board. Each member of the policy group was designated as the lead negotiator for their jurisdiction or sector, representing the partnership and their own entities' interests at the same time, exploring options and testing the waters for feasibility. Throughout this "incremental process," in the words of the chief partnership staff person, legal, technical and political details were negotiated. The negotiations lasted through most of 1978.

The study ultimately led to a proposed plan, which divided the county into six catchment areas, each covered by a center. The core group and the partnership staff were involved in developing ten different staffing options. Each option was diagrammed and rated in terms of accessibility, client flow, coordination of services to clients, financial feasibility, paperwork processing, implementation time, and conformity with state regulations. Another set of options involved exploring ways of financing the construction or acquisition of centers where no buildings were readily available. The partnership core group and staff also worked closely with county staff to develop criteria for dividing the county into decentralization catchment areas and collecting necessary social indicator data to pinpoint areas of need. Finally, they worked with the county staff to develop the formula for allocating welfare department staff to each proposed center, and a timetable was established.

The county commission adopted the plan in resolution form and implementation began. It has proved to be an incremental process involving the extension of the strategy, one center at a time. City CDBG funds were used for building acquisitions, while the county used general fund monies to put managers in the centers. The partnership has been instrumental in facilitating the effort, not only by providing supportive information, but by urging its political allies in the partnership to urge others in the county to be supportive. Eventually, the partnership was able to transfer some of its research functions to the newly created county department of human resources, but the advocacy component of the joint planning process continues. Partners who are sympathetic to the aims of this strategy continue to put political pressure on colleagues representing other jurisdictions. Three of the six centers were established, while the partners continue to provide research and support for extension of this ongoing strategy.

Title XX Allocation Project

The Title XX allocation project began in 1979 and continues through transfer to another planning body. Title XX (now Social Services Block Grant) was a relatively open-ended program that operated almost like a block grant. In Ohio, responsibility for planning was transferred to the county level. This project was initiated at the request of the welfare department. Although there is a statutorily defined welfare and social services advisory board, there was dissatisfaction with the way allocations were made. Decisions were not always needs-based, and allocations were often made to those who screamed the loudest or had the greatest political influence. There was considerable local criticism about the process, with the welfare department and the commissioners taking the heat. Thus, the partnership was asked to design a planning and allocation process that would help the county out.

Both the core planning group and the policy council were involved in considerable negotiations to get actors to provide information and to define their respective roles. The core group performed a research inventory of all Title XX services in the county, developed a minimum needs statement (similar to the minimum capacity approach), developed several indicators of services (e.g., number served, waiting lists), and identified populations at risk. From this information it established a means to set priorities for the need for services. Meanwhile, the policy group met every three weeks to review the work of the core group and to report and exchange views on the political negotiations.

The result was an extensive ten step process that involved:

1. community priority setting;
2. analysis of needs factors for exemptions to competitive bidding;
3. analysis of general needs factors;
4. development of RFPs;
5. competitive bidding;
6. review and evaluation of bid proposals;
7. consideration of evaluation committee recommendations;
8. third party review;
9. consideration of allocation recommendations; and
10. implementation of commission action.

Each step was broken down into specific tasks, documented, and responsibilities assigned. End products of each step were then listed and completion dates set. The entire process for 1980 is illustrated in Table 3.2.

Any technical approach like this has its political dimensions, and the Title XX approach was no exception. Even though the county had asked the partnership to undertake the study, the newly created County Office of Management and Budget felt it should make its own allocation decisions. Moreover, the Welfare and Social Services Advisory Board felt left out of the process. These factors were particularly important for the first round in 1979 since the process had been developed just before deadlines. As a result, the county commissioners felt they could not adopt the entire process for the first year. They decided to allocate ninety percent of the money by the previous method, holding ten percent back to allocate according to the Partnership's recommendations. By the second round in 1980, the process was revised and used in full, with the partnership backing off and letting the Welfare and Social Services Advisory Board and the commissioners follow the sequence. Well into the second year the process was complicated when a new human services director introduced his own ideas about allocations based on his experiences as a county administrator in an adjacent county. The partnership served to

Table 3.2   Task Timetable: Title XX Allocation Project

Timetable	February 1980	March April	May	June
	February 19 Title XX Public Hearing		May 5 CASP Due in District 1 Office	July 1 Contracts Take Effect
1. Community Priority Setting	▬▬▬▬			
2. Analysis of Needs Factors for Exemptions to Competitive Bidding	▬▬▬▬▬			
3. Analysis of General Needs Factors	▬▬▬▬▬▬▬			
4. Development of RFPs	▬▬▬▬▬▬▬▬			
5. Competitive Bidding		▬▬▬▬		
6. Review and Evaluation of Bid Proposals		▬▬▬▬		
7. Consideration of Evaluation Committee Recommendations			▬▬▬▬	
8. Third Party Review			▬▬▬	
9. Consideration of Allocation Recommendations			▬▬▬	
10. Implementation of Commission Action				▬▬▬▬▬

reinforce the importance of the process, provide information, and to expedite the process from behind the scenes. The entire Title XX allocation followed the process during the second year.

After three rounds, the Title XX planning and allocation process can be identified as a success. The partnership spearheaded change from a very ad hoc approach to systematization of decision making. While no longer in the complete possession of the partnership, needs-based allocations have been set in motion and are continuing. The process has helped in negotiating role delineation and in increasing the partnership's awareness of respective roles in the human service community. Funders such as United Way, the county, and the mental health board, are aware of each other's allocations and program directions. Title XX planning data are therefore useful to these other agencies for their allocations processes. The evaluation of Title XX contracts is a step that few social service funders in the country have undertaken. Undoubtedly, the fact that some agencies have been eliminated from previous funding, some have been reduced, and some new agencies have been funded makes it a process that deserves attention, if not respect. The Ohio Department of Welfare is reported to be extremely positive about this process. It feels that the process allows the county welfare department to focus greater attention on other aspects of Title XX, such as contract management. The process has also been adopted by a neighboring county. In all, the Title XX process is indicative of a strong sense of cross-agency participation, extremely high community utility, and partnership willingness to spin off ownership. It also proved to be extremely useful when the community faced the need to make substantial funding cuts. It built a planning capability and atmosphere of intergovernmental cooperation.

Impact Analysis Project

The third partnership project to be highlighted is the study of the local impact of proposed nationally generated funding reductions. Conducted in the first quarter of 1981 and based on the early proposals, it was entitled "Preliminary Assessment of the Impacts of Proposed Reagan Administration Budget Cuts on Human Services in Montgomery County." The project was initiated by the directors group of the policy council, who were concerned about certain specific impacts, such as the number of dollars, the types of people who would be affected, the number of people who would be affected, and which functional areas would be hardest hit. The entire policy council endorsed the project and requested that the staff groups present preliminary results quickly.

The scope of work and division of labor are typical of partnership operations. The core planning group met with the partnership staff to design the study. The programs examined ranged from basic entitlement programs such as Aid to Families with Dependent Children and Food Stamps to special discretionary programs in education and the Employment Opportunities Pilot Project. Ten functional areas were selected to categorize the study. The partnership staff developed a common form for use in data gathering. The work was divided by members of the core planning group who shared responsibility for obtaining information

in the ten areas with other staff from their respective agencies. Each
member of the core planning group was responsible for investigating
proposed statutory and funding changes in his or her respective area.
As work assignments were submitted, the partnership staff collated and
aggregated the data into a draft report. The policy council subsequently
adopted the report after reviewing its merits and suggesting revisions.
Tables III.3 and III.4 present summary data and representative findings
from the study.

Table 3.3   Sample Summary of Initial Impact Assessment

• Changes in Food Stamp and AFDC regulations and reductions in Medicare
  will reduce basic benefits to many lower income families.

• Reductions in funding for health, mental health, social services, educational
  and mass transit programs are likely to heighten the pressure for more local
  tax levies and increased United Way fund raising.

• More than 800 lower income Public Service employees will lose their jobs
  along with an unknown number of persons currently employed by human
  service agencies as a result of the proposed cutbacks, adding to local unemployment roles.

• Loss of the Public Service Employment Program represents not only a personal loss for the PSE participants, but also diminishes the service capacity of
  local governments and human service agencies.

• Reductions in funding for assisted housing programs and the elimination of
  the 312 Loan Program will further increase waiting lists for existing subsi-
  dized housing.

• Reductions in emergency and energy assistance programs and in Food Stamp
  benefits will put a strain on the already limited resources of local food pan-
  tries and emergency service programs.

• Until other resources are developed, service reductions can be expected along
  with increases in user fees.

• More than $50 million will be lost by the local economy as a result of federal
  reductions in human service programs. It is not clear how much increases in
  local defense spending will offset the loss.

• The consolidation of numerous categorical grants into large block grant programs with funding reduced overall by 25 percent will make human service
  planning and programming at the local level extremely complex.

Table 3.4 Summary of Expected Local Financial Losses
Resulting From Proposed FY 82 Budget Cuts

Financial Assitance	**$13,454,165**	**Food and Nutrition**	**$4,761,758**
AFDC	10,692,000	Food Stamps	2,448,000
Emergency Assistance	205,691	School Lunch Program	1,662,000
Energy Assistance	175,452	Summer Food Program	136,557
Social Security		Child Care Nutrition	103,363
—Minimum Benefit	480,00	WIC Program	411,005
—Student Benefits	1,301,022		
—Disability Insurance	600,00		
		Housing	**$1,555,500**
Employment and	**$21,368,121**	Section 8	
Training		Existing	192,500
CETA Consolidation	1,702,215	New Construction	330,000
PSE	9,665,906	Public Housing	N.A.
EOPP	10,000,000	312 Rehab Loans	1,033,000
Mass Transportation	**$0**	**Mental Retardation**	**$580,925**
No cutbacks expected in FY82, but major cutbacks are proposed in FY83 and FY84.		Various programs operated by 169 Board	580,925
Delinquency Prevention	**$279,335**	**Education**	**$3,739,040**
Juvenile Justice	279,335	Title I	721,470
LEAA	124,000	Title IV-B	95,393
		Title IV-C	94,768
Social Services	**$3,767,121**	Adult Basic Education	21,943
		Vocational Education	473,241
Block Grant		Education of Handicapped	423,225
Consolidation		Pell Grants (BEOG)	N.A.
		Guaranteed Student Loans	1,090,000*
Health and Mental Health	**$5,221,707**		
Medicaid	2,894,199	**Total Estimated Loss:**	**$54,727,672**
Preventive Health and Health Services			
Block Grants	2,270,625	*Reflects data from Wright	
Title XX	56,963	State and Sinclair only	

The impact study is, in many ways, a mark of the partnership's structural and procedural maturity. It was conducted in a month's time with fourteen staff from the contributing partners. More importantly, the impact study proved that a smooth, unified effort could be easily made to meet a community crisis. The next step is for a partnership policy council strategy to deal with the cuts and to make adjustments as they change. There is no guarantee that Dayton-Montgomery County is any better able to meet this challenge than any other community, but at least a structure and process is now established to meet it.

Subsequent project work by the partnership indicates new substantive directions but continued interest in capacity development. It has continued to spend more time on investigating the impact of federal and state budget reductions and provided the staff work for investigating the feasibility of combining the various health and social services levies into a combined human services levy. In 1983 Montgomery County voters passed a multipurpose human services levy. The partnership also was instrumental in developing and staffing an Area Progress Council (APC) made up of local business and corporate leaders. APC has reviewed subsequent research and planning work of the partnership, served as a forum for educating the business community on human services, and is helping local agencies develop their management capability to deal with funding reductions and new program challenges resulting from federal and state changes. APC also established a Transition Fund to serve in emergencies when the need for services, housing or food is immediate. The partnership played a major role in assessing the likely local impact of new block grants and changes in categorical programs like Food Stamps and Aid to Families with Dependent Children. Primarily, it monitored federal and state activities, turned the information over to relevant agencies, alerted other local intergovernmental actors, and in some cases provided technical assistance and planning for improved program management. While many other planning groups have suffered because of the elimination of federal funds, the Partnership has held its own and in some ways thrived as a result of funding reductions, as this IGB provides information and services of relevance to the metropolitan area.

ASSESSMENT

The partnership is a forum that brings the major partners in the Dayton-Montgomery County human services system together. It has forged a viable relationship between the area's public and private sectors. The membership criteria for the partnership states that the agency must be involved in community planning, be a funder, and be an "umbrella" or comprehensive agency.[5] As such, it has brought together the most important governmental and nongovernmental actors, those who control the major program and funding resources and have the potential to resolve problems of cross-cutting importance. Its work has focused on intergovernmental problem solving through cooperative action to develop the capacity of partner members.

Several of this IGB's projects have contributed to its development and growth as a viable human service planning body in the Dayton-Montgomery County community. The core planning group's work on the Title XX allocation process helped it develop a comfortable and productive working relationship based on task forces and informal decision making. The specific work products of the Partnership projects have been used by almost every organization and agency in the community's human service system. The original research conducted by the partnership created a firm foundation based on knowledge of the community's current human service system, from which the group has extended its other research efforts. Several of the members reported that this foundation, in conjunction with the federal "seed money" grant project, has done more to contribute to the partnership's continued existence than any other single project.

Understanding the partnership's agenda is a prerequisite to understanding the partnership itself. The group has dealt with such cross-cutting issues as the Title XX allocation process and the Reagan cuts. Since agenda items can be suggested by any member, a project being worked on by one partner often becomes a project for the entire partnership. Discussants reported that this is not considered a problem until the time comes to take credit for a particular project. Should the credit go to the partner or the partnership? When issues are brought to the attention of the partnership, it is often with the presenting partner's own needs or purpose in mind. What happens repeatedly when the partnership chooses to deal with an issue is that the information generated by the research is pertinent to all the partners. For example, the city requested that the partnership evaluate the Emergency Resources Bank (ERB). The evaluation revealed that most of the partners had a stake in the ERB, and consequently in its continuation. Such issues illustrate the interdependencies of the intergovernmental system in addition to helping the partners identify their roles in that system.

Some agenda items brought to the partnership's attention are too politically volatile for one partner to deal with. For example, one discussant felt that a political stance against the Reagan cuts was impossible for the agency she represented. However, if such a stance was taken by the partnership, it would have been politically acceptable to her agency. On the other hand, another discussant reported that the partnership avoids sticky issues that could create conflict. He said the partners tend to be "too nice" by avoiding major problems that might become a bone of contention between two or more partners, e.g., the city and county's problem concerning the deinstitutionalization of mental health and retardation institutions. Even though the opportunity exists for the partners to reveal their own agendas to the partnership, it has seldom been done. The partnership, however, is viewed as a necessary and useful mechanism to deal with unexpected and sudden crisis in the human service arena because it can make decisions in a shorter period of time than the individual partners can. Some believe that coordination resulting from an atmosphere of complete trust has yet to be achieved. Nevertheless, most of the partnership's activities have resulted in information sharing, education of elected officials about human services, minimal joint funding, and a clarification of the partners' respective roles in the community's human service system.

The partnership's consensus-based decision-making process has reinforced the interdependency of the partners in the human services system and helped them realize the complexities of the system. This has been particularly true for the elected officials. The one-on-one consensus-building process has also proved that the group can compromise. The partnership has shown elected officials their importance to the local human services system. As a result, they have been able to work out their respective roles intergovernmentally. Some people feel, however, that more of the most powerful elected officials should participate in the partnership. Several partnership members feel that the officials' advocacy for human services has waned as a result. Nevertheless, the partnership has contributed to elected officials' increasing awareness of the intergovernmental and political nature of the human services system.

Problem solving proceeds along the same lines by bringing the relevant actors together, including those who have the ability to mobilize or make decisions for their jurisdiction. When they are brought together, the issues have already been researched and "trial ballooned" by relevant staff and administrators, and as a result, many compromises and adjustments are made. The protracted process of research and accommodation may lead to a set of less than elegant, but acceptable, products, but there usually is an outcome, such as a strategy, study or plan that the City, County, Mental Health Board or United Way is willing to act on. Solutions are acted upon by having each partner meet its commitment by allocating funds, making an administrative change, or otherwise using its governance or policy authority. As the process unfolds, IGB staff, directors, and policy-makers try to see whether it is really working or needs adjustment.

The partnership has no direct relationship with the state or federal governments, and the possibility of including state or federal representatives in the IGB has never become an issue. They feel that state and federal involvement would destroy the good working environment the partnership has created. Even during the partnership's first three years, when it was funded by an HEW Partnership project grant, there was little federal involvement. The partners view the state's decision-making process as primarily political in nature and as such, antithetical to the partnership's premise of planning and decision making based on needs and priorities. Also, it was felt that state and federal representatives would not be informed on local human services issues, nor would they have the authority to speak or act for their respective governments. Several key actors agreed that state involvement may be critical under block grants. Several actors also reported that the partnership may need to include other planning or funding boards in the county if the state decides to rely on the counties to deal with significant funding issues. The partnership did include major private business through APC to inform them of community problems and solicit their involvement in community human services. As a result, the Chamber of Commerce was invited to join the APC to inform them of community problems and solicit their involvement in community human services. The Chamber of Commerce was then invited to join the partnership in 1982, but it did not. The partnership remains as an IGB that involves local public and private human services intergovernmental interests.

The Dayton-Montgomery County IGB illustrates how major intergovernmental actors can be brought together to face issues of joint concern, develop a community-wide response, and, correspondingly, to build the capability of individual agencies. Cooperative action has developed relationships, mutual respect and understanding. In the process of exploring an issue, elected officials, appointed executives, and staff planners gained appreciation for how complex IGM can be, with its intricate legal questions, local politics, and planning/research techniques. What they learned became the basis for making necessary adjustments. Confronting the specifics of a given problem produced concrete results. The actors also found that as they developed planning and management capabilities that could be transferred to the agencies, they created an intergovernmental atmosphere of "satisfied customers." Another element of satisfaction was undoubtedly taking the political heat off individual politicians and administrators by tackling the tougher issues, like funding allocations. However, the essential political ingredient in IGM was always there. Finally, the IGB used its evolving capability to face new community crises on a joint basis, such as facing federal funding cuts and the corresponding need to bring in the private sector. This IGB was able to use IGM as a means of facing new problems.

Notes to Chapter Three

1. Beth Walter Honadle, "A Capacity-Building Framework: A Search for Concept and Purpose," *Public Administration Review*, 41 (September/October 1981), 577.

2. Dayton-Montgomery County Partnership Project. *Revised First Year Application*, 7.

3. Dayton-Montgomery County Partnership. *Summary of Research Findings*, 1977, 3.

4. *Prospectus: The Dayton-Montgomery County Human Services Partnership*, September, 1977.

5. Dayton-Montgomery Partnership. *Criteria for Membership*, 1978, unpaged.

CHAPTER FOUR

Bringing the Public and Private Sectors Together: The Coalition for Human Services Planning in Indianapolis/Marion County

One of the distinctive features of President Lyndon Johnson's creative federalism was the initiation of new agents into the federal system. Not only did his program bypass the states to reach into local governments and substate districts; it also attempted to involve business and labor, private institutions, and private individuals.[1] Since the 1960s, the system of federal grants has tapped a multitude of public and private agencies who work cooperatively at the local level. As David Walker suggests, creative federalism assumed implicitly that no division of functions between levels was either possible or desirable, and that officials and sector representatives were allies, not adversaries.[2]

In Indianapolis these principles were acted out as new federal and state grants reached into the local government and private human service agencies, building on a strong private sector. Thus, public-private cooperation preceded the attention placed on it by the Reagan administration during the 1980s. In Indianapolis it took on many forms: funding of developmental projects and services by the United Way and local foundations; joint efforts between public and private human service delivery agencies; involvement of business and industry with governments in solving human and economic development problems; and governmental encouragement of neighborhoods', voluntary associations', religious institutions', and employers' roles in community problems. The Indianapolis IGB operates as one of many vehicles to support community-wide, public-private cooperation.

In 1977, Indianapolis established one of the first cooperative public-private human services efforts. The Coalition for Human Services Planning in Indianapolis/Marion County is a voluntary effort of the public and private sector funders of human services "to promote better human services through improved funding coordination, information sharing, and joint planning and development."[3] The coalition's objectives are "to establish incentives and benefits for cooperation, to remove obstacles for cooperation, to establish mechanisms for improved funding/coordination, and to provide technology for facilitating improved funding/coordination."[4] The coalition is composed of individuals from the highest levels of the major funding sources for human services in Indianapolis and Marion County, including representatives from the state, City-County Council, and the private sector (see Table IV.1). The Community Service Council (CSC), a research and planning agency serving the private sector in an eight-county area including Marion County, serves as the coalition staff.[5]

Table 4.1	Indianapolis Coalition for Human Services Planning

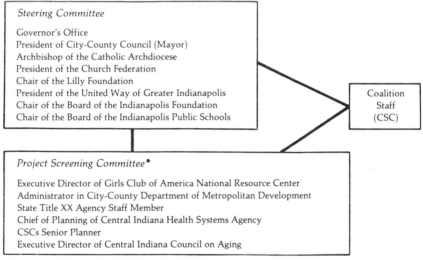

Steering Committee

Governor's Office
President of City-County Council (Mayor)
Archbishop of the Catholic Archdiocese
President of the Church Federation
Chair of the Lilly Foundation
President of the United Way of Greater Indianapolis
Chair of the Board of the Indianapolis Foundation
Chair of the Board of the Indianapolis Public Schools

Coalition
Staff
(CSC)

Project Screening Committee*

Executive Director of Girls Club of America National Resource Center
Administrator in City-County Department of Metropolitan Development
State Title XX Agency Staff Member
Chief of Planning of Central Indiana Health Systems Agency
CSCs Senior Planner
Executive Director of Central Indiana Council on Aging

*Present members appointed to Screening Committee

Indianapolis, the capital of Indiana, is located in the center of the state. Approximately 800,000 persons live within the 400 square-mile area encompassed by Indianapolis and Marion County. In 1970, the city and county governments consolidated to form a metropolitan government known as "Unigov."[6] The Indianapolis community has a very active private sector that helps support more than 900 human service agency programs. During 1978, it contributed forty-six percent of the funds given to seven selected human service agencies.[7]

The city's current human services delivery system evolved from an array of direct funding grants for the provision of human services by local governments, among them CETA, Model Cities, CDBG, and Title XX Social Services. Unigov does not include several important human services systems, such as health and education, because of their size and complexity. Neither does Unigov have a distinct department of human services; rather, the responsibility for human services administration is vested in the mayor's office, the department of metropolitan development, and the department of administration.

During its first years, the coalition spent a great deal of time and energy developing its organization and structure. Its major projects have been an integrated human services planning information system and a unified management structure for public and private multiservice centers in the city-county. Other completed projects include a report on expenditures for human services in Marion County, a human services resource library, and an access services model.[8]

DEVELOPMENT AND OPERATION

IGB Formation

The Coalition for Human Services Planning did not evolve from a federal grant or project; however, there were several coordination attempts, all different that contributed to a general awareness of the need for coordinating human services efforts. In 1974, the National Association of Counties Research Foundation studied Indianapolis' ability to implement the proposed Allied Services Act and recommended that the city "initiate service integration and arrange a cooperative agreement with other agencies providing services."[9] The Indianapolis Division of Planning and Zoning also recommended that the city treat human services problems on a community-wide basis. Yet another attempt at coordination was the Indianapolis Unified Program for Urban Progress, which helped fund the development of the Indianapolis Services Identification System (ISIS). These and other efforts contributed to the timeliness of the coalition.[10]

In April 1977, the chief executives of the CSC and the United Way of Greater Indianapolis approached the mayor with their ideas for the Coalition for Human Services, which would coordinate the efforts of human services planning organizations and major human services funders.[11] Although the coalition was not organized around any one issue, its initiators recognized that no scheme for setting priorities among human services existed in the community, and that there was some duplication of effort by human services funders.

Structure

The first job of the coalition's steering committee was to develop a systematic approach to coordinate efforts for funding human services in the community. The steering committee appointed a technical committee to recommend a structure for the coalition. A subcommittee developed a prospectus outlining several options for integrated planning mechanisms. The prospectus was approved by the steering committee in March 1978 and the following philosophy was adopted:

> The Coalition will respect the individual autonomy and responsibilities of its member organization; no elected, appointed or voluntary official will be asked to abdicate program or funding decisions to the Coalition; the program will serve to help planning agencies and authorities, not replace them; and the Coalition will seek a united position on human service needs and policies to present to state and federal agencies and officials.[12]

Following approval of the prospectus, the technical committee was restructured into an advisory committee with three subcommittees; a technical subcommittee, a communications subcommittee, and a resources development subcommittee. The first major project of the Coalition was the creation of the Human Services Information System (HSIS). The technical subcommittee was charged with developing the work plan for the HSIS project. Because the other two subcommittees were not involved in the HSIS project, they became inactive and were disbanded. Late in 1979, the coalition became involved in the CSC's Neighborhood Services Study (NSS).[13] The coalition appointed an interagency task force to develop a model of access services in response to the NSS. The Access Services Model and HSIS will be described in detail in a subsequent section.

In the fall of 1980, the coalition was reorganized. The advisory committee was removed, leaving the steering committee and a screening committee. The steering committee remains the overall policy-making and funding-decision body, made up of representatives of the major funders.

Staff support for both committees is provided by CSC. From the early stages, it was thought that the missions of the coalition and CSC were fairly consistent and, thus the necessary staff time and support services could be provided by CSC. Also, CSC has the support of the United Way, its funder, to perform such services. CSC designated one staff person who is primarily assigned to the coalition and also supplies major clerical and communication support. Staff work is donated on a project-by-project basis by other coalition members, particularly by the City-County staff and key steering committee members as needed. Finally, one of the coalition's two major efforts, the HSIS, was conducted through a contract with Indiana University.

The three-level system of IGB funding is also quite simple. First, core staff activities are provided by CSC out of its budget as an in-kind contribution. Second, specific projects undertaken by the IGB, such as the HSIS, are funded by having each member of the coalition, or as many as are willing and able, contribute a mutually agreed upon "fair share." In practice, this has only been put to the test once or twice and, while it has worked, the "fair share" often is unequal, with one or two members not contributing at all. The money is held in a restricted CSC account; CSC is the legal contractor with outside vendors. Third, joint-funded projects go through the coalition decision structure, but funds are disbursed from individual funders to the specific participating agencies. Only the application process is a joint venture; recipient agencies are fiscally accountable to each funding source on an individual basis.

Decision Framework and Role of Key Actors

Basic IGB policy decisions are made on an informal basis. When staff or key coalition members place an issue on the agenda, it is discussed and action is taken. A great deal of the decision process has been behind-the-scenes consensus building. The coalition has no written charter or enabling and operating agreements. In 1980, a set of ground rules was established that outlines decision processes. The ground rules say very little about steering committee policy roles, beyond the mandate for quarterly reviews of project proposals. The ground rules also make it possible for the project review to be changed with a concurring vote of five members. But previous informal practice suggests that members are reluctant to follow a process that will lock them into commitments they do not want to make.

There are four steps in the current screening process (see Table IV.2). The screening committee's task is to reduce the number of project proposals submitted for consideration by the steering committee. Before the final ranking, weights are placed on the criteria. Usually, the greatest weight is placed on the following factors: (1) political feasibility, (2) degree of innovation, (3) potential for success, and (4) documented need. Besides the detailed criteria for reviewing possible projects, several criteria have been set for defining the elements of a good proposal and minimal project standards. Also, a number of management issues—fiscal accountability, needs delineation, and potential for success—have to be explicated. These factors are combined into eight categories comprising the overall criteria for joint-funding proposals. The categories have been transformed into a set of guidelines included in solicitations for proposals from community agencies. Weighted rankings of the top 25 projects are then sent to the steering committee for its review. The steering committee has no obligation to adhere to the rankings of the proposals;

however, the screening committee has a written assurance that the steering committee will consider its work for the "possibility of funding submitted projects." The steering committee is scheduled to meet quarterly to review proposals.

Table 4.2   Steering Committee Screening Process

Project Flow

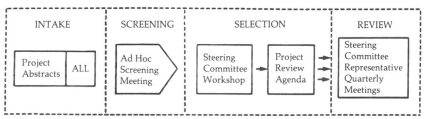

Agenda and Development

For the steering committee, the agenda-setting process has been very informal. Prior to the coalition's reorganization, issues under consideration were those an individual member wishes to place on the agenda. Because steering committee members work at very high levels, these issues tended to come from one or two key members or top staff people. One person reported that he often had to make a few calls before a meeting to let people know what had to be decided.

The funders on the coalition use its structure and agenda for cooperation and coordination—the studies provide important decisionmaking tools, data bases, and a clearinghouse of information—but they always maintain autonomy in their final decisions. Because of an informal ground rule, the coalition has nothing to do with the funding of individual projects, nor does it deal with any joint projects that elicit major objections. It is designed to deal with voluntary joint ventures, based on the knowledge that two or more funders might be involved in the process. This IGB has developed slowly and carefully, avoiding major conflicts or controversies between powerful actors representing key segments of the community. Its work has focused on planning and coordination, involving those who control project funding at decision level and working professionals at the technical level. Unlike other IGB's, it has avoided many projects of major significance, such as examination of federal funding cuts and block grants, it has left these efforts to other bodies. Its projects are concentrated on those that the steering committee can reach agreement on.

PROJECTS

The style and operation of the IBG has limited the coalition's agenda and thus its project undertakings. Two projects, which have been the centerpieces of the coalition's work, illustrate how this IGB operates: they are HSIS and the Access Service Model. Both are successful public-private intergovernmental ventures.

Human Services Information System

From the beginning, the need for a common human services information base was recognized by the coalition funders. Later, in the prospectus, the idea was developed and recommended as the first joint effort for the coalition. The purpose of the HSIS is to provide basic information for human services planners and funders about service needs, current services, funding recipients, funding sources, where expenditures are needed, and so on. The system consists of four components, which are linked by a data analysis group (see Table IV.3). The components include a human services inventory, a socioeconomic-demographic data file, a human services activity profile, and a financial reporting inventory.

Table 4.3   Human Services Information System

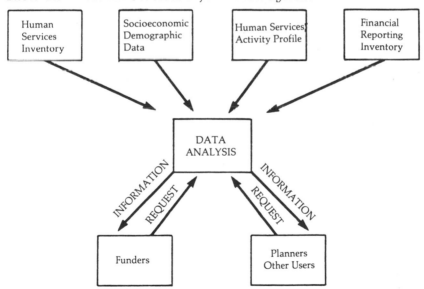

The human services inventory component is the Indianapolis Services Identification System (ISIS) developed by the CSC. It classifies human services into functional activities, allowing for an inventory of agencies providing human services as well as agencies providing supportive services, such as transportation and information-referral. ISIS is automated and can be updated regularly. This service provides uniform, comparative data about human services agencies. It can provide a detailed list of agencies by census tract and by target population. The socio-economic-demographic data file is an expansion of the existing Marion County Data Component (MCDC), which is a computerized information system of social and economic data about Marion County developed by Indiana University. The system has a ranking function and currently uses 1970 census data, but will be updated when 1980 data are available.

The human services activity profile, which is still in the initial stages, will, when completed, provide summary count data on how many people request or present themselves for what kinds of services, what their demographic characteristics are, and whether services were provided or were not available. The financial report inventory has yet to be developed. Its objective is to categorize information according to money expended by agency, by program, and by source of funds. This component will also yield a quarterly report of grants approved or awarded to agencies by funding source and type of program.

The second phase of HSIS involves revisions incorporating 1980 census data and further modification of the MCDC. The activity profiles and financial reporting inventories are proceeding through development. The extension will continue to be jointly funded by the coalition.

The HSIS project illustrates the decision-making process of the coalition as well. Advice to the coalition during the development of HSIS came from the technical subcommittee, chaired by a specialist in data development from the Indianapolis Center for Advanced Research. In addition, technicians from government agencies and private sector funders were asked to provide advice and reaction to drafts. Since much of the information needed to build HSIS was largely imbedded in the agencies, staff people representing the funders needed to engage in extensive negotiations to gain information. Steering committee members were instrumental in getting agency support and information for the program. Most important, steering committee members have ensured financing of the project.

Ultimately, the HSIS will be available to all community funding and human service agencies and thus will provide a common information base for planning, development, and decision making in human services. Such a comprehensive information system will undoubtedly facilitate joint funding efforts as well as cooperative service delivery activities among service providers.

NSS/Access Services Model

The NSS/Access Services Model has a distinctly different history from the HSIS. The NSS is a plan for a continuum of services delivery at the neighborhood level in the Greater Indianapolis Area. It was developed by the CSC, independent of the coalition. The CSC presented the coalition with its study late in 1979. As a result, the coalition appointed an interagency staff group to analyze the funding required for provision of access services in the community. The product of the staff group was the Access Services Model, approved by the coalition in October 1980. At that time, the coalition also agreed to discuss joint funding of access services.

Since Access Services was not a project that originated with the IGB, the coalition got involved in the problem-solving process after the problem had been identified and possible courses of action were researched. Nevertheless, the CSC style of operation, involving a broad base of public and private actors, is similar to that of the coalition. Indeed, if the coalition had initiated the project, most of the actors would have been the same: city-county, state, United Way, and foundations. After the IGB put the project on its agenda with an available model, the key actors negotiated and developed a solution with a sound technical approach that major parties could agree upon and that was fundable by coalition partners. Thus, the IGB was instrumental in moving this important project through its critical stages.

As negotiated, the Access Services Model incorporates several objectives of the NSS:

> To build upon the existing access services administered by the Division of Community Services and delivered by neighborhood multiservice centers (core services); to expand Core Services to include all of the functions connoted by access services including outreach and increased follow-up; to deal with service delivery in presently underserved areas; and, to create increased linkages with agencies providing specialized services or serving specific segments of the community to open the way for increased coordination and broadened funding of access services.[15]

The model is based on the following premises:

> Access services will be delivered by existing service organizations wherever possible; the proposed network of decentralized access service units or teams will serve more clients than existing access-type services; the staff of each access component will function as a team; and, access services will make use of existing service resources.[16]

The Access Services Model could not be implemented without a stable funding base for neighborhood multiservice centers. NSS documented the need for the centers to rely more on "stable" funding sources. Since the coalition's approval of the Access Services Model, the funding of neighborhood multiservice centers has become a community-wide problem. The coalition deferred the implementation of the Access Services Model until the multiservice center funding problem could be resolved. The coalition appointed a special task force to develop funding strategies and recommendation for solution of the problem. A spin-off of the coalition is involvement in the multiservice center funding problem has been the creation of a federation of multiservice center directors. The effort to resolve this problem was the coalition's first attempt to confront a substantive service need.

By early 1983 the coalition had indeed developed a solution to the problem. The steering committee agreed to fund the model by supporting the concept of a central management structure for the multiservice centers. Public agencies and the private settlement houses were consolidated at the administrative level, and funding for the centers was assured by the major funders agreeing to fund their components. By mid-1983 the structure was in place with a single executive officer.

The Access Services Model and the development of the multiservice center funding problem solution demonstrated the coalition's ability to deliver. It proved it could engage persons with expertise in a problem area as they are needed, to appoint special task forces, and to use current or prospective projects to facilitate resolution of related problems as they arise in the community. As the coalition becomes more familiar with its new operating format, it will increase its capacity to deal with the new projects submitted by the screening committee, as well as continue its work with the HSIS and the Access Services Model.

Problems on this IGB's agenda include a social vulnerability study, a combined public-private metropolitan paratransit system for the elderly and the handicapped, an employment and training program for special target populations, and a program for mainstreaming the handicapped in community recreation programs.

ASSESSMENT

The coalition was formed to bring public and private funders together to do joint planning and gather information, to develop an overall philosophy or set of community priorities for funding, and to be more systematic in funding decisions that involve two or more funders. The selective and limited agenda precludes any decisions about single-funded projects. Moreover, it is not directly targeted to community-wide planning or policy development. Indeed, the agenda has been limited to a few very broad issues of concern, such as access services, funding of multiservice centers, and provision of an information base.

Within these narrowly confined issues, the coalition has brought forth some important products and solutions of use by the broader community. Moreover, it has been the prime vehicle for combining public and private efforts in human services, an essential ingredient in IGM.

Admittedly, the coalition developed slowly. It took three years to make the structure explicit, during which reorganization and development of operating principles were the coalition's primary nonstaff activities. "Too much time on process" was reported as leading to a lack of interest on the part of some powerful actors. However, through the organization and work on projects, some relationships have developed. The coalition was reported as being important in opening up lines of communication among the various actors. At the steering committee level, where perhaps the lines were already open, the need to reach decisions jointly accelerated the process and elicited increased participation.

Perhaps the most important communication links were at the second or operating executive level, particularly between the public and the private sectors. Important new working relationships between the public and private sectors were also developed on a "lateral work level" through specific projects. For example, the research staff of the City-County Council and CSC were reported to have gained knowledge and respect for each other on the neighborhood study and the data projects. Indeed, there are reports of several new working relationships developed outside of the Coalition as a result of the forum it provided.

There is concern that the coalition can never be the forum for important intergovernmental decisions because the parties are unwilling to make them over the table. In the words of one observer, "It is the behind-the-scenes maneuver or the back room" that prevails. Others thought that while communication has opened, there remains a lack of trust over "the other parties' agenda." Leadership is considered to be another problem. The real moving forces for the coalition are powerful in their own spheres, but not necessarily overall. There was hope in the early stages that the business and economic elite could be brought in through the human resources section for the Greater Indianapolis Progress Committee (GIPC), but that unit is the least active component of GIPC and has shown little interest. The mayor is nominally in charge of convening the coalition, but he has not felt a strong need to take a leadership role.

Coalition activity surrounding several joint issues, culminating in the crisis over the funding of the multiservice centers, was reported to be extremely important in bringing together the public and private sectors. First, the city was put on the line early when the private sector announced during negotiations over the first joint-funded project that public sector participation was expected on an equal basis. That event, and subsequent decisions, made it clear that the city and other public components had to be partners in a financial as well as a decision-making sense. It thus brought them into the orbit of "funder" in the eyes of the community. Second, the coalition, speaking in unison over the crises such as the funding of multiservice centers, helped make the City-County Council realize that it no longer had the luxury of saying "no" to human services. The unified front has been instrumental in convincing the legislative body that local government has a role to play and that there is local support for it. Third, the previously mentioned working relationships have made it easier for the city's administrative personnel to see important points of interaction between the components at the service level.

The local joint-funding orientation of the coalition has limited state and federal participation. By design, there have been no federal government representatives on the coalition. Most federal funds are seen as either going through the states or directly to the community. A federal official on an IPA transfer to the City-County did put in a considerable amount of staff time in 1980 on the reorganization of the coalition, but his role was not in an official federal capacity. A few officials recognized the importance of the federal government in human services funding, but were unclear as to what position might be designated. The state role has been clearer, inasmuch as the governor appoints a designee to represent state government on the coalition. Usually, that person has been whichever high-ranking staff member chairs the multiagency Interdepartmental Board of Coordination of Human Services. Generally, this relationship has been satisfactory because the representative has the broad-based authority to speak for the governor.

When the city filed an appeal with the state over funding of access services, the coalition was able to present a unified front, with public and private funders attempting to change the state's position. Their attempt helped the State Title XX agency and the city develop a compromise in which the state agreed to fund the counseling in their access services category. The effort proved to be unifying and important for other coalition developments. State involvement is considered essential because of the strong direct fiscal control state government has had over local governments in Indiana and because of the importance of such programs as Title XX for local governments. Coalition partners believe in maintaining regular contact with key state people, if nothing else to inform the state of how its actions can affect the local scene.

The Indianapolis-Marion County IGB primarily demonstrates how public and private actors can coalesce to solve problems of mutual interest and concern. Although the scope and type of problems the coalition has undertaken is limited, it stands as a demonstration of how public and private sectors can engage in creative IGM. Its project work has been both harmful and constructive. Because the major projects—HSIS and Access Services—involved long leadtimes key actors became frustrated with the lack of results that would demonstrate that their time and dollars should be continued. Once breakthroughs were made, however, confidence and patience led to renewed interest.

The difficulties and ultimate successes of the coalition demonstrate some important principles. Sometimes it takes a long time for a group like the coalition to get together because members have to learn to work with each other and respect the autonomy of the governments and sectors involved. It means that results are more important than adhering to structure. The coalition is testing a new structure that both teaches them to work together and attempts to solve problems. As parties become more involved in the process, they see that it will cost them something in terms of effort and dollars. These costs come out of jurisdictional domains and are contributed to a common cause. No matter how much a partner may agree that a given problem is worthy of the group's commitment, a bit of their "hide" is lost, and this does not come easily.

Success also depends on technical work being done at one level and decision work at another. Pragmatism is important, too, as when the IGB accepted fact-finding work previously conducted by CSC and integrated into their process. The need to allow each funder to maintain control over its portion of a project not only respects autonomy, but is a practical management adjustment often needed in IGM.

Problem resolution by the coalition approximated the steps previously identified in which the group convened, agreed upon problems, researched and developed options, selected a course of action and implemented it through the component members. The Indianapolis IGB has been able to use this process to further its interest in jointly funded public-private projects, particularly as it tries to find a way to deal with other questions of critical interest, such as integrating the handicapped and training the unemployed.

Notes to Chapter Four

1. Quoted in David B. Walker, *Toward a Functioning Federalism* (Cambridge, Mass.: Winthrop, 1981), 104.

2. *Ibid.*

3. Larry Carroll, *Coalition for Human Services Planning* (Paper prepared for presentation to persons interested in the Coalition, 1981), unpaged.

4. *Ibid.*

5. *Ibid.*

6. Hester Schultz, *Coalition for Human Services Planning* (Paper presented at the First National Network Building Conference in Denver, Colorado, June 1980), 239.

7. *Human Service Funding Information for Marion County.* (A staff report to the Coalition for Human Services Planning, March 1980).

8. Carroll. *Coalition.*

9. Schultz, *Coalition*, 230.

10. Other community studies included: Community Action Against Poverty's (CAAP's) *Probability Outreach Study of 1979*, CSC's 1976 *Social Vulnerability Study*, and Peat Marwick, Mitchell and Company's 1974 study, *Improving Human Services Funding in Greater Indianapolis*.

11. Larry Carroll, Dan McDonald, and John Riggle. *Integrating Human Service Planning in Greater Indianapolis: A Prospectus*. (Paper presented to the Coalition for Human Service Planning, March 1979), unpaged.

12. *Working Paper, Human Services Information System* (Paper presented to the Coalition for Human Services Planning by the Technical Subcommittee, June 1979), 2.

13. Irvin S. Katz and Rosemary F. Dorse, *Neighborhood Services Study: A Framework for Effective Service Delivery in Indianapolis Neighborhoods* (Community Services Council of Metropolitan Indianapolis, February 1980).

14. *Coalition for Human Services Ground Rules*, 29 September, 1980, 4.

15. Joseph Ryan, Chairperson of the Ad Hoc Access Study Group, *Access Services Model: A Report to the Coalition for Human Services Planning*, October 1980, 3.

16. *Ibid*, 5.

CHAPTER FIVE

Policy Management: The Metropolitan Human Services Commission of ColumbusFranklin County, Ohio

Policy management has become a central activity in IGM. Increased interdependency among governments has generated a need at the state and local levels where services are actually delivered for officials to manage their jurisdictions as a whole and to assure that programs meet community needs effectively and efficiently.[1] An Office of Management and Budget Study Committee on Policy Management Assistance defined policy management as, "the identification of needs, analysis of options, selection of programs and allocation of resources on a jurisdiction-wide basis." It distinguished policy management from program management (the implementation of policy or daily operation of agencies along functional lines) and resource management (the establishment of basic administrative support systems such as budgeting, financing, financial management, procurement and supply, and personnel administration.)[2] Phillip Burgess, among others, has distinguished policy management by its emphasis on: expanded intergovernmental partnerships; reduced burdens placed on grant recipients; increasing local choice-making responsibilities; design of integrated policies and programs; and management of policies, programs, and operations on the basis of jurisdictional (or "place") rather than functional (or "program") criteria.[3]

Such efforts to engage in policy management characterize the Metropolitan Human Services Commission (MHSC) of Columbus/Franklin County. While it has been involved in a broad range of communitywide planning and problem-solving activities, its most notable achievements are in the area of managing intergovernmental programs from a local

perspective. MHSC's work on such projects as developing financial allocation processes, Negotiated Investment Strategy, facilitation of deinstitutionalization of former mental patients, contingency planning to deal
with federal funding reductions, and review of local tax levies stand as
prime illustrations that the process and products of policy management
can work in IGM.

The Metropolitan Human Services Commission is a broad-based organization of local representatives who bridge the various sectors in human
services to deal with community-wide issues of planning, financing, and
delivering services. Established in 1977, the commission's eighteen-member
board of trustees includes representatives from the local governments,
private and public human service funders and providers, and at-large
members who represent education, health, religion, neighborhoods, and
consumer concerns. The commission operates with both professional
executives and elected board members, working together in a policy
capacity, representing the primary local funders.

Columbus, the capital of Ohio, and Franklin County comprise one of
the few urban areas in the northeast quadrant of the United States that
is increasing in population. With a population just over 1 million, the
area's economy is relatively stable; unemployment rates are generally
lower than in other major Ohio cities. Columbus has strong home-rule
provisions. Its charter calls for an elected mayor and seven city council
members. Franklin County is administered by a three-member board.
Its functions are prescribed by state law, including requirements to operate
many human services programs.

The local human services arena is a mix of the public and private
sectors. County government services include the Welfare Department
(income maintenance, Food Stamps, general relief, and Title XX), the
Children's Service Board, and the Mental Health and Mental Retardation Boards. The city of Columbus Department of Community Services
administers CETA for the city and county and administers the nearly 5
million dollars the city spends on human services out of its general
revenue sharing (GRS) funds. The Columbus Metropolitan Area Community Action Organization (CMACAO) is the community's antipoverty
agency. The private sector is funded primarily by the $10 million to
$11 million raised by the United Way and several family and corporate
foundations. The largest foundations contributing to human services are
the Columbus Foundation and the Batelle Memorial Institute Foundation.

MHSC operates with a relatively open style, using research as an
important foundation for its recommendations. Recognizing that there
is a political component to IGM, MHSC has operated with the belief
that all issues undertaken should involve as many parties as are affected,
that "all bases should be touched." Because MHSC has been involved in
several highly controversial issues, this IGB has followed a slow, careful

path, blending high quality technical information with process—essential ingredients of policy management in IGM.

DEVELOPMENT AND OPERATION

IGB Formation

MHSC emerged from indiscriminate problems arising from various sectors in human services. Generally, MHSC appears to have been triggered by a feeling that human services were growing immense, particularly as new programs funded by the federal government were brought into the local community. Initially, this involvement was through Model Cities and the CDBG. Then came GRS, with local groups petitioning for funds from the city. The city's response reflected greater support from the city council than from the mayor. Meanwhile, the county's funding was expanding through support of more programs by the local tax levy, but entitlement programs and reliance on the property tax made growth increasingly problematic. Concerns of the private sector included keeping up with inflation, the future of private delivery systems receiving public funding, and dealing with general community dissatisfaction over the local health and welfare planning council.

A 1975 city council resolution calling attention to "the definite need in Columbus and Franklin County to coordinate effectively and efficiently the numerous social services which are and will be provided to the public" led to the establishment of MHSC.[4] Leadership within the council was taken by a council member, who later became a federal official instrumental in involving Columbus in major intergovernmental negotiations. Behind the scenes, five individuals have played key roles throughout the life of the commission; (1) the director of the regional planning agency; (2) the chief of staff of the Columbus City Council; (3) the head of United Way, who later became executive director of the Chamber of Commerce; (4) a settlement house director, who later was elected to the City Council; and (5) a management consultant, who later became executive director of MHSC. These individuals shared the general concerns of the local funder groups and wanted to enhance coordination and community-wide policy development and planning.

The city resolution was transmitted to the county and United Way and, as a result, a Citizen's Committee for Human Services (CCHS) was appointed jointly by local elected officials and the president of the United Way. The twenty-seven-member panel represented a broad cross-section of the community, including government officials; business, labor, civic and service organizations; and private citizens. It was chaired by a businessman, who is an influential community leader.

In November 1976, CCHS completed its general reports. CCHS's subcommittees presented detailed status reports with recommendations and outlines of actions in most cases.[5] The major recommendations included:

1. The creation of a Metropolitan Policy Body (MPB) "to coordinate the work of individual social service agencies, provide staff support for them in areas of mutual concern, and establish both program and spending priorities on a long- and short-term basis"

2. A provision that the bulk of the work undertaken by the MPB, be performed either on a purchase-of-service basis or "shared staff" basis and that only a small core staff be employed by the MPB to manage its operations

3. The formation of a cabinet of executives "composed of the executive directors of major human service organizations...as a critical link between the MPB, systems and agencies to enhance the coordination and integration of service delivery"

4. The development of a uniform and consolidated service access system for users of social services

5. The development of a community participation process through a network of community councils.[6]

The recommendations were presented and unanimously accepted by the city, county, and United Way.

The new commission began working on specific projects in 1977. The initial thrust followed the recommendation of CCHS on the development of baseline planning information on needs and services. A related attempt was made to develop systematic community priority setting, derived from criteria using both quantified indicators and perceptions of community need. The commission's first attempt to deal with a community-wide problem involved Title XX cash flow. MHSC enlisted several community leaders, including business executives, to propose an alternative means for the state to advance payment based on estimates. The solution they developed for alleviating cash flow problems for many small agencies was accepted and extended to Ohio's eighty-eight counties.

Another early effort was the development of information services to ensure community access to data compiled and used by MHSC and to provide technical assistance to organizations collecting information and designing programs. A resource development program designed to secure additional funds for the local human service community through grantsmanship training, technical assistance, and secure the services of a Washington agent to help identify new federal monies was also begun.

By 1978, the commission had initiated a goal-setting process, which began to formulate goals for human services that reflected a consensus of the community. MHSC took leadership in 1978 in averting a proposed $83 million decrease in Title XX funds for Franklin County, once again calling upon community leaders to impress upon state legislators and administrators the impact of cuts on service delivery. The commis-

sion also convened an emergency human services committee to supervise the development of an emergency human services delivery plan,
which specified public and private roles in the event of a disaster.

IGB STRUCTURE

MHSC's overall agenda and activities are set by an eighteen-member
board of trustees, representing government and various public, private,
business, and labor organizations in the community (see Table V.1). To
date, city appointees have been council members and department directors.
At least one county appointee has been a commissioner. The board of
trustees elects a chairperson, vice chairperson, secretary, and treasurer
at the MHSC annual meeting.[7] The board designates a president, who is
the chief staff person and need not be a. trustee of the commission. The
chairperson presides at all meetings of the trustees. The president acts as
chief executive officer and supervises the business of the commission
and its employees. The code of regulations also stipulates that the president have the power and authority to sign all deeds, mortgages, bonds,
contracts and more. The code enables the board to appoint a committee
of trustees to delegate certain responsibilities as needed.

Table 5.1   Columbus/Franklin County
Metropolitan Human Services Commission

Board of Trustees

1 Mayoral appointee
1 Columbus Metropolitan Area Community Action Organization
   appointee
1 City Council appointee
1 appointee from the Columbus Chamber of Commerce
2 representatives from the Board of County Commissioners
4 at-large members from the Community
1 United Way of Franklin County representative
3 at-large members from the areas of Health, Education, and Religion
1 joint appointee from the Columbus Foundation and the Batelle
   Memorial Institute Foundation
1 Franklin County Board of Mental Retardation and Developmental
   Disabilities appointee
1 representative of the United Labor Leaders Advisory Council

Cabinet of Executive Directors

Columbus Department of Community Services
Franklin County Welfare Department
Franklin County Children Services Board
Franklin County Mental Health Board
United Way of Franklin County
CMACAO
Franklin County Board of Mental Retardation and Developmental Disabilities
Mid-Ohio Regional Planning Commission
Professional Advisory Council
Columbus Department of Recreation and Parks
Columbus Department of Development
Columbus/Franklin County Criminal Justice Coordinating Council

---

MHSC Staff

MHSC's twelve-member cabinet of executive directors serves as the link among the trustees, the funding systems, and the community's service agencies (Table V.1). The cabinet was conceived as a working body meeting as necessary over specific issues and problems. Because the cabinet did not meet very often but participated directly in board discussions on issues of concern to them, the board of trustees made all cabinet members ex-officio members of the board who are "on call" to deal with specific concerns. MHSC also established four standing committees— policy and research, systems operation, community information, and long range issues—with members assigned from the trustees, cabinet, MHSC staff, and other agencies in the community as needed. The standing committee format is expected to increase participation of board and cabinet members.

MHSC is jointly funded by the United Way of Franklin County, the city of Columbus, Franklin County, the Franklin County Mental Health Board, and CMACAO. At the outset, a small HEW Partnership Grant financed a consultant to provide staff support. Monies from the various local supporters are granted to the MHSC in different ways. The city uses GRS funds. The county uses GRS as the match for Title XX, and certain services are contracted to the MHSC by the county under Title XX. The Mental Health Board has the most restrictive contract with the MHSC, stipulating the services for which the money can and cannot be used. The United Way and CMACAO simply contribute specific grants of money.

Decision Framework and Role of Key Actors

All project work undertaken by MHSC is considered and approved by the trustees. Decisions are discussed, debated, and narrowed to a point where most trustees can agree with a position. Since the board is large and can rarely reach complete consensus, issues are resolved by majority vote. However, by the time a vote is called, near consensus is almost always reached.

Various officials, community leaders, and executives are involved in the MHSC by virtue of informal and formal commitments to human services. They consist of community and business leaders who, while not formally represented on the board, agree with its philosophy and support its existence. These people have considerable influence over the business and labor community's involvement with the MHSC. Of the officials who are formally represented on the board, some are more involved and committed than others. The city council is supportive of the MHSC and looks to it to provide the information and expertise necessary for the city to deal with human service problems. The county is not as intimately involved with the commission as is the city, but they have a good working relationship. The United Way is reported as somewhat skeptical of MHSC's ability to be equitable to all the actors involved in the commission. The level of involvement of the other funders and the two private foundations is minimal, unless a particular project or activity requires their cooperation, expertise, or is in their own interests.

The agency executive directors are less directly involved in the commission than the trustees. Their involvement depends on the specific issue and their perceptions of that issue's importance. Directors who are members of the cabinet of executives are obviously more involved than administrators not included by the MHSC structure. MHSC does make an effort to involve administrators on a project-by-project basis when appropriate. In such instances, they are relied upon heavily to supply necessary project data and information.

Agenda and Development

MHSC's work is determined by an annual plan modified periodically by the trustees. At an MHSC annual retreat, trustees and cabinet members decide informally on annual objectives for the commission. The staff then proposes a number of possible projects pertinent to the specific objectives. The board votes on whether to consider the projects and sets priorities for those projects approved. The staff then uses the priority list to develop a detailed work plan for the year. Requests to consider community human service problems come from trustees, cabinet members, the staff itself, and other service agencies in the community. After preliminary research, the request is presented to the board of trustees for consideration in the form of a proposal. If accepted by the board, it is incorporated into the commission's overall work plan.

Projects also are individually funded by the trustees. When a proposal has been approved by the board, the staff prepares a detailed work plan delineating goals, objectives, assumptions, timetables, work activities, data and information needs, and a budget. To prepare a budget for a project, MHSC staff must contact the trustee representatives who have potential interest and a willingness to make a financial investment in the project one by one until the sum of the financial commitments equals the amount needed for the project. Then a comprehensive work plan, including the budget, is presented to the trustees for final approval and sanction.

The process of project development has generally followed a staff-driven, commission-approved format. A project begins with a staff report outlining a study being sent to the commission for its approval. The study is then undertaken by the staff, although data collection may be done within the agencies or by consultants; the staff, however, makes the ultimate decision on the format of the study. When studies are complete, they are sent to the commission in the form of a staff report, subject to MHSC's review, modification, and approval. A MHSC position emanating from a project usually supports the general conclusions or direction of a report.

MHSC staff has to exercise caution in its tendency to accelerate "at a rate that exceeds the lay board's ability to perform their policy-making role."[9] The staff provides the agenda, reports, and project proposals for the board of trustees' monthly meetings. The entire staff is present at these board meetings and the kind of competition fostered by a paid staff challenging the capacity of a volunteer board is considered healthy for the MHSC.[10]

Projects

The problem-solving work of MHSC represents the greatest level of productivity of any of the IGBs examined in this study. Table V.2 lists the reports and publications completed from 1977 to 1980, the years immediately preceding the field examination. This section highlights three projects undertaken after MHSC's developmental stage—the Allocation Process, the Negotiated Investment Strategy (NIS), and the Deinstitutionalization-Group Homes efforts—as well as more recent undertakings. Collectively, they not only illustrate the critical need to involve research and fact-finding in IGM problem solving, but demonstrate different means by which policy management can be invoked at jurisdiction and cross-jurisdiction levels.

Allocation Process

The process for allocation of GRS by the city of Columbus grew out of the experience of reduced funding for human services. The mayor annually recommends severe reductions in human service funding, after which the council attempts to restore the funding to at least the previous year's allocation. However, by 1978 it became clear to the council that some cuts would have to be made. It was thought that even if priorities were adopted and followed, many popular programs would have to be cut and the council would take the heat. There also was a feeling that many of the agencies that might be hit hardest were funded by the United Way, creating a rebound effect on the United Way allocations process. Thus, a more neutral party in the form of MHSC was asked to develop a priority system as a political "buffer" and as a means of meeting true community needs.

During the 1978 city budget-building process, an abortive attempt was made to convene the city, county, United Way, and a MHSC representative to divide areas of responsibility and make respective allocations. Resistance came from a number of sources and the effort died. But the city remained uncomfortable with the pressures to continue funding each project; the prospect was that each agency would take a proportional

Table 5.2   MHSC Reports and Publications

1977	1978	1979	1980
• A Report to the Community on Human Services Needs in Franklin County	• A Report on Income Required To Achieve a Minimum Standard of Health and Decency in Franklin County	• An Assessment of Social Well-Being in Franklin County	• Group Homes and Property Values: A Second Look
• An Inventory of Available Information on Human Services Needs and Socioeconomic Environment of Franklin County	• An analysis of Agency Forms and a Potential Common Intake Form for Use in Cases of Domestic Violence	• Day Care Cost Study	• An Analysis of Physical Health Problems in Franklin County
• An Inventory of Selected Human Services in Franklin County, Ohio	• An Analysis of Financing Options in the Event of Title XX Cutbacks	• A Food Action Plan for the Columbus Metropolitan Area Developed by Hunger Task Force of Ohio staff	• A Case Study: The Development and Implementation of the Metropolitan Human Services Commission of Columbus Franklin County
• First Year Report of Metropolitan Human Services Commission	• Emergency Human Services Plan	• Program Planning Considerations for Exoffenders	• An Exploratory Survey of Mental Health Practitioners in Franklin County
• Program Profiles	• Impact Analysis of Title XX Cutbacks on Franklin County	• Program Planning Considerations for Displaced Homemakers	• Review of the Food Stamp Program Operated by the FCWD
		• Property Acquisition Study	
		• Recommended Social Services Allocation Policies for the City of Columbus Department of Community Services	
		• Report on Program and Fiscal Reporting Requirements	
		• The Non-Effect of Group Homes on Neighboring Residential Property Values in Franklin County	

cut and no sense of priority would have been met. The commission was again asked to develop a process for 1979, which it did on an interactive basis with the city council staff and the city Department of Community Services.

Since GRS operates as a relatively open-ended process, there were few legal considerations that had to be worked through. The city was relatively free to make allocations according to its own priority-setting process. Since the decisions were highly political and a number of agencies with community standing were likely to be reduced, extensive discussion and negotiations were required. At one level, MHSC staff and selected trustees had to reinforce the views of certain city council members. Extensive behind-the-scenes negotiations were held with the United Way to ensure that its allocations committee understood the impact of new city decisions. While the United Way was concerned about the effects of this new process and did not really support it, it was involved in all stages of the process. At the agency level, continuous briefings and discussions were held throughout the process with key agencies and those who were likely to be affected. Whenever possible, these discussions were held with representatives of the city administration, city council, MHSC and the United Way. Thus, agencies were able to examine the process, and having advance notice of its likely impact, had some opportunity to modify the proposal. The technical proposal was forged by confronting jurisdictional and political considerations.

The resulting proposal included a set of criteria and principles for the application of those criteria.[11] As a follow-through step, a set of suggestions for funding were adopted, based on a matrix format for application of criteria. MHSC staff and the city did independent rankings based on the allocation system, which were carried forward to the council. With some minor alterations, the council supported the allocation's process through adoption of two resolutions. By the time these resolutions were adopted, it was late in the budget cycle and the council decided to delay the process for a year.

The 1980 budget year brought the prospect of even greater cuts. Thus, the negotiations continued. To put the allocation system into place, the allocations process was developed into specific point recommendations and RFPs were sent out by the Columbus Community Services Department. A three-step process was followed:

1. criteria were applied to each program, scores were tabulated, and rankings were established;
2. the city discussed the priority rankings with each agency, both as a general system and the ranking of the agency's proposal; and
3. scores were assigned to the proposals and a set of recommendations were made and forwarded to the council.

Throughout the process MHSC provided review and comment. The council generally followed the recommendations in 1980.

About fourteen programs in eleven agencies were not refunded. A number of other agencies only received inflation increases. The commission's decision to terminate two other programs in a twelfth agency was based on management evaluations and criteria, not on program criteria. Twenty-two agencies received continued funding of all of their programs. Among the agencies receiving cuts, one did not have all of its programs terminated and continues to receive some funding. A phaseout has been funded for all eleven agencies that received complete cuts.[12] The MHSC-generated city GRS priority allocation process has continued in subsequent budget cycles.

According to the MHSC, some important successes and changes have resulted from implementation of the allocation plan:

1. the decisions were made based upon programs, not agencies;

2. increases averaging seven percent were permitted in programs maintained at full funding to meet inflation and full programming needs;

3. some shifting from lower to higher priority programs occurred with the addition of three new programs; and

4. a rationale was provided for the decisions that served as the basis for negotiations with agencies and the final recommendations, which were accepted by the council.

Negotiated Investment Strategy

MHSC's involvement in NIS was part of a larger intergovernmental problem-solving effort with Columbus; Gary, Indiana; and St. Paul, Minnesota. NIS is a labor-management process, in which intergovernmental actors who sit on federal, state, and city teams attempt to negotiate and bargain out their differences. The tricity efforts, centered around economic and community development, have been supported by the Kettering and Ford Foundations.[13] MHSC became involved in the Columbus effort because its president was a member of the city team, representing human service interests.

Since the larger effort centered on community development, the city was somewhat reluctant to include human services on the NIS agenda. However, MHSC mobilized support for including some issues. The board of trustees charged the cabinet of executives with identifying a set of issues. After a preliminary list was agreed upon, the cabinet approved them. Then, selected trustees and executives began informal negotiations with city officials. Ultimately, the mayor agreed to a limited number of issues.

MHSC's framing the issues at the local level was the first NIS step toward presenting issues to the state and federal teams. The particular issues included:

1. Changing the AFDC state plan for increasing federal-state reimbursement for foster care, thus reducing the local property tax burden;

2. Changing the state Medicaid plan to broaden reimbursement services to facilitate deinstitutionalization;

3. Securing special waivers under the Older Americans Act for "special needs" transportation out of nutrition programs; and

4. Developing improved access to services by allowing federal spending for intake/case management where it was restricted.

The second step was to carry these identified issues to the local negotiating team for agreement and forward them to the state and federal teams. The third step was to receive initial federal and state responses to the local position. The fourth step required the three teams to negotiate and synthesize the entire range of issues that might be dealt with. The fifth step was agenda-setting; some issues were dropped because of their complexity, while others were easily settled by administrative interpretation. All four of the human services issues were carried forth. The sixth step involved the actual negotiations on a tripartite basis. The federal and state teams had to check decisions through their own line program authorities. Local representatives generally were sanctioned to act by their respective administrations. The seventh and final step was the fruition of the negotiations through an agreement signed by the three parties involved. All four human services issues were negotiated through to reasonably satisfactory resolution.

Involvement of MHSC in NIS not only solved some nettlesome local human service problems, it also provided openings for the resolution of other problems. The entire experience taught the locals the process of dealing with state and federal officials and opened new doors with intergovernmental generalists who deal with human services. The affected agencies and governmental units developed new services and funding modes and relieved the local tax burden. The IGB gained new maturity and adeptness in honing out future solutions with the state capital and federal offices.

Deinstitutionalization and Group Home Zoning

MHSC's deinstitutionalization efforts were based on work done by the mental health board in 1977-1978, before the commission had a staff. The state legislature had passed a facilitative home zoning law that superseded existing restrictive local ordinances, even in home rule communities. After enactment of the state law, an effort to place a group home for the retarded in one of the higher property value neighborhoods in Columbus was thwarted, and legal action was threatened. An investigation of group homes (through examination of property values) was initiated by a Mental Health Board-generated task force when it received a small foundation grant for the MHSC-staffed Community Education Program. Its work continued into 1978, when the program funds expired. The study work was then transferred to MHSC and immediately broadened beyond mental retardation to include all group home populations. The commission study investigated procedures for starting group homes and examined three basic components: (1) licensure, (2) standards of operation, and (3) the effect on property values. The commission received cooperation and access to information from the Franklin County Board of Realtors for the latter component of the study. The study results were presented in a neutral fashion, particularly the procedural standards and licensure information.[14]

The property values component of the study titled, "The Non-Effect of Group Homes on Neighborhood Residential Property Values in Franklin County," involved rigorous statistical analysis of real estate transactions, which occurred before and after the location of eight group homes. Using the time that a parcel remained on the market and sales price as a percentage of list price as indicators of value, no statistical difference was found in the "before" and "after" measures of property values.[15] Although the results were considered conclusive, critics charged that the study was deficient in defining location date because neighborhood awareness was likely to be tied to the purchase date of the facility. Thus, MHSC replicated the earlier study started by the mental health board using the date of occupancy as the pivotal event. Five of the original eight group homes were retested and it was found that three homes showed no statistical difference in property values, and in two cases property values actually increased.[16]

The group home studies were completed in early 1980, at a time when the Columbus City Council was under pressure to pass a very broad, group zoning ordinance under the new state law. After extensive hearings and consideration of the studies by MHSC, the city council passed, and the Mayor signed, an ordinance that set criteria for group home zoning. The ordinance was a negotiated compromise between the proponents of unrestricted zoning and the proponents of restricted zoning. Unrestricted group home location was allowed for the elderly, mentally retarded, children, and the physically handicapped. Locational restrictions were placed on the mentally ill, substance abusers, and exoffenders. The criteria framed in the ordinance were delegated to the Board of Zoning Appeals for specific application. While a politically realistic compromise, the group home ordinance was considered a victory for the coalition of interests that supported it. Community activists generally thought that the MHSC studies were essential, providing hard data to the council. The council subsequently reinforced its earlier decision by refusing to hear appeals from the zoning board, pointing instead to the criteria set up in the ordinance.

The activity surrounding zoning led to an interest in the real impact of deinstitutionalization. There was particular concern over the impact of exinstitutionalized individuals on the local human services system. Attempts were made to get lists from the state agency of patients discharged from area mental health and mental retardation facilities and to follow their service patterns. These efforts caused several problems. MHSC experienced difficulty in tracking most clients and, because a case management system was not in place to follow clients, a lot of data were lost to the study. Also, the study met with resistance from client advocates who thought that following clients was a violation of their rights. Thus, while interesting, the results are considered inconclusive. Generally, the two studies suggest that most of the local impact is within the mental health or mental retardation system itself and that clients do not "spill over" into other human service programs.[17] As a result of data difficulties, this portion of the deinstitutionalization effort has been tabled. Originally, the elderly and exoffenders were at the focal point of the next deinstitutionalization effort, the elderly because of the NIS refinancing successes. MHSC, however, thinks that it must continue to refine the study methodology before pursuing this effort further.

Deinstitutionalization work continues through MHSC's slide-and-sound presentation to community groups. MHSC uses its research as a neutral introduction to a potentially emotional issue. Meanwhile, study methodology development continues, as it is expected to for some time, with MHSC research continuing to support decision-making information.

MHSC's subsequent work has generally followed on its developmental projects in policy management. In addition to improving the data base for deinstitutionalization studies, the IGB plans to expand some of its earlier work into longer-ranged efforts. A unified agency audit process and a unified budget and reporting form have been developed.

Work on the impact of the budget cuts went beyond dealing with the crisis of the moment. This intensive look at the human services system and its capacity lead to new efforts in developing a comprehensive planning and allocation process through a contingency planning process. This relatively sophisticated policy management process involves interjurisdictional efforts to: (1) analyze the impact of funding decisions; (2) identify which services should be maintained, reduced, terminated, or redefined; (3) formulate alternative local funding strategies that can replace federal and state sources; (4) determine alternative services delivery strategies; and, (5) develop an advocacy role at the state level.[18] One significant outcome of this process was that in making negotiations to direct funds towards areas of priority, a children's services levy passed in November of 1982 contained a provision whereby $1.8 million of the $9.6 million raised would be earmarked for public/private priority setting. The 1.6 mill levy was structured on the anticipated loss of revenue from federal and state funding reductions. By early 1983, the Franklin County Commission established a policy whereby all human-services-related public agencies eligible for a property tax levy are required to submit their proposals to MHSC for review and determination of the size of the levy.

As a result of the economic crisis of 1982-83, MHSC facilitated several efforts to deal with emergency situations. For example, the city and the county jointly funded a transient's shelter to house and protect Columbus's and Franklin County's homeless citizens. MHSC provided staff support to the city's Emergency Assistance Task Force, which cooperated with the private sector in a community-wide food drive. MHSC also helped with a coordinated effort by family service agencies to create an emergency family shelter.

MHSC has also been involved in intergovernmental monitoring and advocating. A committee is responsible for monitoring state activities with block grants and other human services programs. MHSC leaders have been lobbying for legislation creating a state-to-county block grant pass-through arrangement which gives local boards and county commissions decision-making authority. MHSC has also taken a proactive role regarding other state human services proposals. It has provided expert testimony about the effect on allocation of resources of earmarking Social Service Block grant funds at the state level and on the financial impact of allowing mental health and mental retardation boards to use medicaid dollars to finance commnity services as long as they provide the matching funds. The IGB demonstrated that this change in the language of the state legislation would not cost the state any money, but wold provide approximately $600,000 in new resources for mental health and $2 million for mental retardation. The language was subsequently changed by the legislature. Thus, this IGB's forward momentum further demonstrates its ability in policy management, intergovernmental negotiation and other aspects of IGM.

ASSESSMENT

MHSC has had a significant impact on the community's human services. It has produced a considerable volume of solid research reports in a short time. A number have led to direct action. The elite of the community openly advocate for human services and MHSC. The commission is unique because it combines the qualities of maturity, visibility, and credibility to solve significant human services problems. For these reasons, MHSC has contributed to the community's overall intergovernmental sophistication.

Whether it be for a given jurisdiction, like its city allocation plan, or across jurisdictions, as in the case of NIS and contingency planning, MHSC has become a forum through which parties representing local governments and sectors can manage their major intergovernmental human services concerns through policy management. This IGB has convened the major local actors, identified major issues of a cross-cutting nature, and engaged in processes that have emanated in integrated policies and programs. From its inception—when the citizens committee recommended that such a group engage in these activities—the commission has been designed as a forum for policy development. In its early days, it had to take on other work to develop credibility and political acceptance. It began to establish itself through program planning, training and consultation work for local agencies and jurisdictions. But after a few years the IGB began to help local officials manage intergovernmentally through numerous studies and processes developed to meet local needs. Moreover, policy management through activities like priority allocations, NIS, deinstitutionalization and contingency planning helped develop an essential capacity to manage for the community before state and federal governments. MHSC has thereby demonstrated the importance of translating local support and capacity into an intergovernmental negotiating ability.

A significant moving force behind the creation and backing of MHSC has been the need to gain broad-based community political support. Both the private and public sectors have relied heavily upon political connections and considerations for decision making in human services. This political atmosphere fosters a great deal of tension between the major funders and actors in the human services arena. MHSC is considered a buffer between these political pressures and the decision-making processes. As such, MHSC has not always agreed with local politicians. Through extensive, intimate working relationships and mutual respect and understanding between local politicians, the commission has promoted the political support necessary to make important recommendations.

Relationships with elected officials vary with each jurisdiction. The city's relationship with the commission was established early and was closer than that of the county when MHSC responded to a request from the city to design the GRS allocation plan. This early and close connection may also be due to the fact that the city had legislative and administrative staff to work with MHSC, whereas the county did not. Although the county's involvement with the commission evolved more slowly, it now has a consistent relationship and shares well-defined expectations with MHSC. Five commission projects have reinforced relationships with elected officials. These are: (1) the City Allocation Plan, which removed political heat from the city council concerning its past decision-making processes for allocating GRS funds to human services; (2) the city's zoning ordinance for the location of group homes, which designed criteria for establishing group homes in residential areas that were palatable to most city residents; (3) the refinancing project through NIS, which found ways to maximize the amount of open-ended, federal-state monies and free up more constrained local monies for other uses;[19] (4) MHSC review of proposed county levies, which provides local administrators and legislators with an independent review of adjustment to the local tax structure; and (5) the contingency planning process, which gives local officials an important process by which they can manage by "place" on the basis of local needs and priorities. The obvious advantages in these projects are foremost among the reasons why MHSC has the support of local elected officials.

The private sector has not been as involved in developing and using the products of the commission as has the public sector. This is attributable to the somewhat different nature of private system politics. The private sector fosters a close relationship between funders and providers, whereas the public sector has to be publicly accountable for its decisions. Throughout the country, the private sector uses political ties and business relationships to maintain its strong and continued existence in communities. Private sector funders, such as local United Ways, view organizations like MHSC as a threat to their autonomy, and some of this feeling exists in Columbus. As a consequence, the United Way of Franklin County is reported by respondents to be among the reluctant partners of MHSC. However, the two private foundations have placed MHSC in a "go between" role; the foundations send a number of service providers' grant proposals to MHSC staff for review and comment prior to formal consideration by the foundation trustees. In this way, the commission has influenced service providers' relationships with the private sector. Of course MHSC has affected the community's entire human services system by establishing a forum for public and private sector relationships and by allowing them to meet and openly discuss common concerns.

MHSC has nevertheless indirectly influenced the way agencies deliver services, albeit with great care because of the need to respect jurisdictions. The city allocation plan, contingency planning, refinancing, and resource development have all influenced the amount of money flowing to particular services, and thus have affected the mix of services. Some discussants reported that MHSC should strive to deal with services delivery more often, whereas others felt the commission's activities should be limited to coordination efforts at the policy level. One reason MHSC chooses not to affect services delivery more is that the private sector funders do not want MHSC involved in their services delivery. They would consider such action an encroachment on their independence as human service agencies. Furthermore, some trustees hesitate to become more involved with services delivery because of their concern that MHSC has more information and power than the individual component members. As a result, they have been threatened by MHSC and are reluctant to broach the "really tough" issues, such as differential costs of services, program evaluation, and elimination of unnecessary services. One discussant put it very succinctly; "joint management may be antithetical to each jurisdiction's needs."

Although state and federal officials are not included on the board of trustees, the MHSC staff maintains regular communication with important human services actors at the state and federal levels. MHSC staff and the cabinet of executives also educate lay people on the board in providing the necessary knowledge base to make intelligent decisions. They use this knowledge base, plus the staff's intergovernmental connections, to facilitate state and federal policy decisions that have been necessary for the success of some projects. The NIS process is the most obvious example. The MHSC president maintained an ongoing dialogue with DHHS regional officials and the Office of the Deputy Undersecretary for Intergovernmental Affairs to enable NIS federal approvals to proceed quickly through appropriate channels. The refinancing of the AFDC foster care component required constant communication with the state department of Public Welfare. MHSC recognized the complexity of the human service system and that any planning and coordinating entity must intervene at many levels before its impact is noticeable. Multilevel intervention requires a great deal of time, patience, and most importantly, "people power." One person described it simply as "stealth."

The work of this IGB underscores some important principles in IGM. MHSC's relative success has not been due to playing an exclusively political or a technical management game. It has played both and played them well. Trustees, executives and staff have developed a knack for involving a lot of relevant people in the process. Constant checking and touching bases for political feasibility, while the affected parties check technical work steps, has been important. But most important, this IGB has demonstrated a time honored principle of politics *and* management; that it is important to bring the important actors "into the tent," and possibly make adjustments with them, rather than having potentially hostile actors on the outside attempting to "bring the tent down." The high quality of the technical work, despite the fact that it is often politically negotiated, has lent the IGB a certain professional credibility that has no doubt carried it forward as it engaged in interlocal and state-federal negotiations. It demonstrates how good products can enhance IGM processes with capacity. Its propensity to educate and involve the highest level political, economic and community leaders in activities they are best suited for—advocating informing, and adjusting—once again shows that sometime it is important for managers to use other officials to help solve intergovernmental problems. The ability to solicit accommodations from state and federal funders did not come automatically. Rather, it was based on learning, developing abilities and ultimately gaining confidence in such processing. Finally, MHSC demonstrates how important it is to make interjurisdictional adjustments in IGM. In nearly each of the projects, there was a need to take a step back and look for avenues of accommodation between the parties. It began with MHSC's early decision not to engage in cross-jurisdictional planning until it was established and accepted. More important, work on projects like NIS, contingency planning and deinstitutionalization demonstrates how interjurisdictional adjustment is at the heart of IGM.

Notes to Chapter Five

1. Robert Agranoff and Alex Pattakos, "Human Services Policy Management: A Role for University Institutes," *Midwest Review of Public Administration* 12 (December 1978), 259.

2. Study Committee on Policy Management Assistance, "Executive Summary," *Public Administration Review* 35 (December 1975), Special Issue, 701.

3. Phillip M. Burgess, "Capacity Building and the Elements of Public Management," *Public Administration Review* 35 (December 1975), Special Issue, 706.

4. City of Columbus. *City Council Resolution. No. 66X-75.* Approved 24 February, 1975.

5. Citizen's Committee for Human Services. *Final Report and Recommendations* (Columbus, Ohio, CCHS, 1976), 4.

6. Barry Mastrine. "The Development and Implementation of the Metropolitan Human Services Commission of Columbus/Franklin County, Ohio," (Paper presented at the First National Network Building Conference, June 1980), 147-148.

7. *Amended Code of Regulations of Metropolitan Human Resources Commission,* 1980.

8. *Ibid.*

9. Mastrine, "Development and Implementation," 163.

10. *Ibid.*

11. Metropolitan Human Services Commission. *Recommended Social Services Allocation Policies for the City of Columbus Department of Community Services.* 11 September, 1980, 4.

12. MHSC. Long Range Planning Allocations.

13. Mastrine, 161.

14. MHSC. *Property Acquisition Study,* August 1979.

15. MHSC. *The Non-Effect of Group Homes on Neighborhood Residential Property Values in Franklin County,* August 1979, 1.

16. MHSC. *Group Homes and Property Values: A Second Look,* August 1980, 8.

17. MHSC. *The Impact on Human Service Resources Associated with the Discharge of Persons from Central Ohio Psychiatric Hospital in Franklin County, Ohio During 1980,* March 1981, 55; MHSC. *The Impact on Human Service*

Resources Associated with the Discharge of Persons from Institutions for Mentally Retarded and Developmentally Disabled, March 1981, 16-19.

18. David A. Connell, "Dealing with Fund Reductions through Interagency Contingency Planning," in *Human Services on a Limited Budget*, ed. Robert Agranoff (Washington, D.C.: International City Management Association, 1983), 199.

19. Mastrine, "Development and Implementation," 161.

CHAPTER SIX

Coordination Through a Council of Governments: The Pueblo Human Resources Commission

The growth of federal assistance, coupled with the proliferation of local governmental units and substate functional programs, made coordination a popular IGM strategy. During the 1970s coordination was most likely to be written into enabling legislation or to become part of official policy. One formal manifestation of this attempt to get governments and quasi governments to work together is the substate regional planning and development organization, or councils of governments (COG) movement.

COG is a term used for a variety of organizations representing several governments, governed by elected officials of member governments, with a staff paid by member fees and grants and contracts. COGs were perhaps strongest during the 1970s and early 1980s, created by federal regional planning grants and regional clearinghouse functions under U.S. Office of Management Budget Circular A-95. Under this 1969 order, state and substate areas were given broad powers to review, coordinate and plan for federal programs.[1] The success and effectiveness of COGs varied considerably across the country; some complied minimal with federal requirements while others actively combined local needs and priorities with a federally-driven process. The Pueblo Human Resources Commission* (HRC), a component unit of the Pueblo Area Council of Governments (PACOG), is an IGB that has been relatively successful in

---

*The name of HRC was changed to Pueblo Health and Human Services Commission in 1984.

meeting local coordination and planning needs through a combination of an A-95 and its own processes. HRC's distinctive competence has been coordination through planning and grants management, backed with strong elected official support. In many ways, it proves that a COG can perform an important role—in this case in human development and services—in helping local governments understand and operate a bewildering array of federal, state, and local programs.

The Pueblo Human Resources Commission operates under PACOG through an eighteen-member commission appointed by the elected officials on PACOG. Commissioners are citizen activists in the community who come from several walks of life; about half of them work in public programs. Most HRC work is done by its staff, headed by an executive director who is appointed by HRC. Since it was formed in 1972, HRC has been involved in several notable intergovernmental issues of planning and coordination, including: review, allocation recommendations, and monitoring of GRS funds; staffing the A-95 clearinghouse review of health and human services grant applications; development of coordination, particularly within "sectors" of human services; providing staff support, information, and advice to elected officials; offering technical assistance for agencies; engaging in intergovernmental negotiation on behalf of governments and agencies; and development of a planning system. At one time HRC also operated programs. With the exception of its sponsorship and oversight of the Area Agency on Aging—itself essentially a planning and coordination unit—HRC no longer operates any programs.

The city and county of Pueblo comprise the southernmost metropolitan area in Colorado, with a population of about 140,000 people. More than eighty percent of these people reside in Pueblo, an industrial city that includes a large steel mill (which closed after this research was conducted), CF&I, which employs over 6,500 people, two major federal government installations, the largest stage mental hospital in Colorado, and a state university. The rest of the county is primarily farm and ranch land. The Pueblo city and county governments are the dominant local governments, there is little population in incorporated areas outside Pueblo City. The city is governed by a council-manager form of government, with seven council members elected on a nonpartisan ballot. Because there is no mayor, the council president serves as ceremonial head of government. The county is governed by three commissioners elected on a partisan ballot and administratively served by a county manager.

There are over 250 public and private human services agencies in Pueblo with the usual public/private array of services. The Colorado welfare system is a combination county-administered and state-operated system, but in essence it is a state system. The state department of social services, through its county offices, administers the usual array of income maintenance programs, Medicaid, Food Stamps, and Title XX. In Colorado, Title XX is spent almost entirely within the Department of Social Services; there is little contracting through other state departments or with private agencies. In Pueblo, a large number of private nonprofit agencies have turned to local government GRS for the type of social services assistance Title XX provides elsewhere. Twenty percent of city and county revenue sharing, about $800,000 annually, has been allocated to human services agencies. The United Way program raised $700,000 in funds in 1980, with nearly half coming from CF&I donations. The United Way once had a separate Health and Welfare Planning Council, but it merged with a United Way Planning Committee in 1976. Many agencies are funded by both local government and United Way, and cooperation between these two funders is increasing.

DEVELOPMENT AND OPERATION

IGB Formation

The Pueblo Human Resources Commission is a product of earlier efforts in the physical planning area. Prior to the development of PACOG, there was a Pueblo County Planning Commission, operated primarily with HUD 701 funds. In 1971, the governor divided the state into twelve management and planning regions, and the establishment of councils of government was encouraged. When Pueblo elected officials set up their COG, neither the city nor the county had its own planning staff; instead, they both relied on the work of the old Regional Planning Commission (RPC). Since there already was a physical planning group, the elected officials thought it necessary to have a social planning group to deal with the growing number of federal and federal-state social programs. Thus, within a year of the creation of PACOG, there were two commissions—RPC and HRC.

The chief force behind PACOG and HRC was the Pueblo city manager, who served in Pueblo from 1966 to 1984. In the early 1970s he believed that the COG needed to develop a social element in its planning to parallel the physical side. The initial goal was to do comprehensive social planning. However, very soon after HRC was created, a new thrust was evident. Several local groups sought local government financial support from GRS and CDBGs. Elected officials had no sound means of judging the adequacy of proposals, the extent of community need, the extent to which a proposal would duplicate existing services, or the degree to which service gaps existed. Decision-makers needed a mechanism to investigate these issues in the local system, listen to applicants, and sift out recommendations. Thus, the need for a review of allocations within the context of planning led to the development of a two-tiered system, in which a citizen's group—HRC—and its staff became responsible for review and recommendations.

Formation of HRC was a fairly easy effort. Its creation was "negotiated" through the members of PACOG and voted on. Commissioners were appointed by PACOG, and they still are. The new HRC developed a search-and-screen process for an executive director for HRC appointment. In short time, the new commission was staffed and the initial work began.

Early HRC project efforts set it on a course that delayed general planning. Work soon began on A-95 review—the Project Notification and Review System. The A-95 process eventually became a routine part of HRC and despite the absence of a comprehensive plan with which to make such judgments, proposals are scrutinized within the general context of the commission's and PACOG's perceptions of "community needs." Work on revenue-sharing allocations and contract monitoring was another important early effort. Some isolated coordination efforts were also made, particularly in response to issues arising from the allocation process.

IGB Structure

The membership of PACOG consists of all seven members of the city council, all three county commissioners, one member each from District 60 and 70 school boards, and one member of the water board. These five represent every unit of government in Pueblo County.[2] PACOG's thirteen members act on a variety of matters relating to planning and coordination, and operationally they have relied on four commissions: the Pueblo Development Commission, the Pueblo Clean Community Commission, the Regional Planning Commission, and the Human Resources Commission.

In 1981, PACOG operated with the four commissions, each under a relatively independent direction (see Table VI.1). The city manager is the nominal executive director, but he deliberately exercises little substantive leadership, leaving it to the four commission leaders and their staffs. The four commissions appeared to relate to PACOG in a similar way. However, major change was undertaken in PACOG in 1982 when both the development commission and clean community commission were transferred to private auspices. This did not affect the two remaining commissions.

HRC is made up of eighteen citizens appointed by PACOG for staggered terms. The chair is elected by the members of the commission who come from all segments of the community. While not necessarily community leaders, these members are well respected and knowledgeable citizens. They give an important citizen's review dimension to community human resource decisions.

Table 6.1   Pueblo Area Council of Governments

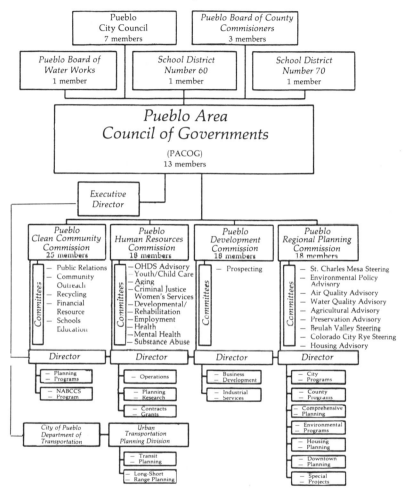

Most HRC funding has come through PACOG. Each of the five-member governments pay COG dues and then a single allocation is made to HRC to finance its operations. Since the bulk of the dues are paid by the city and county, most of HRC's money comes from these two government bodies. Of course, most of the work performed directly benefits them. A federal grant provides additional funding for planning and coordination work.

Decision Framework and Role of Key Actors

HRC, as a group, does most of its work through standing committees. An executive committee made up of officers provides administrative guidance and conducts business between meetings. A special federal grant steering committee, consisting of categorical or program are representatives, was created to oversee and comment on activities relating to planning (see Table 6.1).

Elected officials are very involved in the work of HRC because city and county officials must act on recommendations of the commission. All major actions are transmitted for a decision. Decisions are made either by PACOG or the respective government, but it makes little difference since all PACOG decisions ultimately return to the affected unit of government. The process guarantees high-level decision-maker involvement.

Current HRC operations reflect the way PACOG elected officials function. Although PACOG is made up of five different units of government, the ten city-county elected officials appear to be key members, particularly with regard to HRC. Since only the two general purpose governments directly fund human services programs, they have a special relationship with HRC. They formally work with HRC in three ways. First, as ten of the thirteen members of PACOG, they are a powerful block in any formal processes, such as voting. Second, the city council and the county commissioners hold regular monthly joint work sessions, where HRC issues are discussed. Third, the city and county also work individually on an informal basis with HRC. The city holds weekly informal work sessions of its own, in which HRC-related business is covered. In addition to these informal means, HRC staff work on elected officials' requests on an individual basis.

In late 1982 the informal lines of authority between the elected officials and HRC staff were made formal. PACOG assumed the official policy-making role of HRC by having the staff report directly to COG. Since PACOG is the prime agent for human services system changes and staff have moved informally closer to the actual decision-makers, it was made official. HRC officially adopted the advisory role it actually had all along, reviewing proposals and making recommendations to PACOG.

United Way involvement with HRC is increasing, but is still considered indirect. As a COG, there would be no way to provide a seat for a nongovernmental group like the United Way in the top decision-making body. However, United Way is ordinarily consulted before HRC appointments are made, and at least two persons sit simultaneously on the United Way board and HRC. There is also regular contact at the staff level. One HRC staff member sits as an ex-officio member of the United

Way Allocations Committee. At the administrative level, a formal working agreement (Table VI.2) signed in 1981 specifies regular working meetings at both administrative and staff levels and pledges to share information and work towards joint planning and allocation.[3]

Agencies are frequently called upon to work with HRC. Any time an issue is of specific interest to an "umbrella agency" or a set of individual agencies, agency representatives are asked to lend their expertise. In the past few years, there has been considerable contact over interagency coordination by functional area. In 1979, the HRC assisted in the development of the Pueblo County Human Services Coalition, which is made up of directors of over twenty-five leading provider agencies in Pueblo. Originally brought together for coordination across functional areas, the coalition functioned as an advocate. Since then it has become involved in a number of substantive projects, including the development of a resource directory, an information and referral service, and the preparation of position papers on a number of community issues.

Agenda and Development

The HRC agenda-setting process is open and accessible. Issues can be brought to the attention of HRC by elected officials individually or by their respective legislative body, PACOG (officially), or by the city or county manager. Issues also come from human services agencies or groups of agencies. Citizens can suggest issues for the agenda, but they are carefully screened to ensure that individual "casework" is not done. Often a state or federal action or proposal will trigger an issue that requires consideration. Finally, the commission itself identifies matters of concern, particularly at its annual work retreat. They may come complete with priorities, whereas issues from other sources tend to be dealt with on an ad hoc basis.

Policy decisions by HRC ordinarily follow this sequence:

1. The issue is transmitted to the commission from one of the several sources identified above.

2. A preliminary analysis is performed by staff to see if HRC should become involved.

3. If it appears to be appropriate, the issue is brought before the commission at its regular meeting.

4. HRC considers the issue, and if it decides it is appropriate, the issue officially becomes an agenda item and is included in the work plan.

5. The policy issue goes back to the staff for research, to an HRC committee, or to a special group of agency representatives (if it is a very specialized issue). In the latter case, if an "umbrella group" (i.e., a lead organization, such as the Community Mental Health Panel, or a planning

Table VI.2 "Management Letter of Understanding"

This "Letter of Understanding" entered into this 5/7/81 day of March 1981, by and between the Human Resources Commission (hereinafter referred to as HRC) staff and United Way of Pueblo, Inc., staff (hereinafter referred to as United Way.)

WHEREAS, HRC and United Way are responsible monitoring and planning agencies for Human Services; and

WHEREAS, HRC and United way staff are involved in making recommendations for Human Services Programs; and

WHEREAS, HRC and United Way are involved in the resource inventory for Human Services; and

WHEREAS, HRC and United Way are responsible for receiving and reviewing reporting systems and Needs Assessment;

NOW THEREFORE, in consideration of the above and of the following and of the mutual covenants and agreements herein contained, HRC staff and United Way staff agree as follows:

1. Continue to share information on a monthly basis regarding contracted Human Service Agencies.
2. Coordinate Planning Activities of Human Services in Pueblo County.
3. Constantly share and update resources available for Human Services.
4. Jointly review and work towards similar reporting systems and allocation procedures for Human Services.
5. Shall meet on the 1st Tuesday of the month at 10:00 to discuss the development and implementation of the above items.
6. Notices of meetings, correspondence and agendas shall be mailed to the following adresses:

HRC	—	#1 City Hall Place Pueblo, CO 81003
United Way	—	229 Colorado Avenue Pueblo, CO 81004

IN WITNESS WHEREOF, HRC staff and United Way staff have executed this Agreement as of the day and year first above written.

Human Resources Commission
City and County Government

By_____
          Executive Director

United Way of Pueblo County Inc.

By_____
          Executive Director

council, such as the Child Care Council) exists in a particular categorical area, the issue may go to that group for consideration.

6. The HRC staff gathers and organizes relevant information to present to the commission.

7. The research report on the issue is considered by HRC. Ordinarily, the staff plays an important role in sifting and presenting the information. Information is presented in a condensed review form by participating staff and HRC members ask them questions. Action is taken by HRC, either through consensus building or by an official vote. In most cases, group problem solving is by voting. HRC, with eighteen members, is considered large and it is felt that it would be impossible to reach consensus most of the time.

8. After an action is taken, it is transmitted to PACOG or to the city council or the county commissioners, depending on the origin of implications of the action. If the action is administrative in nature, it is transmitted directly to the person making the inquiry.

Elected official action by PACOG has proceeded more informally. Staff generally bring recommendations to the affected governmental unit— usually the city or county—or to the COG as a whole. Issues are normally forwarded for consideration by the city or county managers. Usually, they will first be discussed at the informal working sessions in which HRC staff are present to answer questions. If the issue needs formal action, it is then put on the official agenda of the body that needs to take action.

The HRC agenda has been driven by the wishes of its funders, the elected officials. A lot of the work is systematic and well thought-out, although HRC staff also perform "fire fighting" or problem-solving work for PACOG officials. In any event, HRC's agenda has been largely what PACOG wishes it to be. The agenda has included some very difficult issues, including recommendations to deny fund requests or the pursuit of agency consolidation. HRC has also made many suggestions for new service avenues which, because of cost implications, have not always been welcomed by local officials. In short, it has been the vehicle for working out many tough issues that elected officials would otherwise have confronted on their own. This response posture has slowed HRC's entry into policy or comprehensive planning because planning is a more difficult, long-term procedure for elected officials.

PROJECTS

An examination of any annual report of PACOG/HRC reveals its basic orientation to coordination through planning and project review, blended with intergovernmental negotiation and assistance. Projects highlighted here—A-95 review, GRS allocations, and sector planning and coordination—exemplify how a COG can play a major role in human services development through problem solving at the local level. As the project accounts demonstrate, achievement has come about through staff work, agency participation, and general purpose government official support.

A-95 Review

As mentioned, A-95 provides state, regional, and local organizations, agencies, and individuals with the opportunity to review and comment on applications for specific federal programs; it also allows them to coordinate their policies, plans, and programs with those of the applicants.* The A-95 review and comment process have not been considered by PACOG as merely routine—as has been the case with many other COGs—but as a serious process that attempts to match proposals with local policy development. In brief, the process is similar to most substate clearinghouse efforts, with notification, review and comment, and follow-up phases. HRC serves as the preliminary review agency for PACOG. A very detailed review manual has been prepared for applicant agencies, and local clearinghouse reviews are based on a common format; project description, goals and objectives, budget information, impact on Pueblo County, linkages with Pueblo County agencies, and evaluation/measurement guidelines.[4] HRC expects sufficient lead time for staff analysis and local agency comment before the commission reviews proposal projects at its regular monthly meeting. Reviews are based on written staff reports and action is taken by HRC. Review decisions are then forwarded to PACOG for formal action. Sixty-four reviews were conducted in 1980: twenty-four of those concentrated on Pueblo County; thirty-three were statewide; four state/regional in scope, and three were entirely national in implication. PACOG supported the action of HRC in all but eight cases.[5] The greatest number of reviews (thirty) came in the health and aging areas.[6]

The A-95 review process has been supported by the staff who, in turn, have encouraged both the commission and PACOG to take the process seriously and use it as a part of an overall approach. Originally, A-95 was considered a minor step toward bringing tax dollars back to the community in the form of new programs. But staff reviews have attempted to examine applications in the light of what elected officials have articulated as community goals. Perhaps the most important issue has been the need for coordination between agencies and efforts to avoid

---

*(Note: A-95 was replaced in late 1983 by Executive Orders 12372/12416, which gave states the flexibility to design their own intergovernmental review and comment processes.)

duplication. As long as discretionary money is available, elected officials feel strongly that service gaps can best be filled with local dollars after state and federal sources have been exhausted. Of course, local politics is also part of the formula. Somehow key support groups and other interests are factored in. Staff reviews may also consider the needs or program directions as articulated by the growing number of functional area "councils" of providers. As the new planning system is developed, it is expected that reviews can be conducted within an improved information context. In these ways A-95 review is considered to be an important element in policy development and management.

GRS Allocation Process

The GRS allocations process works through HRC staff who offer direct allocation recommendations, contract development, contract monitoring, and technical assistance for the city and county. The monitoring and technical assistance functions also involve HRC's oversight of the large "delegate" agency programs operated by the various governmental units. In funding other agencies, the city and county actually make the allocations and HRC operates as their staff arm in administration of GRS funded agencies. All human services GRS money goes to nonprofit agencies outside of government: the local governments operate no programs. HRC also plays a related role in providing staff work and advice in human services-related CDBG funds, but there is no accompanying administrative function.

The GRS process operates on an annual cycle that includes six phases:

1. Planning, in which needs assessments and resource inventories are made of the community to identify new program needs, areas of potential duplication, service gaps and so on. Agencies themselves are expected to update their needs assessment and resource inventories. Whenever possible, information is sought from various community advisory councils about their perceptions of needs and priorities. Also, the inventory and needs assessment efforts associated with the OHDS grant will be used at this stage.

2. Meetings are held with the two groups of elected officials to review GRS procedures, dates, available funds, as well as to receive input on suggested areas of interest and emphasis.

3. Public notice is made of the availability of GRS funds, and RFP packets are made available to potential applicant agencies. Proposals are expected to follow a common format, including a complete budget and information on governance and organization. A 29-item list of criteria for proposal evaluation is included in the RFP.

4. Proposals are reviewed by the HRC staff, who make recommendations to the commission. At the commission meeting, during which allo-

cations are considered, the same criteria are independently applied and reported back to the full HRC. If differences exist, they are discussed and ironed out, and recommendations are made to the elected officials.

5. City and county officials make their final allocations during their respective budget process, by each jurisdiction.[7]

6. Contracts between the funding unit of government and the agency are drawn up by HRC and signed. In addition, fund accounts for each granted agency are established, administered by the city and county, and monitored by HRC. This process ordinarily operates on a calendar year cycle, with contracts being drawn up in December and starting dates in January (see Table VI.3).[8]

The monitoring phase begins when the contracts and fund accounts are established. An extensive "contracts and monitoring manual" places in writing all of the expectations agencies are required to follow.[9] Early in January, HRC staff hold individual meetings with contract agency representatives (director and board chair) to discuss the contract and its implications. This annual meeting is a requirement before the first quarterly "advance payment" is made. At this time, quarterly reporting requirements, due dates, conditions, and assurances are discussed. About thirty agencies are involved from year to year, and another eight to ten agencies are normally funded on a single-year basis. The quarterly reports become the initial input for agency oversight. For the three largest agencies that receive the bulk of the money—called delegate agencies because they conduct major programs as agents of the city, county, and PACOG—both field and desk audits are made. These agencies are the Community Action Program, Head Start, and the Area Agency on Aging. At least once a year an on-site visit is made that examines agency management, services delivery issues, client flow and levels of client services, and community perceptions of agency performance. Other agencies are generally not field monitored because of the staff work load. Desk monitoring is followed based on the quarterly reports. Both desk and field monitoring are conducted with a guide containing questions and measures of performance on governance, fiscal administration, financial accounting, property management, personnel, facilities management, planning and budgeting, management information, staff qualifications, service delivery indicators, and community relationships.[10] Findings from the monitoring are transmitted to the agency in writing and during meetings. In 1980, over 82 monitoring meetings were held with agencies to discuss problems in the areas of programming, fiscal matters, or statistics. In many cases a meeting can lead to an easy adjustment and the issue is resolved. If an agency is unable to follow through on a recommendation, technical assistance is provided by HRC staff to develop a solution. In the rare case that an agency will not follow a suggested practice or accept technical assistance, HRC will take the issue up with appropriate elected officials.

Table 6.3 Pueblo Human Resources
Commission Revenue Sharing Process

Planning	Program Development (Meet With Elected Officials)	Program Development	Human Resources Commission Makes Its Recommendations And Forwards To Elected Officials	Resource Allocation By General Purpose Governments	Funded Allocation Contract Development
Jan.–April	April	May	July	Oct.–Nov.	Nov.–Dec.
Needs Assessment	Elected Officials City County	Requests for Proposals General Revenue Sharing	Human Resource Commission Recommendations	General Revenue Sharing	City / County
Resource Inventory				City County "Earmarking" S S Community Board Organization	Fund Accounts PHRC

Public Participation

The allocations and monitoring role HRC plays in the city-county process places it in a strategic position with elected officials and community agencies. Ordinarily HRC and the elected officials reach a mutual understanding of what the GRS process is to address, with varying agendas of provider agencies and general government to be worked out. HRC is the essential go-between in this process.

Sector Planning and Coordination

The planning process, supported by a grant from the Office of Human Development Services (OHDS), U.S. department of Health and Human Services, is expected to be a major link with other HRC activities. Basically, the project is to expand and make effective the coordination, communication, and planning process for human services. The planning process is expected to deal with the following service areas: aging, criminal justice, education, employment, drug and alcohol, veterans services, mental health, health, child care, women's services, advocacy services, and volunteer services.[11] Four action steps, or objectives, have been determined as essential in carrying out this process.

1. Streamline and link the human service maze to increase the amount of direct services to families.

2. Identify multiple and coordinated approaches that have a holistic emphasis of treatment to families.

3. Develop a human services plan that includes comprehension of the relationship of agencies to sound service delivery, of cross-program nature and accountability, and of the impact on the family unit.

4. Review the perspective of strengthening the family unit in service delivery, the client linkage to family, and the overall emphasis of dignified treatment, easy access, and quality of life issues.[12]

Considerable efforts already have been made toward meeting the first three objectives. A number of developments have occurred in the area of coordination, particularly in substance abuse and the children's services areas. HRC was instrumental in getting the drug and alcohol providers and board members to develop the Substance Abuse Council. This council, with staff assistance from HRC, is working toward the development of a continuum of combined services, including detoxification, out-patient care, and a half-way house. In addition, agencies represented on the Substance Abuse Council are planning to develop prevention activities on a joint basis. In the child care area, HRC was instrumental in getting all the day care agencies to develop the Child Care Council (CCC). This was an integral part of the overall coordination efforts related to the OHDS grant that grew out of the GRS allocations process. Several small agencies were submitting vastly different proposals, particularly in terms of costs, and it was a difficult situation for both HRC and the elected officials to understand. As a consequence, CCC developed a joint application process in which each agency has standardized wage scales, career ladders, job descriptions, and fee scales. While each agency maintains its own budget, all now have the same goals and objectives, making it much easier to allocate. In addition, all CCC day care providers submit to a field program audit team of one person from a peer agency, one outside person, and one HRC member. CCC also engages in joint auditing and group purchasing and has developed standardized parent handbooks and enrollment packages. CCC is now going beyond this joint activity to do needs assessments and planning and in the process will bring in other child-serving agencies. Other coordination activities are being developed in women's services, youth services, volunteer services, employment services, and mental health services.

A second aspect of the planning effort is resource development. One resource element is the creation of a central library on human services information at HRC headquarters. Another is the Conference Series of workshops for the commission itself, agencies, and elected officials. Also, a steering committee was formed as a condition of the OHDS grant, which is composed of representatives of the twelve functional areas who oversee all planning activities.

Planning functions are the third aspect of sector planning and coordination. Most of the planning work to date has been in service inventories and needs assessment. When the inventory work was initiated, several external taxonomics were explored and a hybrid "grid system," encompassing twenty different services and eight clientele groups, was adopted. Using the information supplied by the funded agencies, United Way, and state and federal sources, a matrix of services and funding sources was generated. The entire planning and research staff of HRC will analyze these data, and a report will be made to HRC and elected officials. This information will then become one important component in the planning system. The needs assessment effort is planned to be a secondary analysis of the needs assessments performed by agencies and functional area councils. Outstanding needs assessments will be filled in with key informant surveys, to be used when the 1980 census data are available. This approach was selected to avoid duplication of effort and because of limited research resources. The initial needs assessment process is planned to be available for the next GRS allocations process. It is expected that this process will be updated annually. After the needs assessment is completed, it and the resource inventory will be used to conduct a qualitative analysis of gaps and overlaps in services. These steps will then be documented in a Blue Series manual, as part of the information sharing component of the grant.

The planning process in Pueblo is designed to be consistent with the HRC approach. It builds upon the work of existing agencies and is linked with the allocation process. It can also be an important source of information for the A-95 review process. Perhaps most important, it builds upon previous coordination efforts, in response to both agency needs and elected officials' wishes.

HRC/PACOG has built on these efforts through other relevant initiatives. A special task force on human services changes was formed to review local implications of federal funding cutbacks, block grant implications, and other new challenges. In addition, in 1983, HRC/PACOG began two new efforts at developing public/private linkages with business and labor for local comprehensive planning and between local public/private interests and the state and federal governments. The latter is to serve in an advisory capacity representing a broad base of interests, reviewing changes and recommending mechanisms for shifting priorities, defining agency responsibilities, delivering services and phasing out programs. Thus, future HRC efforts extend their approach, using the planning process to improve coordination, achieve some agency or process consolidation, and to provide improved decision-making information.

ASSESSMENT

Since the Pueblo IGB is part of a COG, its work is explicitly intergovernmental. As a substate planning area, it has an agenda that includes both comprehensive area-wide planning and individual problem-solving efforts. The initial aim of PACOG/HRC was social development planning within a local context using federal A-95 authorization and control over certain federal funding streams that pass through general purpose governments. HRC staff and commissioners found that because of their close ties to the local elected officials and managers who controlled these funding streams, they had to work on problems and adjustments, delaying attempts at comprehensive social development planning. But within a decade, HRC has moved towards this aim in the work it has accomplished, not so much by the development of a comprehensive plan to match individual decisions against, but by making its problem-solving projects more systematic. Movement in this direction includes the way PACOG/HRC has used A-95 review, the GRS allocation and management process, planning and coordination by subsectors of human services, its work in bringing various sectors together, and in negotiation and advocacy with state and federal governments. As local officials and HRC staff and commissioners approach intergovernmental problems, they have developed means that enhance their ability to understand and manage the human services system in a more coordinated fashion.

HRC activities have thus shaped its character as a brokering, coordinating and decision-making body. As a nonservice delivery agency primarily funded by local sources it has diligently responded to the needs of elected officials by providing some means of decision-making support. Projects are recognized as essential and responsive, however limiting. The character of its planning appears to be a functional area-by-functional-area basis. At this stage in HRC's development, overall policy development or comprehensive social planning is not yet part of project efforts; however, planning and development activities, such as the major effort in streamlining child care agency relationships with general government, may "bubble up" into a more general, if not more comprehensive, planning role for HRC.

HRC obviously has extremely close ties to local elected officials. The commission's work on allocations, A-95, and coordination has not only provided an important information service, it has been an extremely important political buffer for the city council and the county commission. In the process of investigating, reviewing, and reporting, HRC gathers reams of documentation, engages in dozens of small meetings with agency administrators and board members, and listens to hundreds of hours of testimony. These activities allow the commission to provide a forum for detailed and considered opinion inaccessible to most elected officials. Elected officials feel this is an extremely important function, since their need to deal with other areas, such as roads, water, sanitation, and public safety prevent as detailed a look at human services as HRC can provide.

The information service is reported as particularly important politically when new agencies or programs emerge in the community. Elected officials can rely on staff reports to get them "off the hook." For example, when a new drug program applied to the city for out-of-cycle GRS funding, the application was turned over to HRC, which investigated the program and alternative funding sources. Its report noted that there was, indeed, a need for such a program, but that state funds were available. Local funds were not recommended. Funding recommendations from HRC make it much easier for elected officials to say "no" since their final decision is preceded by staff research and a citizen board. Of course, the HRC process can cut both ways: a positive recommendation can provide crucial political support. In all the HRC functions, information of a neutral, supportive, or critical nature makes it easier for the council person or commissioner to render an informed decision.

The commission and staff also provide an important point of focus between the various human services interests and elected officials. In many ways, HRC is the "funnel" through which service delivery agencies, the United Way, and state and federal officials deal with local elected officials. When an intergovernmental, public/private, or agency/government issue in human services is put on the agenda, PACOG as a group, or an individual unit of government represented on PACOG, makes it an HRC function. Constant reinforcement of this process over a decade has made the commission recognized and respected, if not always welcomed.

State and federal relationships with HRC have been generally positive and constructive. HRC staff have provided important brokerage functions between local agencies and organizations and the two governmental levels. In this regard, a lot of the contact has been with counterpart generalists in the governor's office and the HSS regional office and, through time, to program officials. Brokerage has occurred over new funding sources and interpretation and adjustments in rules and regulations. In addition, HRC staff have been active at both state and federal levels in demonstration projects. HRC staff participated in the OHDS planning requirement simplication effort and in providing technical assistance in planning, allocation, and coordination to the energy-impacted communities of western Colorado. In general, the work of HRC is valued by generalist state and federal officials; they consider it an important reference point and means of contact. Relationships with state human services agencies and programs have been mixed. Agencies are sometimes uncomfortable with HRC as an interpreter, or broker, of programs. They feel the "double-barreled shot" of the local program official and HRC sometimes puts them in a difficult, if not tenuous, position. On the other hand, HRC feels that this type of brokering is essential if it is to represent general government issues.

The work of PACOG/HRC demonstrates the variety of intergovernmental problems that emerge as a result of growth and complexity in the system. In a general sense, the city and county managers and elected officials have sought to understand that system and manage it in a coordinated fashion that is responsive to funder program aims and local needs. After a decade, they no doubt recognize that this is a difficult task no magic managerial processes apply. Rather, success requires incremental steps, such as A-95 review with a local purpose, regarding GRS as a program, and enticing various functional areas to plan and coordinate. Pueblo also demonstrates how important it is for elected officials and top administrators to buy into, participate in, and use their power in the IGM process. They are needed to make the necessary adjustments work. Moreover, without a key decision-maker agenda to be played out, plans would perhaps have been more elegant, but probably in "the closet." With official interest, however unsystematic, an agenda with meaning can be played out. At the same time, Pueblo again demonstrates how important staff-level research can be in supporting officials' decisions. The problem investigation stage was not taken lightly; evidence of legal feasibility and technical possibility proved to be valuable tools to combine with political judgment. Armed with case, or problem-specific, information matched with perceptions of local directions, if not written plans, PACOG/HRC has been able intergovernmentally to manage human services programs.

Notes to Chapter 6

1. Raymond A. Shapek, *Managing Federalism: Evolution and Development of the Grant-in-Aid System* (Charlottesville, Va.: Community Collaborators, 1981), 60.

2. Pueblo Human Resources Commission, *A Human Services Planning Cycle Model: Strategies for Development, Implementation, and Transferred Replication of Human Service Technology*. Pueblo, Colorado, HRC, April 1981, 7.

3. "Management Letter of Understanding," Communique between the Human Resources Commission Staff and United Way of Pueblo, Inc., Staff, 5 May, 1981.

4. Pueblo Human Resources Commission, *A-95 Review Process Manual*, Pueblo, Colorado, HRC, undated, 15.

5. Pueblo Human Resources Commission, *1980 A-95 Review: Year End Report*, Pueblo, Colorado, HRC, 31 December, 1980, 4.

6. *Ibid.*, 5.

7. Pueblo Human Resources Commission, *Contracts and Monitoring Division*, Pueblo, Colorado, HRC, 1981, Sec. 4, 1-4.

8. *Ibid.*, Sec. 1, 1.

9. *Ibid.*, Sec. 2.

10. Pueblo Human Resources Commission, *Monitoring Guidelines*, Pueblo, Colorado, HRC, undated.

11. HRC, *A Human Services Planning*, 22.

12. *Ibid.*, 18.

CHAPTER SEVEN

Achieving Service Delivery Reform: The Baltimore Blueprint

Reform efforts designed to change public services rarely survive program and administrative alterations to affect the way services are delivered. The Baltimore project departs from this model in that its primary focus is to identify and change barriers to services as they impact clients. Its philosophy and approach proved to be both a distinguishing characteristic and a major weakness that stalled progress of the IGB.

The service delivery approach is distinguished by its direct focus on the nexus between the human services provider and the individual client/consumer,[1] in order to counteract such problems as fragmentation, inaccessibility, discontinuity and lack of accountability.[2] Service reform is an intergovernmental strategy identified by the federal government since the early 1970s. The former Department of Health, Education and Welfare, for example, called for a "wholistic approach to the individual and family unit" as a strategy.[3] The Blueprint philosophy was formed around services delivery approach principles; reform identification must begin at the service delivery level where the client meets the practitioner; reforms must result in a definable improvement in the delivery of services; all three levels of government must simultaneously participate in the design of reforms and come together as equals; reforms must be implemented and tested in a real setting; a high degree of participation and consensus is essential for successful and lasting reform; and reforms must initially focus on effectiveness within systems before addressing broader, cross-cutting issues.[4] As this chapter demonstrates, this IGB was able to effectuate a number of delivery level reforms. However, without simultaneous attention to program and administrative changes, it proved difficult to make them last or affect the system beyond the Blueprint's target area. Moreover, it demonstrated that however difficult working through political and legal accommodations may be, they are worth the effort. Management of affairs between jurisdictions is rarely effective if only technical arrangements form the task orientation.

The Baltimore Blueprint is an IGB made up of federal, state, and local government signators, which identifies human service delivery reforms and tests those reforms in a target area of the city in the form of an experiment. The Blueprint catchment area is Southwest Baltimore, an area of 40,000 people in fifteen neighborhoods. The community has a low-income, racially mixed population and twelve public schools, two social service centers, two hospitals, one community health center, and numerous other service agencies.[5] The project focuses on reforms in a wide range of human service programs by identifying and examining ways to improve the effectiveness of the practitioner in meeting clients' needs.

Baltimore, Maryland, is the nation's ninth largest city and one of the oldest cities on the eastern seaboard. With a population over 780,000, the city has recently undergone a renovation of the downtown area. Commercial enterprise is being stimulated by the Baltimore Economic Development Corporation, a private agency for business wishing to build and finance their operations in Baltimore. Besides containing twenty-one percent of the state's population, Baltimore is the only city in Maryland with a separate governmental jurisdiction merging city and county functions. Therefore, the city is the only local provider of public human services.

The local human service structure mirrors that of the states. In 1970, the governor created a Department of Human Resources as a cabinet-level agency combining welfare, social services, employment and manpower training, and other human services into a single organization. Another cabinet-level agency combines public health, mental health, mental retardation and related health services.[6] Similarly, Baltimore's mayor created an Office of Human Resources that links the same human services. The office does not deliver services directly, but serves as the city's human services coordinating vehicle.

The Blueprint has implemented its philosophy by engaging local level actors in a team approach. Policy teams identify service delivery problems and possible reforms, implement subsequent improvement, and evaluate their effectiveness. Examples of a few of the reforms are a WIN registration/appraisal reform, a clean-up campaign for school playgrounds, and an improvement of the juvenile justice arraignment process. The policy teams institutionalize the reform process and use it to resolve nettlesome service delivery problems.

DEVELOPMENT AND OPERATION

IGB Formation

Baltimore's Office of Human Resources (BOHR) initiated several projects designed to strengthen the management and delivery of human services prior to the Baltimore Blueprint. One such project is the city's Human Service Reporting System, which provides an annual inventory of city-sponsored services and identifies the number of people served and the costs of services by standardized categories and by age groups.[7] Two other projects designed by BOHR preceded Blueprint. The Home Visitor Project attempts to unify in-home services across service systems such as health, education, and social services. Under this project, services are now provided by a generalist caseworker.[8] The other project, called Operation Mainstream, is a specific welfare reform for families with single parents who want to become employed.[9] Another development, which led to the creation of the Blueprint project, was an HEW official's Intergovernmental Personnel Act (IPA) mobility assignment for research on human service delivery at the local level. The IPA selected Baltimore as the site for investigation. He identified several fundamental weaknesses of the human service system after nine months of direct observation of client and service worker interaction in several program areas. The concept of a comprehensive intergovernmental human-service-delivery-system reform strategy developed from this research.

The Blueprint's formative stages occurred during most of 1978. During this year considerable negotiations took place among the city, state and the U.S. Department of Health, Education and Welfare. The latter was initially reluctant to get involved at the local level, but the project was ultimately sold as a demonstration project. Once the federal government agreed to participate in and fund the largest share of the demonstration, it made state and local financial participation easier.

The three-party negotiations culminated in an agreement signed in December 1978 by the mayor of Baltimore, the governor of Maryland and the undersecretary of HEW. In addition to identifying the service delivery focus of the demonstration, the agreement emphasized the three-level cooperative nature of the project and the importance of continuing commitment at those levels. Further, the agreement specified the "...intention to stress negotiation, the development of consensus, and accommodation to the interest of the participating organizations."[10] Finally, the agreement emphasized the need to increase understanding of specific reforms and the usefulness of this approach to intergovernmental cooperation in identifying and testing reforms.

The Baltimore Blueprint was officially established in January 1979, with the HEW official receiving another IPA assignment to the Blueprint as executive director. Thus, the Blueprint was formed to identify several deficiencies in the delivery of local human services, as well as an effort to mesh the political environment with the bureaucratic environment. The project was proposed as a process of "bringing together" agency personnel at the city, state, and federal levels to design a comprehensive income, employment, and social service strategy in a major urban area and as a structured experiment in designing a model human services system flowing from that process.[12]

IGB Structure

In accordance with its basic memorandum of agreement, the Blueprint operates with a board of directors, the seven policy teams, the Blueprint staff, the citizen council, and a research panel. Table VII.1 provides a graphic description of the project's structure. The mayor of Baltimore, the governor of Maryland, and the undersecretary of HEW each designates a representative to sit on the board of directors. The president of the citizen council holds the fourth seat. In 1982 the Board was expanded to ten members; they are: the president of Southwest Merchants' Association, a representative of the Greater Baltimore Committee, the Chair of the Advisory Board of the state Department of Social Services, a representative of the mayor's Professional Advisory Women's Group, the deputy secretary for mental health from the state health agency, and the state delegate (representative) to the legislature from the Blueprint catchment area. Chairmanship of the board rotates every six months. The board meets as necessary to review the various activities of the policy teams. Usually, there is agreement and sanction of the agenda, so formal votes are not considered necessary.

Four senior staff people serve as liaison personnel for the board of directors. Full-time positions in the mayor's office and the governor's office link the board with other city and state officials. Two HEW officials, each on a part-time basis, keep the undersecretary's office informed of Blueprint activities. The liaison personnel are responsible for facilitating management decisions of Blueprint operations with relevant officials at the three levels of government.

The mechanism created to generate changes in the system is the policy team. Seven teams were organized to address service delivery issues in major human service program areas, such as education, employment and training, health and mental health, housing and community development, income maintenance, juvenile justice, and social services. A major part of the formation of the Baltimore Blueprint was establishing the policy teams.

Financial support for the Baltimore Blueprint is provided by several sources, include the city of Baltimore, the state of Maryland, the U.S. Department of Health and Human Services, the U.S. Department of

Table 7.1   Baltimore Blueprint Organizational Structure

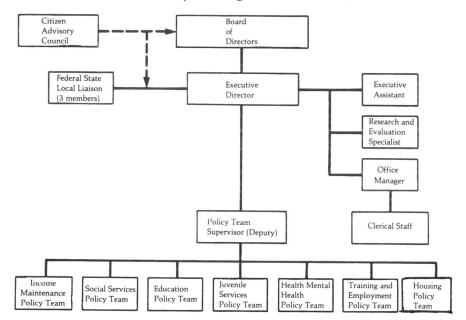

Labor, the U.S. Community Services Administration, and the U.S. Department of Education. The first five sources give grants of money to the project, whereas the department of education contracts for certain services. By comparison with the other IGBs in this study, the Blueprint is well funded, with nearly half a million dollars in grant funds and contributed full-time staff in its peak funding year. These funds pay for the main operation of the project; when a specific reform or project needs program funding changes, the policy team negotiates with appropriate parties for the necessary arrangements.

Decision Framework and Role of Key Actors

The day-to-day activity of the Blueprint project takes place on the policy teams. Each team is composed of representatives of a service system (e.g., social services) from the city, state, and federal levels. Supervisors, administrators, and line workers are included as well as community organization representatives from the Blueprint citizen council. Each team is managed by a policy team coordinator who is a full-time Blueprint staff member. The teams meet regularly, as a whole and in subgroups, to engage in the reform process. Much administrative support for the Blueprint is provided by team members and their respective agencies. The executive director and deputy director supervise the seven coordinators and policy team activities. The Blueprint staff provides the necessary coordination services, organization, and technical skills for the policy teams, the board, and the Blueprint citizen council.

Citizens and community organizations participate through the citizen council, which is composed of community leaders from most of the thirty community organizations in southwest Baltimore. A community specialist serves as the link between staff and the council. The president of the council is a member of the board of directors and other council members serve on the policy teams to provide maximum community support and input for service delivery reforms.

A final component of the Blueprint is a research panel of six persons with extensive qualitative and quantitative social service research skills, who provide technical assistance to the project. The panel meets quarterly to review the project and recommend design and operation improvements. Blueprint staff also contract with consultants in communications, organizational development, and evaluation as the need arises.

Officials' involvement with the Blueprint project is mixed. The mayor's office and the director of BOHR have a vested interest in the success and continuation of the project. Since the reforms deal with specific service delivery problems, there have been few opportunities for the active involvement of state and federal officials. The city, state, and federal participants have been restricted in their use of Blueprint reforms as a key to solving intergovernmental problems. In contrast, members of the policy teams represent three levels that are intimately involved with the Blueprint project. Even agency directors who are not on the teams are indirectly involved when reforms require their cooperation. In 1982, the Blueprint formally altered their process to include reforms initiated by agency and department directors. The Blueprint has become a forum for agency administrators at all levels who seek cooperation through the informal communication networks established by the project.

Agenda and Development

As established in its organizing document, policy teams were formed around a five-step process:

1. Problem Identification: review of problems and reforms, setting priorities, and establishing work plans.

2. Problem Validation: identification of the barriers to the service delivery problems identified in Step 1, as well as potential solutions that appear to be in substantial control of policy team members.

3. Reform Definition: identification of the action or actions needed to effect the change.

4. Reform Implementation: carrying out the interventions identified in steps 2 and 3.

5. Reform Evaluation: assessing the impact of interventions on changes in the service delivery system.[13]

This process is used by every policy team for every Blueprint reform undertaken.

Therefore, the main operation and agenda-setting process occurs during policy team activity. Service delivery problems are identified and brought to the teams by team members, administrators, and Blueprint staff. The team considers five criteria in the selection of a problem area for reform:

1. Does the problem affect a large number of service recipients?[14]

2. Can the problem be resolved within the service delivery system with available resources?

3. Can problem resolution be planned, negotiated, and implemented in a short time?

4. Will problem resolution have an immediate effect on reducing barriers to effective service delivery?

5. Will problem resolution improve worker/client relations?

If the team decides that the problem meets these criteria, it begins a process of on-site validation of the problem, and subsequent procedural steps are undertaken.

Several changes are initiated by the policy teams for each problem they tackle. Usually, the teams divide into subgroups to deal with the issues encompassed by one problem area. Reform evaluations or assessments are designed after an improvement has been initiated. Improvements have dealt exclusively with system or program reform. Table VII.2 provides a listing of reforms undertaken by the Blueprint. It identifies a representative reform from each of the seven teams, the problem addressed, and the type of intervention. As can be readily surmised, the policy teams deal with changes in the system at a level that most directly effects the target neighborhood. Consequently, issues of program coordination, policy management integration of services, and other policy-level issues have not been addressed, and major policy decisions have not been made by the board of directors.

Project development has required considerable documentation and dissemination of information and training. During its second year, Blueprint began publishing the *Baltimore Reform and Response*, a newsletter primarily distributed in Blueprint's catchment area to facilitate community pride and participation in the project. A few papers documenting the project's design and structure have been written, and, each policy team has documented its meetings, proposals, reform evaluations, and other such materials extensively.

The Blueprint staff has identified a crucial need at the service delivery level for concrete help in managing programs and creatively supervising

Table 7.2 *Exemplary Baltimore Blueprint Reforms By Policy Teams*

Reform	Problem Addressed by Reform	Description of Reform Goal	Intervention
Social Services Policy Team			
Service Intake	Staff at Clarence Bishop and Federal Hill Centers lacked the procedure, tools, and training to properly conduct the service-intake function and client problem assessment.	To create a new service-intake procedure that both provides clients with understandable, reliable information about what services are available and also assists intake workers in assessing the client's needs and making appropriate referrals.	Introduction of: (1) written guidance for service-intake function, (2) written guidance for client problem assessment, (3) a uniform procedure for client problem assessment, (4) training necessary for the service intake function.
Date Problem Identified: Sept., 1979			
Date Reform Implemented: Sept., 1980			
Date Reform Evaluated: Feb., 1981			
Income Maintenance Policy Team			
Waiting Room Reform	Clients at Clarence Bishop and Federal Hill Center may wait to see a line worker from thirty minutes to four hours.	To move clients through the waiting room effectively, meeting both their needs and the staff's needs to do an efficient job so that the waiting time is reduced. To allow workers to schedule their time by reducing interruptions.	Introduction of: (1) an appointment system in all but emergency situations, (2) training for waiting room personnel, and (3) bimonthly meetings for clerical supervisor and waiting room staff.
Date Problem Identified: April, 1980			
Date Reform Implemented: March, 1981			
Date Reform Evaluated: May, 1981			

Juvenile Justice Policy Team

Arraignment Process

Clients may receive inadequate legal representation because they do not have sufficient contact with an attorney prior to their appearance in court.	To improve the quality of legal representation to youth and their families by insuring that the family is aware of the services of the Public Defender's Office and by facilitating contact with an attorney prior to arraignment.	Introduction Of: (1) a notification of the right to an attorney and the availability of the Public Defender which is included with the summons, and (2) a change in the interaction between the Public Defender's Office and respondents.

Date Problem Identified: Feb., 1980

Date Reform Implemented: May. 1981?

Date Reform Evaluated: Jan., 1982

Employment And Training Policy Team

WIN RegistrationAppraisal

A two-day registration and appraisal process results in a high "no show" rate for appraisal appointments, adjudication, and the possible loss of the client's social service grant.	To simplify the participation of clients in the intake stage of the WIN program as a means of providing better manpower services by reducing the registration and appraisal time from two days to one.	Introduction of: (1) a new appraisal procedure with reduced paper work, and (2) training for staff in using the new procedure.

Date Problem Identified: May, 1980

Date Reform Implemented: Dec., 1980

Date Reform Evaluated: July, 1981

Health/Mental Health Policy Team

Access to Alcoholism Services

Despite the severity of the alcoholism problem in Baltimore, primary care facilities do not offer services which would facilitate the identification of alcohol-related problems and the referral of clients in need of alcoholism related treatments.	To improve the availability of services to people, especially youth, with alcohol related problems in the West Baltimore Community Health Care Corporation (WBCHCC).	Introduction of: (1) training for medical staff in the identification of alcohol-related problems (2) a protocol to be used in the identification of these problems, and (3) an alcohol counselor stationed at WBCHCC on a part-time basis.

Date Problem Identified:

Date Reform Implemented:

Date Reform Evaluated*:

Education Policy Team

Parenting

Date Problem Identified:
Dec., 1979

Date Problem Implemented:
April, 1980

Date Reform Evaluated:
May, 1981

There is a significant lack of parent involvement in their children's scholastic activites.

To increase student achievement by increasing parental involvement in working productively with their children.

Introduction of:
(1) parenting classes for parents of children, and
(2) a variety of activities involving parents.

Housing Policy Team
Code Enforcement

Date Problem Identified:
Feb., 1980

Date Reform Implemented:
June, 1980

Date Reform Evaluated*:

Housing inspectors do not talk to the complainant before or after the complaint is handled, causing confusion and frustration for citizens.

To develop ways to allow citizens to know the status of their cases when they make a complaint to the inspectional division of HCD.

Introduction of:
(1) a revised complaint form which includes information concerning the complainant's desire to be kept informed as to the disposition of her/his case, and
(2) cards which inspectors leave with complainants giving the inspector's name, telephone number, and a time when he can be reached.

* Not evaluated at time of field research.

Source: Policy Team Summary, Baltimore Blueprint, 1982.

operations. As a result, the teams have had to engage in orientation and training sessions for frontline workers and supervisors to understand, support, and carry out the reforms. The staff has developed ongoing activities to determine training needs generic to all seven systems—needs that are system-specific and reform-specific—in order to design training and orientation programs for human service personnel. These activities will become more crucial as the complexity of cross-cutting reforms and initiatives escalates.

PROJECTS

More than twenty reforms have been initiated by the Baltimore Blueprint policy teams. The education team was the first to organize and served as the prototype for the others. The first reform goal of this team was to improve school performance by removing obstacles that prevent good teaching through a school-based problem-solving process. Several school-specific projects resulted from this general reform goal. Likewise, the other six teams identified a broad problem area, which then led to specific program improvements, such as a new service-intake procedure, improved information dissemination to line workers, a waiting room reform, improved legal representation to youths and their families during the arraignment process, a simplified WIN registration or appraisal process, improved access to alcoholism services, efforts to increase parental involvement in school activities, and the reorganization of classes so teachers have a more homogeneous group of students.

Foster Care Reforms

Two policy teams—the social services teams and the juvenile justice team—addressed the problem of foster care. The social services team was engaged in developing and piloting the Foster Care Aid Demonstration Project, which was staffed by volunteers and allowed foster care workers time to carry out casework services. After assessing the success of this project, the Maryland Department of Social Services plans to implement it systemwide. The juvenile justice team, on the other hand, developed standards for the recruitment and selection of foster care homes for the Maryland Juvenile Justice Administration, which operates its own foster care program. The juvenile justice team identified several inadequacies in the Maryland Department of Social Services Foster Care Program standards.

Neither team consulted the other about its efforts to improve foster care programs or attempted to coordinate the two programs' services in the Baltimore area. This was a pervasive problem due to the program-specific reforms being implemented by the policy teams, particularly in the absence of approaches to services integration, such as policy development or linkages. It is a major reason why the board of directors wants the teams to begin addressing cross-cutting issues. Another reason for the board's decision to redirect the teams' efforts is that previous reforms have not required the participation of the board members or specific policy-level interventions that fall under the Blueprint's original problem-solving design. Two recent reforms—adolescent pregnancy and welfare and school enrollment—have been initiated to address program linkages.

Adolescent Pregnancy Reform

The Blueprint recently received a grant from the Maryland Department of Health and Mental Health's Office and Maternal and Child Welfare to develop an adolescent pregnancy prevention strategy and to test that strategy in southwest Baltimore. The staff decided to create a special adolescent pregnancy subcommittee to be chaired by the health/mental health team coordinator. Because adolescent pregnancy is a problem that cuts across several service systems, the subcommittee is composed of members from the health/mental health, education, and social service policy teams. Other subcommittee members represent the Center for Maternal and Infant Care, the Baltimore City School System, the Maryland Department of Social Services, and other appropriate professionals. Table VII.3 outlines the work program established by the policy team. It illustrates how project work is conducted by this IGB. In this case the subcommittee reviews major adolescent health, education, and social service programs to ensure that each program meets its objectives and is mutually supportive of the other programs. Based on this assessment, the subcommittee proposed the necessary service delivery and policy changes, implemented them, and evaluated their effectiveness. The subcommittee pays particular attention to the interrelationships of the agencies and develops contractual agreements with the agencies to *specify* the nature of the service and the sequence of events among the agencies as they work with female teenagers and their families.[15] The next step was the interactive forging of agreements on specific interventions at the policy level. This required interactions, negotiations, interpretations, and accommodations by city, state and federal officials.

TABLE 7.3 Teenage Pregnancy Prevention Strategy—Work Program

Blueprint is committed to using the existing programs which currently are focused on teenage pregnancy. We are also committed , in a partnership arrangement, to insuring that the existing health, education and social services programs are functioning effectively and are actually serving people's needs. Finally, we will want to insure that each of these programs is effectively linked and mutually supporting one another at the service delivery level.

As soon as the new policy team on adolescent pregnancy is formed, the team will undertake the following activities:

1. A review of each major adolescent health, education and social service program to *insure that product of the program matches the objectives of each program* and that teenagers and their families are satisfied and supportive of the service.
2. A review of each major adolescent health, education, and social service program to *insure that each program is mutually supporting one another at the delivery level.*
3. Based on the work done in (1) and (2) above, the policy team will assist each program to make whatever changes are necessary to improve services delivery to teenagers and their families.
4. As the activities described in (1), (2) and (3) are getting underway, the second part of the strategy will begin. Blueprint believes that there are two *initial* ways to create a new environment which will increase the communication and support to families and the community: First, increase the Single Parents Services of the Department of Social Services and focus the new resources on an intensive intervention strategy in the Blueprint target areas. These resources, of course, would be aimed at teenagers *already pregnant.* Second, select a junior high school in the Blueprint area and develop a special and intensive program aimed at working with students and their families around adolescent and pregnancy issues. Particular attention will be paid to those students who may be most likely to become pregnant. The policy team will develop an index of predictors of pregnancy. These will include:
   —families in which an adolescent has already become pregnant and in which there are other teenage children
   —single parent families
   —families with children who are significantly below grade level or have high absenteeism
5. It will be the responsibility of the policy team to develop a detailed work program for each of the four stategies above.

Welfare and School Enrollment Reform

A second example of a cross-cutting issue is being addressed jointly by the education and income maintenance teams. It is a change in the current policy requiring high schools to verify student enrollment in order for families to receive welfare payments for their children over sixteen. The policy mandates schools to determine whether the teenager is enrolled *and* attending classes (parents often enroll their teenagers, but do not encourage them to attend). This problem, identified by a school administrator on the education team, is not beneficial to the teenager, the parents, or the schools. A meeting was therefore scheduled between the appropriate school system and income-maintenance program administrators.

Considerable interaction and discussion ensued, in which each administrator expressed his jurisdictional positions, consulted with administrative superiors and legal counsel, and brought interim solutions to the policy team. Throughout the process it was clear that all parties stood to gain: students who were not actually attending school could be dropped from the welfare rolls, reducing costs; the threat of ending payments would help parents encourage children to attend classes; and school officials would benefit by more regular student attendance. Students would also benefit educationally from more regular attendance and aid formulas would be bolstered. These incentives kept the parties actively seeking workable solutions.

The result was an agreement for a coordinated computer data program between the city schools and the welfare department to document and track whether or not the student is enrolled and attending school. Families will not receive payments for those children 16 and over who are not attending school on a regular basis. The short-term effect of this reform is expected to be a decrease in welfare payments while the long-term effect is hoped to be increased school attendance.

There are several noteworthy features about the policy team reform process and its contribution to the Blueprint's overall framework and design. Each team gained experience and sophistication in problem identification and validation, reform definition and implementation, and implementation assessment, and the time it took for the team to complete these activities shortened. The problems and issues addressed by the teams have become more substantive in nature. Because the reforms are implemented and evaluated by members of the teams who represent agencies from the entire city, several of the reforms have had a spillover effect, such as the education team's special education procedure.

Since the Blueprint will continue to address cross-cutting issues, future projects will be aimed at "how to do more with less" measures, such as streamlining regulations, redeployment, and repackaging of services. Two recent Blueprint projects are (1) combined intake services for the workfare program and (2) a private sector commitment to provide low-cost services to individuals not eligible for Title XIX (Medicaid) after it is capped. The Baltimore Blueprint would like to prove it can pay for itself with the savings from the reforms it initiates.

ASSESSMENT

The Baltimore Blueprint is the only IGB studied that has been discontinued. During its last year and one half it operated entirely on special project funds; Blueprint discretionary funds were withdrawn by the federal government in late 1981. It died in 1983 when the federal government chose to discontinue any program and financial involvement. The easy explanation is that a new national administration wished to disassociate itself from a project forged under a previous regime, and thus chose not to fund it. While such motivation may be a contributing factor, another explanation goes closer to the heart of the model. The Blueprint appeared to be in trouble more than two years before its demise. The Blueprint model, with its emphasis on service delivery may be able to shed additional light on IGM processes.

The Blueprint was founded on the premise that meaningful change must flow from the interaction of those responsible for creating human service policies and those responsible for implementing those policies. The plan was for the early reforms to deal with specific service delivery problems to facilitate dialogue between the community and practitioners and city, state, and federal policymakers. This dialogue was to create the appropriate environment or context from which meaningful and substantive reforms could be achieved. The Blueprint believed that the context must be rooted in service delivery issues and reflect the real world as it exists, because it is the context, not the individual reform, which will have a lasting effect on the services clients receive.[16] Once the context was firmly established, the Blueprint planned to begin addressing cross-cutting policy issues.

To many observers, the Blueprint never got beyond creation of the context. The teen pregnancy issue is a case in point. It was identified as a problem to be addressed in the initial 1978 Memorandum of Agreement for Blueprint consideration. A policy team did not address the issue until the spring of 1981. An evaluation of the Blueprint, sponsored by the U.S. Department of Health and Human Services, stated that too much time and effort had been spent on process; that the twenty or more reforms was a relatively low amount of productivity for the dollar, staff, and volunteer effort expended. Investment in process building was recognized as appropriate, but overexpended in this case.[17] By 1981 the board of directors had decided that enough time had been spent on "creating the context" for change and should begin considering the coordination and integration of services issues. The problem was that while the Blueprint had identified and processed some reforms that impacted service organizations and clients, there were few products that impacted, or were of benefit, to the participating jurisdictions.

In effect, the Blueprint kept IGM decisions down at the staff and operative level. For the meaningful life of the IGB, agency administrators and representatives of federal, state, and local government signators felt they were kept out of the process. IGB service delivery reforms primarily involved Blueprint staff and agency staff working on policy teams. This created a tenuous relationship with top governmental officials. Designated officials found themselves having to reexert their program control at different points, use the threat of withdrawal of funds, and attempt to muscle top staff out of the project. As a result a lot of the IGM rhetoric was over staff versus board control rather than over policy changes. Since it is top officials who ultimately make intergovernmental decisions (on an actual or a delegated basis), it is important to bring them into the process at critical stages.

Turnover of top officials supporting this demonstration project no doubt weakened its base of support. As a model project, the key actors had to be sold by the local driving forces as well as by the federal officials who devoted more than three years to Blueprint. After initial reluctance, the original representatives entered the project with high hopes and considerable excitement. All high-level administrators left within two years because of changes in federal and state administrations; the director of BOHR took a position in Washington. New appointees did not have the interest, understanding, or investment in the project. Indeed, they began to question whether federal, state, and local government agendas were compatible with the Blueprint's design and approach. During its last eighteen months the board of directors wrestled with these key issues. IGM actors need to reach at least some agreement that their energies and efforts to meet and solve problems are worth the effort. This requires constant reinforcement by their involvement in the workings of the process.

Blueprint has been criticized as just another federally encouraged and funded experiment that failed. To term the project a failure is too harsh a judgment; it was a demonstration with a number of significant successes. Blueprint was primarily federally driven, but it would not have occurred unless state and local government officials had agreed to participate in the problem-solving process. Indeed, it was these officials who took the initiative to "fix" the Blueprint in its last two years by making it address policy level questions. Federal funds did pay the lion's share of Blueprint's bills, unlike the other IGBs, which are primarily locally funded. The small amount of state and local funding in Baltimore may have made it harder to respond to state and local needs; when governmental actors pay they *expect* to participate and have their agendas met. Moreover, the long term stability of other IGBs are no doubt products of the shared participation of the key intergovernmental actors, financial and otherwise. Blueprint perhaps demonstrated this in reverse.

The Blueprint demonstration, however, made some very positive contributions to intergovernmental networking and service delivery reform. A major success was the creation of an extensive network among community leaders, practitioners, and city, state, and federal officials. It was the only project of its kind to bring together actors from every major human service system, including education, housing, and juvenile justice. As one source stated, "some heavy politics have been played out" during the establishment of the project as well as during the policy teams' reform process. Maintaining dialogue between the actors is a feat that deserves considerable respect. Through the process of creating the Blueprint, solid political connections were nurtured that helped the project. When something needed to be done to carry out a particular reform, the changes were initiated through the informal network channels. This evolutionary process, whether natural for this type of model or not, has led some to believe that Blueprint's original political foundation was undermined. For example, city representatives wanted to have more control over the project and the federal government wanted it to serve as a prototype for federal policy implementation.

The Blueprint developed strong relationships with the city's human service agencies, particularly with those agencies represented on the policy teams. These relationships had to be encouraged and nurtured in the beginning. The program managers and the agency directors were skeptical about the project and resisted early reforms that required a change in operating procedures. Gradually, the agencies learned that the teams could act as a buffer between the agencies and the state and federal officials with whom they had problems to discuss. Discussion, they found, could take place without animosity. Increasingly, the project became a credible forum in which the agencies could air their problems and discuss cooperation toward resolution of those problems.

The Baltimore Blueprint's relationship with the community was a key component of the project and of its success. In order for the services delivery reforms to be relevant to the clients, service problems had to be identified and articulated by them. The Blueprint citizen council was the formal mechanism for citizen involvement in Blueprint activities. The community specialist also made a concentrated effort to maintain citizen participation on the policy teams. The specialist was responsible for developing a broad-based community strategy to engender a feeling of pride and involvement in the neighborhood. The Blueprint publication, *Baltimore: Reform and Response*, was a major part of that strategy. The newsletter was circulated through the Blueprint service area to inform residents of the project's existence, its purpose, and the needs for their input. The Baltimore Blueprint was premised on the belief that change cannot occur unless people become involved in the change process, care what happens, and think that they can make a difference. Although there were differing opinions about when citizen participation should be incorporated in the project, (e.g., Should it begin before or after operations are established?) all agreed that it was essential to the project's achieved success.

Perhaps the most important aspect of Blueprint's success was that the project dealt directly with service delivery issues. One concern about intergovernmental decision-making bodies is that broad-based policy decisions never filter down to the services that are delivered to the client.

The Blueprint was designed to work from the client and line worker level to the policy-making body. This vertical filtering may be inhibited by the fact that the reforms were confined to a small catchment area, and thus overall policies were not adopted on a jurisdiction-wide basis. Because the reforms were not policy issues and were limited to a specific area, policy-makers on the board did not have to address policy issues and, as a result, adjust their decision-making processes. In other words, board members were not compelled to change the system.

An outcome of the teams' reforms and other Blueprint efforts has been the discovery of a need for management skills, rather than new policies for service delivery. If this is true for all human service systems and programs, perhaps an intergovernmental problem-solving model or decision-making body is not the appropriate vehicle for improving services. In this case, management training and procedure orientation for front-line workers and their supervisors would lead to better service delivery. This has been the approach taken by the Blueprint.

However, some major human service problems transcend program management and involve conflicting policies at the city, state, and federal levels. Resolution of such policies is the reason Baltimore chose to have all three governments involved in the project. This objective was not emphasized while the Blueprint staff was concentrating on the implementation of service delivery reforms. The representatives from the three governmental sectors needed to have a vested interest in the Blueprint reforms for their interest and support to remain high. The delay in addressing cross-cutting issues shortened the time for teams to produce some viable reforms at the policy level, a lesson the other IGBs found they had to adopt.

Notes to Chapter Seven

1. Robert Agranoff and Alex Pattakos, *Dimensions of Services Integration* (Rockville, Md.: Project SHARE Monograph Series, 1979), 13.

2. Neil Gilbert, "Assessing Service Delivery Methods: Some Unsettled Questions," *Welfare in Review* 10 (May/June 1973), 25.

3. U.S. Department of Health, Education, and Welfare, "Services Integration Next Steps," Secretarial Memorandum, Washington, D.C., 1 June, 1971.

4. Thomas P. Coyle, "Baltimore Blueprint: Creating the Context," 1980, 2-3.

5. *Ibid.*, 4.

6. Thomas P. Coyle, "A Concept Paper for the Development of a Model Intergovernmental Human Service Delivery System Focusing on Families," 6.

7. Coyle, "Concept Paper," 8.

8. *Ibid.*

9. *Ibid.*

10. *The Baltimore Blueprint: A City, State and Federal Partnership in Human Services, Memorandum of Agreement,* 19 December, 1978, 2.

11. *Ibid.*

12. Coyle, "Concept Paper," 10.

13. The Baltimore Blueprint, 10-15.

14. Coyle, "Concept Paper," 10.

15. *Ibid.*

16. Coyle, "Baltimore Blueprint," 3.

17. Larry Bialis *et al., Evaluation of the Baltimore Blueprint,* Urban Systems Research and Engineering, Cambridge, Mass., 1983), 10.

CHAPTER EIGHT

An Intergovernmental Partnership Approach: The Human Resources Commission of Seattle-King County

A group of Seattle-King County officials has demonstrated what an intergovernmental partnership can do. Under such a partnership, federal and state governments do not necessarily use their legal and fiscal powers to preempt or centralize local powers; they facilitate and work with local governments and related interests in solving major problems. In such a strategy, Zimmerman suggests, centralization and decentralization continue to operate side by side because of concerns over the transfer of fiscal resources, constitutional and legal powers, and because of states' special responsibilities to ensure that the actions taken by one local government do not cause problems for other governments or abridge the rights of minorities. In such a partnership approach, joint action by actors at different levels will often be needed.[1]

Such joint action has been the hallmark of the Human Resources Coalition (HRC) of Seattle-King County, an IGB that believes that meaningful intergovernmental problem solving is based on bringing all of the relevant actors to the table. Intergovernmental cooperation in the northwest region has received national recognition in human service circles. Some have suggested that it has been engendered by the inspiration and leadership of the longtime head of the federal region office (Region X) of HSS, who is known for creating an atmosphere of federal responsiveness to state and local problems. The state of Washington, particularly through its Department of Social and Health Services (DSHS), has also been a willing and active partner in these innovative efforts. Region X has been a leader in several of the national experiments that involve intergovernmental innovation, ranging from regional organizations in human services to combined grant programs. The spirit of cooperation and interchange is especially evident in Seattle-King County, where governmental officials have taken advantage of mobility transfers, through permanent changes of positions between governments, and by overlapping participation on advisory boards.

The Human Resources Coalition of Seattle-King County represents major funders that engage in general problem solving of joint interest. Coalition partners include the city of Seattle; King County; the state of Washington, Region 4 (King County) DSHS; Region X, DHHS; U.S. Region X, U.S. Community Services Administration (CSA); and United Way of King County. In late 1982, two changes affected the coalition's structure: a representative of the Pacific Northwest Grant Makers Forum was added and the CSA representative was discontinued because that agency was abolished. Operational since June 1979, HRC has engaged in a limited agenda surrounding isolated issues requiring joint problem solving "in which success is achievable and measurable."[2]

Seattle is the major city in the northwest United States, with a population of approximately 500,000 people. King County has a total population of 1.2 million people. The area is the major shipping, commercial, and manufacturing center of the region. The city operates with a mayor-council form of government and the county is governed with a nine-member county council and an elected county executive.

Human service delivery in Washington is state-oriented, with most services either delivered or funded by a large "umbrella" agency, the Department of Social and Health Services. This structure includes health, income maintenance, social services, aging, and all other major human service programs with the exception of employment and education. Community mental health, drug abuse, and alcoholism services are contracted out by the state, primarily through counties. The county human service unit is part of a Department of Rehabilitative Services, which is primarily correctional. The Human Services Division provides direct services related to involuntary mental treatment; aging, in which the county contracts with the city of Seattle as the Area Agency on Aging (AAA) designee; and mental disability, in which the county administers state dollars in mental health and developmental disabilities, which are then contracted out to private agencies. The city of Seattle Department of Human Resources (DHR) not only administers the AAA for the entire county, but operates a series of "little city halls" where emergency services are provided, sponsors a Veterans Action Center, oversees day care, and operates youth programs relating to employment and juvenile concerns. Neither the city nor county has put revenue sharing dollars into human services to any significant degree, presumably because of state-imposed limits on local government revenue raising but also because human services are seen as predominantly a state responsibility. However, the city of Seattle has spent most of its twenty percent declining share limit of CDBG funds on human services. The private sector is primarily represented by the United Way of King County, which raised $18.6 million in 1980 and funded 111 agencies. In addition to its planning and allocations committee, United Way sponsors a council of planning affiliates made up of 180 public and private providers, which deals with general planning on a community-wide basis.

Compared to other cases in this study, the coalition is by design a low-keyed, low-budget operation, devoted to deal with those problems that all members can agree on. It has no permanent staff, offices, or budget, and the chair rotates among the partners. HRC can point to several actions that have led to changes in the intergovernmental human service system: the development of a common data base for planning, a computerized information and referral service, development of emergency housing services, a coordinated transportation plan for the elderly, creation of a plan for implementation of the energy assistance program, and a plan of action for housing the mentally ill in the community. HRC has not engaged in any community-wide planning. Its efforts have followed a problem-oriented planning and coordination mode.

DEVELOPMENT AND OPERATION

IGB Formation

Antecedents to HRC developed through informal cooperation between governmental actors and between the public and private sectors. About three or four years before HRC was officially launched, a group of administrators participated in a set of informal lunch sessions in which common problems were discussed. Major participants in these sessions included the county budget and planning director, the city director of human services, the regional director of DSHS, the associate executive of United Way (responsible for planning and government relations), and regional HSS officials. Meetings were irregular, with no set agenda, but discussions tended to focus on joint planning and other areas of common concern. During this period there was considerable turnover among actors, but the ad hoc group remained together on an irregular basis, up until the development of the coalition.

The essential actors who formed HRC built on previous working relationships. The most instrumental individuals were the HSS regional head, his intergovernmental and congressional affairs officer, the new director of the Seattle Department of Human Resources, the United Way associate executive and the regional DSHS director. With an overwhelming state human service presence, the state was considered a key actor in this effort, and the regional administrator was supportive. Discussions about the formation of HRC were facilitated by the city director, although other key individuals played very active roles.

Although a particular issue was under discussion at formation time, it was agreed that general coordination and problem solving led to HRC development. The city director thought that one way to get people to cooperate was to develop a common data base which elected officials and other decision-makers could use. He felt there was a lack of communication between officials and that decisions would be more rational if they were based upon shared information. A commitment of money by the county, state, and United Way was requested to go along with a city contribution. This effort could not immediately be accomplished, and the federal government was asked for help. Funding was not immediately forthcoming, and it was then decided to form some kind of body to collectively look at common problems. Thus, the concept of cooperation was triggered by the data base efforts, but was immediately broadened to include some form of service planning.

Formation of HRC continued by bringing in other actors. The county was said to have been reluctant to joint the partnership, but it finally agreed to join. At the federal level, it was decided by the regional office of HEW to make the Office of Human Development Services a representative, since its programs are the broadest in scope. The Community Services Administration was asked to join at this point, since CSA programs are also broad and have a significant local impact.

The parties were then brought together to establish the structure. Staff from the city, state, and United Way developed basic working papers for the coalition and a presentation was made on three alternative models used in other cities. The other models were not seriously considered, and the group zeroed in on the staff paper. A Working Agreement was signed by the mayor, the county executive, the president of United Way, and relevant state and federal administrators.[3]

IGB Structure

HRC operates through two mechanisms—coalition members and task forces. The coalition is composed of two members from each signator. Only three positions are specifically named in the agreement: director of the city department of human resources, county director of budget and program development, and the United Way planning and allocations director.[4] The full coalition membership includes:

> the director of the city department of human resources,
> city office of policy and evaluation human services planning director,
> county director of budget and program development,
> county manager of human services,

United Way planning and allocations director,
United Way planning director,
CSA regional director (until 1982),
CSA Washington state liaison (until 1982),
HHS director, office of intergovernmental and congressional affairs,
HHS director, office of human development services,
DSHS region 4 director,
DSHS region 4 planning director.

Representatives of the metropolitan area private foundations developed their own working group, the Grant Makers Forum, to coordinate their efforts. That group was asked to send an ex-officio representative to HRC. It replaced CSA as a full partner in 1982.

Table 8.1 Seattle-King County Human Resources Coalition

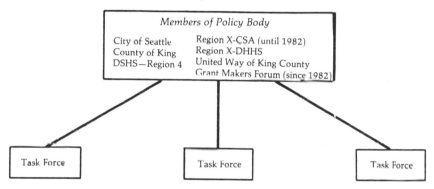

Administrative operations at the Seattle-King County Human Resources Coalition are conducted simply. The basic working agreement refers to a convenor, to be selected every six months by the members on a rotating basis. The convenor is actually referred to as a chair and is responsible for arranging meetings and recording meeting minutes. Staff operations are limited to the joint staff time contributed while working on various HRC task forces and to accompanying clerical support, which is usually supplied by the office of the task force chair. The chair supplies an additional small measure of clerical time for official correspondence, record keeping, and notification, but this resource commitment is not considered burdensome because it rotates.

HRC is financed entirely from in-kind contributions. At no time has an organization budget and paid staff complement been seriously considered. There is a strong feeling that this may upset the delicate cooperation and contribution base. As one person suggested, "If we got a grant, someone would have to sign off and be responsible, and we would have to decide who it would be, and then someone would be top dog, and there goes the equal partners idea." HRC has been responsible for bringing new money into the community, but it has been services money chan-neled through the appropriate delivery agencies. Some people feel that at some point external funds may have to be sought for one or more of their larger projects. At this time they will have to face the issue of where the money goes.

Decision Framework and Role of Key Actors

The agreement states that the method of operation is by ad hoc proj-ect groups, to be led by one of the members, with staff commitments and other resources expected. Coalition members are urged in the agree-ment to communicate with each other on planning processes, to plan jointly whenever possible, and to agree upon service areas for analysis and problem solving.[5] HRC organizational guidelines further specify that only designated members of the six organizations may vote—a quorum consists of at least one member from each signator—and that all actions and recommendations must be approved by unanimous vote. Member-ship is limited to policy making and funding organizations with major responsibilities across the human service system. The working docu-ments specify a few "field of service" issues, such as transportation and emergency services, but the content of the agenda is to be incorporated into an annually developed "limited priority list of unmet needs of serv-ice delivery problem areas." The autonomy of each partner in funding decisions is also affirmed.

The actual work of HRC is done through task forces. When the part-ners decide to work on an issue, a lead agency is designated. Ordinarily, a member from the agency is selected as the chair and is responsible for convening and coordinating the work of the task force. Task force mem-bers are designated by the coalition, although a task force chair may request that any individual be designated by the HRC chair. A specific scope of work and timetables are developed. Task forces are also given a written problem statement to work on. These groups are ordinarily made up of one or more staff persons from member agencies. On occasion, staff from nonpartner agencies are brought in, if it is felt their expertise is needed.

After a task force is convened, a common reporting format is developed and the work is divided among the members. The work steps may involve collecting agency information or interviews conducted by task force members. At this point other agency personnel may be brought in to help. The information is reported back through the task force chair and collated for task force consideration and recommendation to the coalition. The chair is responsible for preparing and presenting the report. After a task force as reported, it is disbanded, since all task forces are ad hoc in design.

Staff assigned to HRC task force work are reported to be highly qualified individuals. They tend to be chief assistants to department heads or staff directors. Given the nature of most task forces, they also tend to be planning and management specialists, although program people have also been included. Since most of the staff involved in HRC work are at a relatively high level and generally work for politicians, they are sensitive to the political, as well as the technical, aspects of their work. The key to task force success was reported as the quality of staff contribution; that is, the leadership ability of the chair to define and orchestrate the work and the chair's key staffs' ability to see that it is carried out. When these two qualities are present, the task force generally goes well; when they are absent its work falters. The HRC has experienced both situations.

Coalition members are expected to attend, and most do. Only one member of the partnership was reported as a reluctant partner with a minimal attendance record. Because the quorum requires at least one representative from each member agency, it has been necessary on occasion (where some partners are absent) to reach agreement by telephone. Strict member attendance rules by designated positions are considered important because they ensure that the persons who deliberate issues are right next to, and presumably speak for, the top decision-makers. Elected officials themselves have not participated in HRC work, nor is their involvement in solving the type of problems the coalition works on considered necessary. HRC has held strictly to the rule of funder participation only: several provider groups have petitioned for membership and all have been denied. Also, no provider agency administrators or contractees have participated directly in the work of HRC.

Agenda and Development

HRC agenda-setting and decisional processes are very simple, since they follow its basic Agreement. Issues are either identified at the annual day-long retreat or when any member chooses to introduce an issue, and then is discussed as possible agenda items. If there is unanimous agreement that the problem should be investigated and confronted, it becomes an agenda item. A few items are quite general in nature and do not require intensive investigation. These are decided upon by the members after discussion. Most issues, however, are turned over to a task force.

After some months, task force reports, including a proposed course of action, are presented by task force chairs. The coalition then considers the issue again as a proposed HRC position. Because of the unanimity rule, every effort is made to reach complete agreement. A formal vote is rarely taken. On most issues unanimity is easily reached after some discussion. On a few issues, if a member says he or she cannot formally vote or take a position, the issue is tabled as an HRC concern and left for individual members. Examples of agenda issues that have been particularly difficult to deal with include joint transportation problems caused by private sector objections to possible consolidation efforts and issues that would place state and federal administrators in the position of having to lobby. For example, in 1982 federal government representatives selected themselves out of a funding reduction impact task force on the grounds that it would not be advisable given the national administration's perspective on state and local responsibility for decision making. In general, it is felt that divisive issues should be avoided in the interest of maintaining the coalition.

The limited agenda of HRC has been a mark of its success to most actors. Most members feel that it can and should only deal with problem-solving concerns of mutual interest in a nonthreatening way. The interests of any member should not be threatened. They feel the unanimity rule helps cement relationships and preserve the coalition; overall cooperation and dialogue should not be threatened by any one issue. Thus, a number of issues, such as joint transportation and unified reporting and accounting, have been pushed off the agenda. However, the limited agenda is a source of frustration to some who feel that complete agreement and over-concern for sector autonomy means that the group focuses on the less important issues. But most of the group seems to feel that expectations should be kept modest, that problems should be addressed where there is mutual agreement, and that expectations will always be met if this recommended course of action is followed.

HRC has survived changes at the elected official level, including new national, state and county administrators. There has been, however, relative stability among the human service administrative actors who regularly participate in the coalition. The basic structure and working procedures have been developed, and original goals have been pursued. While its agenda is admittedly limited, it has developed plans that have led to actions. The partners were able to quickly assess the impact of national budget cuts, as well as state DSHS budget reductions. The coalition also supported Project Transition, an effort to mobilize the business sector for local help in meeting federal and state funding reductions.

PROJECTS

Coalition work efforts began with a full work plan, building on the common data base started earlier by individual partners. Task forces were formed to deal with youth employment and preventive services, emergency housing, mental health, and transportation for the handicapped and elderly. Finally, a planning task force was set up as the mainstay of the coalition. Its charge was to develop a means for coordinating the planning processes of all the partners. Common data base work, which is highlighted below, has proved to be such a long-term project that its almost considered permanent. Other HRC projects highlighted in this section—housing and energy—are examples of how projects come and go, as HRC identifies issues, task forces operate, and issues are acted upon.

Common Data Base Project

The work on the common data base is the oldest and longest-standing project of HRC. As mentioned, it was one issue that brought the parties together. The data base effort continued some pre-coalition efforts to establish a computerized information and referral service (I&R) for King County. This effort was seized upon by HRC and was a first test of its viability. After nearly a year of negotiations over funding, the I&R system began operating in January 1981 as a joint venture between United Way, the city of Seattle, and King County. The project has been initially funded by $140,000 from United Way, $45,000 from the city, $60,000 from the county (later reduced to $30,000), $15,000 from a foundation, and $17,500 from HHS, channeled through DSHS. The county had some doubts about the benefit of I&R to them and the state DSHS office would not let Region 4 participate until the federal money was channeled through the state. While the I&R project really began before HRC was officially formulated, it received the enthusiastic support of the new coalition, and its members were instrumental in moving it along. The I&R experience led directly to the data base experience.

The Common Data Base task force met for about six months in 1979. Ten staff persons representing the partners officially sat on the task force, which was chaired by one of the United Way members. Other persons participated by invitation of one partner or another, primarily other agency staff people. A total of thirty people attended meetings. The charge was to address three issues related to the development of a common data base; development of common program definitions, development of a common listing of client characteristics, and development of a common financial reporting system. The diversity among experiences and interests was so great among those involved that there was no unanimous agreement by all attending on the issues. The most basic agreement was reported to be "on the importance of the subject matter under discussion."[6]

In terms of program definitions, the task force agreed in principle that the partners move toward the United Way of America Service Identification System (UWASIS) taxonomy as a means of overcoming the problem over time. There was also recognition of the difficulties of some partners moving in this direction. Action has been taken by CSA, which has formally moved toward the UWASIS taxonomy for all CSA agencies in Region X. The task force assisted CSA in implementing this system of program definitions. Orientation to UWASIS has also been provided to Region 4 DSHS staff, but the program definitions have not been adopted.

Common client characteristics and broad service identifiers were also recommended and agreed upon by the coalition for use in joint planning. The city of Seattle and United Way have designed a common data base using UWASIS as the classification scheme and common forms for agency reporting. An approach was designed that maintained the integrity, i.e., format of the basic data collection system so that aggregation of information is possible, yet allowing for subdetail according to partner specification. City data are processed under contract by United Way using a common electronic data processing program.

Less progress has been achieved in the area of financial reporting. Formats vary considerably because of different governmental reporting requirements. The state of Washington's system is the key to reporting required by DSHS, King County, and the city. On the other hand, United Way felt it must remain with the Standard Financial Chart of Accounts established by the American Institute of Certified Public Accountants and used by the IRS 990 reporting for nonprofits. While the two systems are not completely incompatible, the task force was not in a position to reconcile the differences. The only recommendation that came out of the task force was a stance of opposition to any new financial reporting formats and encouragement to the partners to move toward the existing standard chart of accounts.

The task force chair recommended that the groups be disbanded and that each partner appoint a representative from the coalition to meet quarterly to review and discuss opportunities for further progress. The common data base issue was reported as complex, raising a number of difficult issues the committee could not resolve. The work on these three issues has continued on an intermittent basis. It led to a limited number of tangible results, and provided several indicators of cooperation and joint effort; however, it also pointed out some very real barriers to joint effort, and thus, is an area of continuing concern. The work on this project demonstrates how difficult it is for intergovernmental actors to reach agreement on occasions when difficult jurisdictional adjustments need to be made. The political willingness appeared to be present, but technical and legal concerns prevented complete success.

Housing and Residential Care Project

The task force on Housing and Residential Care for the Mentally Ill focused on the need for residential beds for persons returning from state hospitals and other clients requiring some type of protected living environment. The task force met during the last half of 1979 and coalition action was taken during 1980. It was chaired by the county human service representative, and all coalition members were represented. The task force was assisted by an assessment study undertaken by the county with city help. Hospitals and the county jail were surveyed to determine the number and type of persons needing placement. Residential facilities were also surveyed to determine how many placements were actually made and what types of clients were placed, and staff opinions on placement barriers were ascertained. The task force also made use of a study of nursing home clients. The findings of the two studies formed the basis of task force discussions.

The report had three basic conclusions. First, almost one-half of the persons who need long-term residential care are not receiving it. Second, mentally ill persons with difficult behavior problems represent the most critical need and, in fact, have no appropriate place for long-term care. Third, quality of care is lacking as well as quantity of care[7] The report then presented a model residential care continuum, (Table VIII.2) ranging from acute/emergency housing to independent family living with case management.[8] The report concluded with a strategy for implementing the continuum and several recommendations for action, most of which related to new or expanded services or the establishment of new housing facilities.

After a great deal of discussion and political negotiations, most of the recommended actions were accepted by the coalition. The county study and the *Housing and Residential Care Report* were used by the state in establishing future funding priorities. Fortuitously, a statewide referendum was passed in 1979 that allows $25 million in state money for community facilities to serve the handicapped. The coalition has used its task force efforts to secure commitments of $2 million of that money to construct five community residential facilities to serve the mentally ill in King County. The state DSHS is trying to find operations money for these new programs when they open. When the facilities open, it will provide much needed relief for the overcrowded jail. The Housing Needs for the Mentally Ill task force demonstrated how sustained effort could lead to joint action based on mutual adjustment, in this case with the state and the county as the principal actors, but with major support efforts from the other federal, city, and private sector actors.

Energy Assistance Implementation Plan

In the fall of 1979, the director of the city department of human resources, who was then chairing HRC, suggested that the coalition form an energy task force to help prepare an implementation plan for the federal-state Energy Assistance Program (EAP). The coalition was viewed as a good mechanism to pull together the various actors and develop a

Table 8.2   A Model Residential Care Continuum for Adult Mentally Ill Persons® in King County

Level of Client Need
Disability/Dangerousness

(more) ←   → (less)

PROTECTION/STABILIZATION.   MAINTENANCE/REHABILITATION/REINTEGRATION

(Stabilization and protection may be necessary here too but are not the primary focus)

LEVELS OF CARE

Intensive/Restrictive
(more) ←   → (less)

ACUTE/EMERGENCY CARE — Short-Term
- JAIL | HOSP
- Long-Term program for most difficult recidivists
- EMERGENCY SHELTER/TEMPORARY HOUSING

INTERMEDIATE CARE — Long-Term
- NURSING HOMES – MH
- INTERMEDIATE PSYCH. FACILITY
- ALTERNATIVE PROGRAM/NATURAL SETTING

SUPERVISED LIVING
- CONGREGATE CARE FACILITY – MH
- CONGREGATE CARE FACILITY – MH – TRANSITIONAL
- FOSTER FAMILIES – MH

SEMI-INDEPENDENT LIVING
- CLUSTERED LIVING
- INDEPENDENT/NATURAL FAMILY w/CASE MANAGEMENT

INDEPENDENT LIVING
- ABLE TO OBTAIN NECESSARY SERVICES ON OWN

* To work properly this model must also include case management and client care monitoring components which assure proper client entry and flow between levels and types of care, and followup of clients who leave care to reengage them if necessary.

plan given the short time period for plan preparation and the program's low administrative costs. The group consisted of shared staff from each of the coalition's partners. The county, Region X of OHDS, Region 4 of DSHS, and United Way all contributed planners; the city contributed a DHR administrative staff person who chaired the committee; and Region X of CSA contributed its contracts coordinator.

The joint-planning process began by identifying those agencies eligible for EAP funds. The city DHR planned to subcontract with three agencies, while the state DSHS planned to contract directly with two county-wide, not-for-profit agencies. The task force decided to set up a single information and referral source for the county by contracting with the Community Information Line (CIL), which provides I&R for the entire county. One number was designated for all I&R concerning the EAP. The CIL would refer individuals to the appropriate agency for energy assistance according to their geographic location in the county. All posters, public service announcements, booklets and the like advertising EAP listed one number for the county. Thus, the joint actions have amounted to a mutual strategy.

The project has continued as planned since its implementation in 1980 and is considered a success. One advantage of this joint-planning process is that the county was able to be involved in a federal-state program they otherwise would not have. The HRC also prepared a report to Washington's congressional delegation on the nature of the EAP implementation plan, its design, and the community's response. The report was included with a letter in support of EAP's continuation. Committee members report that the delegation's response to their project was both positive and prompt.

In addition to its more recent work in assessing and dealing with the impact of federal and state funding reductions and involving the private sector in local human service emergencies, HRC has been active on other fronts. A task force was formed to investigate and report on the advisability and potential of a series of youth program management centers. Under such a plan, all youth service management and administrative activities would be consolidated into a single operations center. Youth services was selected because the city and county are considering disengagement from these programs. Another initiative involves HRC examination of options whereby the state might legislatively transfer resource allocation responsibility to counties. A task force is examining such pass-through practices in other states. This, and other work, demonstrates how HRC has developed into a focused working group, exhibiting functional degrees of trust and accomplishment.

ASSESSMENT

HRC illustrates how true intergovernmental partnerships develop, in this case through a formal IGB; although the formal workings mask considerable and essential informal networking activities. The work of HRC on such projects as the common data base, housing for the mentally ill, and energy assistance demonstrate that, although parties must sometimes limit their agendas and do not always achieve success, if a group keeps working at issues some successes will be forthcoming. Most important is the notion that constant interaction and persistent attention to agreed upon problems can indeed pay off through intergovernmental accommodations. In most of HRC's work, results have been a product of coming to agreement on the issues, development of decision-making information, reaching agreement on the issues, development of decision-making information, reaching agreement on actions through multiparty accommodation, and carrying out those actions. It is a process that has worked because of the personal and pragmatic relationships that have evolved in an atmosphere where politics is not a "dirty word," where there is willingness to get into the "nuts and bolts," and where there is no reticence to speak up for or to protect one's interests.

HRC has been instrumental in developing a number of beneficial interactive relationships among human service funders and policymakers in King County. First, there are formal contacts made possible through meetings and other coalition events. While most of the players knew each other before HRC, familiarity has come about because of the formal working relationships. Second, task force involvement has brought top staff from different agencies in direct working contact with each other. This has led to operational as well as personal familiarity; the partners have become much more aware of each other's procedures, planning and data systems, and so on. Third, in cases where the coalition itself has felt reluctant to act, task force and HRC deliberations have led to a number of bilateral or trilateral formal actions. In these cases, HRC gets little credit for such actions, but discussants feel that the coalition has directly or indirectly stimulated these actions. Fourth, the coalition has facilitated numerous one-to-one informal information sharing or problem solving. For example, Region 4 DSHS and United Way now informally share information about agencies they both fund. Similarly, the city and the county can get instant federal interpretation of a federal-state program without going through the state. And fifth, participation by coalition members and staff on other advisory bodies enhanced interaction. For example, federal and local officials sit on the state's Region 4 citizen planning committees, giving them a better understanding of state processes. Members and staff have also been active in United Way. In all, HRC has cemented many working relationships that were informal or tenuous to begin with, making the partnership concept very real.

Relationships with elected officials have not been as direct as in other locales. Since HRC's focus is on smoothing out jurisdictional planning, allocational, and service problems at the administrative level, less direct elected official involvement is required. However, most of the members of the coalition work for politicians and many are top administrative appointees. As such, they are not only sensitive to political concerns but feel they can call on the elected officials if they are needed. HRC work has largely avoided involvement in provider agency politics or major local government political issues. HRC problems to date have not required a great deal of elected official input, nor have they submerged the coalition very deeply into political waters.

Public-private sector relationships in King County are considered good, at least among the participants in HRC. There is virtually no negative undercurrent between United Way and the public sector. United Way has always played an essential leadership role. Public sector members not only value their participation, but feel that United Way has developed a number of useful processes—such as in allocations and technical assistance and training—that other partners should adopt. United Way has served frequently as a conduit for outside funds, particularly private funds, that have then gone to delivery agencies. In the case of the computerized I&R project, United Way has not been reluctant to stand up to the public sector as a full and equal member of IIRC, objecting to positions and approaches that threaten its interests. Out of this synthesis have come constructive approaches, mutual understanding, and cooperative ventures.

State and federal government relationships are also considered to be good. During the founding period, formal state and federal coalition membership was viewed as an automatic reaction to the close working relationships and overlapping participation that had developed over the years. Because of the long-standing experience and encouragement of improved intergovernmental relationships, the state and federal governments were not seen as the enemy, but as actors with different and legitimate interests. These interests do not tend to be seen as aggrandizing bureaucracy, but as the inevitable need for regional administrators to carry out statutory intent, an elected administration's wishes, or instructions from headquarters. Federal and state officials see their role as smoothing out these messages and trying to accommodate them to local wishes. State and federal officials are more constrained to take positions when they have lobbying implications. Frustrations are reported over state involvement since the regional office is often powerless to act on many important state decisions that effect HRC business; they are either made in Olympia or local decisions are overturned there. For example, contracts to deliver services by private agencies are monitored at the regional level, but they are made at the state level. Region 4 officials were reported as extremely understanding and cooperative with HRC interests but can only act on limited service delivery packaging arrangements without going to the state capitol. The biggest federal government problem was reported as intermittent interest on the part of one partner. But despite these admitted reservations, state and federal participation is on a full partnership basis, and cooperation is consistent.

The coalition has dealt with a number of issues of community importance and has done much to improve relationships among the major funders while selectively approaching cross-cutting issues. The existence of HRC has not done a great deal to change relationships among providers and local, state, and federal governments, nor with the private sector. Those relationships were pretty much in place before HRC and have continued as usual. The model, with a limited agenda and limited partners, did not intend to change these relationships. Nevertheless, it has become an important forum where people can get together around the same table and discuss issues, allowing different jurisdictions to build familiarity and trust. Its constructive nature in developing relationships is considered a direct result of having to work on specific issues, rather than mutual talk sessions about being more coordinated or more cooperative.

The HRC model is a demonstration of how federal and state officials can work together with local officials in a problem-solving partnership. It has demonstrated how shared interests can emerge from working together on agreed upon problems. Additionally, its work demonstrates the importance of pragmatically working through adjustments or mutual strategies among relevant jurisdictional representatives. This IGB has proceeded by involving top level administrators—those who appear to have sufficient authority delegated from elected officials—at a policy level. At the same time staff work has been performed by those who are at a level where they possess the technical knowledge that can be blended with political and jurisdictional considerations. This combination—one group looking at legal program responsibilites and developing planning or service models that reflect extant knowledge and the other group forging staff work into interjurisdictional and political accommodations—seems to work well. HRC experience also suggests that this is not an absolute formula for success; in many cases intergovernmental actors must do what they can, such as the limited accomplishments in the data base project. The latter typifies many intergovernmental situations, where there are difficulties in making adjustments. In these cases, parties often need to salvage what they can, hoping the experience can lead to later successes. In the case of this IGB, considerable success did follow many times, such as the Energy Assistance Project, where HRC efforts led to the development of an interdependent, mutual strategy for administering a new program. Finally, these two projects indicate how difficult it is to characterize intergovernmental work, in that it is so cumulative and pragmatic.

HRC has followed its original design to engage in intersectoral funder problem-solving and create many beneficial cooperative spinoffs. It has also demonstrated that a donated and shared staff task force method can work and that, with the right commitment, an important forum can be created without budget, staff, or a great deal of fanfare. It now has a few years of experience in process and products and appears ready to meet future challenges in human service funding and programming.

Notes to Chapter Eight

1. Joseph F. Zimmerman, *State-Local Relationships: A Partnership Approach*(New York: Praeger, 1983), 169-70.

2. Seattle-King County Human Resources Coalition. *First Annual Report* 1979-80. Seattle, 1981, 2.

3. *A Working Agreement Between County of King, City of Seattle, Region 4 Department of Social and Health Services, State of Washington, United Way of King County, Region X of the U.S. Department of Health, Education, and Welfare, Region X of U.S. Community Services Administration for Joint Human Services Planning, Service Delivery Coordination, Monitoring and Evaluation.* Seattle, Washington; April 1979, 1.

4. *Ibid.,* 2.

5. *Ibid.,* 4.

6. Seattle-King County Human Resources Coalition, *Common Data Base Committee Report,* Seattle, January, 1980, 1.

7. Seattle-King County Human Resources Coalition. *Report of the Task Force on Housing and Residential Care for the Mentally Ill.* Seattle, November, 1979, 3.

8. *Ibid.,* 4-13.

CHAPTER NINE

IGB Experiences in
Six Metropolitan Areas

A series of case studies only has meaning if the cases are woven together into a comprehensive analysis. Understanding of IGM processes is extended in this chapter through a summary assessment of the cases in the light of the research questions. The lessons of each case study were compared to determine a common explanation that can be used to characterize the nature of problem solving in IGM. As mentioned in chapter 2, the key to systematic use of case studies is to preserve a chain of evidence through analytic steps, including explicit citation of particular pieces of evidence. Therefore, the analysis will carry forth case evidence, summarizing the IGM process by addressing the central questions that guide the research.

Case generalization will attempt to put focus and meaning on the IGM process. The first section focuses on case study implications, addressing IGB formation and operational questions. The next section attempts to address the unique contributions of IGBs. Then the focus shifts to the central research questions of how and why officials attempt to solve their intergovernmental problems through IGBs. In chapter 10, a more general discussion of problem solving as an IGM approach is presented, as are study and research implications.

IGM AND THE IGBS: WHAT THE CASE STUDIES SUGGEST

This section will highlight general patterns that characterize all six IGBs and contribute to our understanding of IGM. The discussion centers on the first two research questions listed in chapter 2: What factors lead officials representing governments and the private sector to successfully work together? Why do officials who work in close proximity with each other find the need to regularize their patterns of activities into formal structures?

Confederal bodies

While each of the IGBs is different in form and has somewhat different operating characteristics, they all share structural and operational elements. All six problem-solving bodies are confederal in nature; they bring together the vital human service actors in such a way that no one actor or partner has rank or authority over another and each of the jurisdictions is respected. Most of the partners on these IGBs are major human service funders. The funders, and in some cases local elected and administrative officials, serve on the decision-making mechanisms of these bodies, which encourage open agendas. They are open in the sense that any partner may introduce a problem or issue for consideration by the local structure and each partner may share his or her own agency's agenda with the decision-making body. While the structures encourage this sharing of individual agendas, they also recognize and respect sensitive territorial issues, and agendas are usually formed by mutual agreement. This combination of trust and respect contributes to the responsive nature of these local structures.

Officials' involvement

Each locale developed a different means of involving or engaging elected officials in its activities. For example, elected officials' involvement in Pueblo is regular and detailed because city and county officials initiate many HRC actions and the COG is required to act on recommendations of the commission. Columbus and Dayton, on the other hand, include a city council member and a county commissioner on their boards. Others, such as Seattle, use indirect representation through top and administrative appointees. Of course, the degree of elected official involvement will vary with the community and the officials themselves. The important point is that their attention and participation can be captured at a policy or decision level.

Public-private interaction

The IGBs are also important vehicles for pulling together the public and private sectors. The structures provide for both the direct involvement and equal participation of private actors in a system where the public sector obviously outnumbers (and outfunds) and could dominate the private sector. There are direct benefits as well as spin-off effects from this. For example, Columbus, Indianapolis, Dayton, and Seattle formally convene the public and private actors as partners. There are obvious tensions from conflicting interests which will never be resolved; however, the structures relieve some of the tensions and allow the actors to explicitly define their roles in and expectations of the human service system.

Jurisdictional negotiations

Trust in the decision-making bodies has increased proportionately with the decrease in tensions between the jurisdictions and sectors. As a consequence, the local structures have evolved into a "go between" role in negotiations with the public and private sectors, as well as between pairs of governmental jurisdictions. Columbus, Indianapolis, Pueblo, Baltimore, and Seattle are all good examples of how IGBs are used as vehicles during intergovernmental and public/private negotiations. One specific case is when the private sector in Indianapolis refused to put up the money for the information system until the public sector came up with its half first. Another example is the Columbus MHSC's involvement with the state department of public welfare in facilitating the relief on local tax dollars for services eligible for federal monies. As these decision-making structures became more credible in their respective communities, more and more of the actors and agencies used the IGBs to bargain with actors from other sectors.

Political support

Another function IGBs play is that of a political buffer. The Columbus MHSC contribution to the group home-zoning ordinance is a prime example of how the individual projects and data produced by these groups help remove political pressure from local decision-makers. In the area of allocations, the projects have helped remove the heat of saying no from local officials' decision-making processes, as in the case of the Dayton Partnership's Title XX allocation process.

Decision by consensus

The decision rules used by the six local structures are also important to consider. Consensus is the mode of operation because it reinforces the partnerships and influences reluctant partners to agree, or go along with, majority decisions. Consensus is often facilitated when the staff makes individual contact with the partners prior to a formal meeting or vote. Whether consensus is produced aboveboard or behind the scenes is not important, but rather the fact that consensus can be achieved at all by these intergovernmental problem-solving organizations. If money is involved, the groups recognize that agreement and participation are more important to the IGB than money. For example, the city of Dayton remained a partner despite its unwillingness to contribute actual dollars to the partnership until 1982; it chose to make "in-kind" contributions. Some governmental units in Seattle have been reluctant financial partners, particularly because of difficult financial problems, but they are considered equal partners. All six localities realize that for the structures to survive, decision-making processes have to be tempered generously with compromise.

Responsiveness

The structures have also developed mechanisms for being responsive to the top decision-makers. By attacking one at a time problems generated by persons representing multiple jurisdictions, the partners have a chance to slowly test the structure, their role in the structure, and the kinds of work products the staff is capable of producing. The partners gradually become confident enough to delegate more work to the staff. Responsibility to decision-makers is also enhanced through the formal and informal decision-making processes created by the IGBs. Informal mechanisms, such as annual retreats and information-gathering sessions, are very important for creating an atmosphere in which the partners can participate with minimal threat to their individual autonomy.

Complexity

Another characteristic of the six IGBs is that all of the structures attempt to reflect the complexity of the political and human service systems. For example, Baltimore's structure represents the service delivery system and Seattle's structure illustrates the interaction between political and administrative decision-makers. Pueblo's relationship to local politicians is extremely close to the HRC's structural and financial ties to the Council of Governments (COG). In Dayton and Columbus the tie is more indirect through overlapping membership. It is important that the structures enable the partners to impact the system at all levels for rapid and effective problem resolution; however, no two local structures will ever be organized alike because of the unique nature of the political and human service systems.

Mixed federal and state involvements

The participation of federal and state officials is sometimes direct and sometimes indirect. Federal and state officials are most directly involved in the Seattle and Baltimore projects. Columbus and Pueblo have fostered more informal relationships, particularly between generalist officials, whereas Indianapolis and Dayton have engaged in less extensive contacts with state officials and have even less contact with federal officials.

Where federal and state participation is active and important to the structure, it has reduced the feeling that they are "the other guys, the enemy." Participation by officials from these two levels of government facilitates rapid interpretation of rules and regulations, bringing the groups closer to the root of the problem rather than leaving them bogged down with unimportant details. Particularly in the case of Baltimore, federal and state participation on the policy teams lead to discussions without animosity, enabling issues to be placed directly on the table so problem solving could ensue.

Indirect service delivery involvement and effort

Provider agency participation with the IGBs has been more indirect than that of federal and state officials. The decision-making bodies are composed of human service funders who feel they need to maintain some distance from the agencies they fund. The structures do help service agencies understand how the system works, who has what role in that system, and where they fit into or impact that system as service providers. More importantly, IGBs help local human service decision-makers work out sectoral problems. In cases where the IGB has not done well at this, projects have lost some credibility in the eyes of the decision-makers.

With most of the IGBs there is a greater indirect than direct effect on service delivery. This is because the decision-making bodies are composed of major human service funders who have more of an impact on the mix of services than actual service delivery. Change at the service delivery level is, however, considered an important activity of these bodies because it directly affects clients. Most local actors concluded that service delivery reform should not dominate the agendas of their groups. In the case of the Baltimore Blueprint, for example, some critics felt there was too much focus on service delivery. As a result, they feel their reforms did not impact the human services system at a policy level. At some point, problem solving has to move beyond services delivery and management to address conflicting policies at the local, state, and federal levels. Thus, it is a mix or balance of service delivery and policy changes that most effectively impacts the human service system and ensures jurisdictional coordination and cooperation.

Critical project results

Most important, the individual projects have meant a lot to the IGBs. The projects are tangible results of the groups' work efforts. They have produced direct benefits, such as a shift away from dependence on the local property tax in Columbus, a redirection of Title XX funds in Dayton, and agency consolidations in Pueblo. Project reports have also produced spin-off effects by being included as input data in other agencies' plans. In this way, the projects have increased the amount of available human service decision-making information within these localities. At some point, these data may become part of future community-wide and strategic human service plans.

The six IGBs also consider the projects proof of their ability to produce a report, consider alternatives and consequences, and solve a problem. These activities test the individual structures; they are a reaffirmation of the actors' commitments to the decision-making bodies. The projects are also a test of the interjurisdictional nature of the human service system and a means by which the actors can work through that system. In fact, many partners bring their own agendas to the IGBs in hopes of working through the complexities of the system. When this happens, it is not important whether or not the IGB gets credit for the project, but that the actor trusted and used the structure to work through a particular problem. The projects have thus facilitated openness, trust, and cooperation within the problem-solving structures.

Pragmatic adjustments

When each of the IGBs is viewed in terms of its objectives and within the constraints of its situation, the general success in dealing with specific intergovernmental issues is evident. Even though the original design for Columbus, Dayton, and Pueblo called for comprehensive system planning, all the structures ended up as problem-solving entities. This does not suggest that these IGBs were less successful in achieving their aims. Rather, one can infer that they took a detour to ensure organizational and procedural viability. It appears that the interjurisdictional, political, technical, and complex nature of the human service system necessitates (at least initially) a problem-solving mode as the means for cooperation and coordination. The specific human service problems various actors have a vested interest in keep the structures together and the actors involved. On the other hand, comprehensive planning requires an intricate knowledge of the system as a whole and an understanding of how the different sectors work together. This appears extremely difficult, particularly when there has been no money or incentives for comprehensive human service planning. Consequently, the IGBs tackle specific problems one at a time and explore a new dimension of the system with each new problem. However, it is entirely possible that at some point the information and understanding gained from the individual projects will filter up the decision-making chain and become part of a more comprehensive planning strategy. Indeed, as the cases suggest, several IGBs were beginning to develop more comprehensive attempts to understand the interdependencies of the various systems, as the several jurisdictions attempted to cope with funding reductions and renewed emphasis on public-private partnerships.

WHAT THE IGBS DO

A picture of the structure and operation of IGBs emerges from the case studies and the preceding summary account. Additional understanding of intergovernmental problem-solving roles will be accounted for through a brief summary of the general activities undertaken by the IGBs. In focusing on this issue, the discussion attempts an analysis of the third research question; how are these PS structures, i.e., IGBs, different from more traditional government structures? Generically, IGB work involves constructive action designed to change agreed upon intergovernmental discrepancies. Focus is almost always on community-level problems that are difficult or impossible for a single government to undertake. The types of problems or actions engaged in by the IGBs appear to fall into the following categories:

Service delivery changes

One of the most important IGB activities is use of their governmental and private sector leadership roles to trigger various changes in the local service delivery system. Most of the work at the Baltimore Blueprint and the decentralization project in Dayton illustrate this, although all of the IGBs were to some extent involved in such activities. Ordinarily these changes affected the arrangements by which services were delivered rather than altering the mode of service delivery itself. In each case the IGB proved to be the catalyst for getting relevant jurisdictions or agencies to make accommodations that would change the way they organized local services.

Community crises resolution

This role emerged in broad perspective as federal funding began to be reduced and the economic recession of the early 1980s affected a number of metropolitan areas. IGBs became the logical entities to help with the human dimensions of economic problems. As a result, many governments found themselves working together to find food, shelter, and other emergency services for those affected. Other crises were not economic. In Indianapolis and Columbus, respectively, it was a community-wide crisis generated by need to develop a coordinated paratransit system for the elderly and handicapped (generated when the state and federal governments refused to fund any programs until coordination occurred) and to somehow deal with large numbers of ex-mental hospital patients. In these cases the IGB provided the formal and informal impetus to get the disparate actors together for they were dealing with crises for which the solutions involved many interests.

Seeding and spinning off new services

Because of their metropolitan-wide perspectives, somewhat neutral orientations, and abilities in dealing with systematic complexity, IGBs have been vehicles to plug the gaps in service delivery in their communities. The work of a number of IGBs in organizing shelters and food banks, which are subsequently run by others, are cases in point. IGBs have also been active in developing new services for others to operate dealing with domestic violence and special children's services. The effort to secure housing for the mentally ill in Seattle is another example. The IGB does not operate such services, but it uses its role to create a new services delivery coalition or build on an existing one that can operate to fill new needs.

Catalysts for seeking new or different funding for the community

This role is obviously tied to the previous two, as IGBs attempt to find new sources of funds for identified service needs. In addition, they have attempted to leverage existing funds into new areas of community need. As new sources of public dollars have leveled off, this search has focused on the private sector but has also included competitive public dollars, such as those for emergency services. The Columbus IGB's NIS process to change funding formulas and Seattle's funding of new housing slots for the mentally ill are examples of this, as are the many cases where IGBs sought private dollars to fill gaps in real or anticipated public cutbacks. Again, this role stems from the IGBs neutral and metropolitan-wide perspectives. In this case the funds acquired or redirected are of immediate benefit to the operating jurisdiction.

Intergovernmental advocacy

In this role the IGB represents the community generally or one of its jurisdictional interests before other governments in order to effect a change of local benefit. Advocacy occurred either as a byproduct of other efforts or was a focused intergovernmental campaign. Illustrative actions include state lobbying for local pass-throughs of block grants, seeking or averting funding formula changes, favorable federal grant interpretations, or getting other jurisdictions (e.g., the state) to care for ex-mental hospital patients. In these cases the IGB has taken the lead for and with various jurisdictions in making important adjustments in the system that would benefit one or more jurisdictions and, presumably, the community as a whole.

Partnerships with area coordinating bodies

In a number of cases the IGBs have found they can improve the working of the local human services system by engaging in joint action with local service delivery coalitions. Two formal examples include the work to improve sector coordination in Pueblo and the Access Services Project in Indianapolis. In other situations, the role has been less formal, such as efforts to work with providers in domestic violence, children's services, mental health, and emergency services. The specific activities vary, ranging from encouraging improved communication to the joint development of focused plans for a particular population (e.g., handicapped children). The IGB can do a great deal to encourage existing coordination bodies to take on these expanded roles, in as much as they represent funders of individual agencies participating in the service delivery coalition.

Major funder information sharing and allocations

This IGB role—that of local funders working together—is perhaps one of the most significant. It provides an opportunity for city and county governments, special purpose governments, United Ways, foundations, and sometimes state and federal funders to assess what each other is allocating and, where possible, to make allocations according to a reciprocal formula that takes into account community needs and priorities. The GRS process in Pueblo and Columbus, Title XX in Dayton, the project funding process in Indianapolis and the contingency planning process in Columbus are examples of this role. Other IGBs were directly involved in similar activities. In each case jurisdictions retained their funding autonomy, but the process allowed for valuable information sharing and exchange.

Building capacity to understand and jointly manage the human services system

The IGBs offered an opportunity for a jurisdiction-wide perspective in a major function of government and of nonprofit agencies. Since each jurisdiction has a part of the human services action, the IGB provides a vehicle for an overall perspective. The Indianapolis HSIS system and Dayton's study of funding reduction consequences are two illustrations of this role. Less formally, much of the IGB work in performing services inventories, needs assessments, project plans, agency capacity studies, and helping smaller agencies and coalitions to help themselves is also representative. These activities contribute to the IGB's ability to oversee the entire system and to move it toward overall metropolitan goals and perspectives.

Community-wide planning

Although this has been one of the most elusive IGB roles, the IGBs have consistently sought to develop plans that merge jurisdictional interests into plans of a metropolitan orientation. The work in sector planning and coordination in Pueblo and contingency planning in Columbus come closest to describing this role. In other cases, IGB expected to engage in this type of activity, but have had to put it on the back burner while they became established and dealt with specific problem-solving projects. Some IGBs, such as Baltimore and Seattle, do not seek this as a role. For those that do see community-wide planning as a goal, it should become easier now that they have accomplishments to build on.

While not every IGB engaged in all of these roles, they became involved in most of them. Together, these roles characterize or identify the distinctive competence of the human services IGB.

THE SEQUENCE AND PROCESS OF PROBLEM SOLVING

The focus now shifts to the intergovernmental problem-solving process itself. Again, using findings from the IGBs, we will attempt to explain how the process worked in all six metropolitan areas, how the normal obstacles to coordination were overcome and the essential factors in reaching success. Specifically, the following research questions will be answered: What IGM sequence or process appears essential for the resolution of problems by IGBs? What factors or conditions are essential for solving intergovernmental problems? What lessons in overcoming the common barriers can we learn from the governmental coordination successes of the IGBs? These are the central research questions involved in this study, in that they explain the nature of PS and how it unfolded in each particular context.

A Problem-Solving Sequence

As was indicated in chapter 1, PS is generally understood to follow a sequence. The sequence adapted for intergovernmental purposes is: convening of decision-makers, identifying the problem, developing a course of action, implementing the decision, and monitoring the decision. This sequence became the framework in which specific problem resolution situations—the IGB projects—were investigated. Each of the seventeen projects or "mini cases" was broken down step by step to examine the degree to which each project followed the proposed sequence. The steps then were combined across the cases. The details are, of course, contained in the cases which are also documented elsewhere.[1] Further illustration from the cases that highlights the process is provided in the next section on IGM conditions. The general findings are reported here.

In order to demonstrate how the case evidence was structured to illustrate the PS sequence, Table 9.1 summarizes the information for one exemplary project from each IGB. The projects that have been selected are: Negotiated Investment Strategy, GRS Allocation Process, Decentralization Strategy, Housing and Residential Care for the Mentally Ill, Access Services Model, and Welfare and School Enrollment. Selection was for parsimony and demonstration purposes. These projects represent the more common routines in IGM that are faced in many communities: adjustment of categorical grant programs (Columbus), allocating unrestricted financial assistance (Pueblo), using a combination of funding sources to meet community needs (Dayton), redirecting program efforts in a functional area (Seattle), developing joint operational models (Indianapolis), and reforming administrative practices to achieve a program result (Baltimore).

Each of the five proposed steps is identified along the lefthand side of the chart and the specific activity that parallels that step for each project has been entered into the appropriate box. A horizontal reading of Table IX.1 reveals that, although the specifics are quite different, the activities are similar enough to fit under the common identifier. A vertical reading indicates that, in sequence, the steps make up a common PS format. Similar sequences were found to exist in the other eleven projects, although in some cases the pattern was altered slightly by previous work on projects outside of the IGB or procedures introduced by nonIGB partners. The sequence will now be explained in greater detail.

THE PROBLEM-SOLVING SEQUENCE

First, pertinent actors and other involved parties were convened into decision-making bodies, in this case the IGBs. The fact that they are permanent bodies of decision-makers and administrators distinguishes them from task forces, study groups, or blue-ribbon committees. In every case, the groups were brought together because of a problem, whether it was a sense of the need to coordinate for a given purpose or a specific issue such as an information system, grant allocation, or teenage pregnancies. Members understand the political implications of the problem areas, possess knowledge of human service programs, and, most importantly, have the authority to speak for their organization or jurisdiction. Considerable time was spent designing a structure and developing comfortable working relationships, but in each IGB these two functions were performed with regard to specific issues. Whether the original aim included the establishment of a broad-range program of coordination, a common information system, or a comprehensive planning program, in all cases continuity flowed from the initial consideration of a specific problem.

Second, the parameters of a specific problem were identified. Project staff and planning staff members from the "primary" or "sponsoring" jurisdiction, and perhaps key resource persons who were not decision-makers, researched the problem area and presented the findings. Generally,

Table 9.1   *The Problem-Solving Sequence*

	Columbus/MHSC Negotiated Investment Strategy	Pueblo/HRC GRS Allocation Process	Dayton/HSP Decentralization Strategy	Seattle/HRC Housing and Residential Care for the Mentally Ill	Indianapolis/CHSP Access Services Model	Baltimore/Blueprint Welfare and School Enrollment
Problem-solving sequence						
Convening of Decision-Makers	MHSC Executive Director made member of city team, preliminary discussions with mayor, other officials	HRC staff bring elected officials into process	HSP bring city and county officials together, Private sector also involved	HRC places on agenda; loans staff to project	Coalition meets and recognizes the problem	Policy Teams address school verification of AFDC children 16 and older
Identifying the problem	MHSC cabinet framed set of human service issues where federal and state requirements were unsuitable to local needs	HRC staff needs assessment and resource inventory/ identifies absence of priority-based funding for GRS allocations	City and county desire more multi-service centers to increase access to services	Shared staff investigate need for protected living environments, survey facilities and report to HRC on needs	Interagency staff group analyze funding requirements	Research problem, regulations, standards, and administrative practices

Developing a course of action	Issues agreed on by local negotiating teams, forwarded to state and federal teams. Teams synthesize issues	HRC staff identity program needs and service gaps and elected officials review GRS procedures and priorities	HSP study feasibility/ develop plan for staffing, financing, facility options, and social indicators	Report presented as model residential care continuum and strategy for implementation	Model proposed by staff; adopted by coalition	School and AFDC staff agree to track by coordinated computer data programs
Implementing the decision	Tripartite negotiations and agreement signed by officials of all three levels	HRC reviews applications for GRS funds and makes recommendations to elected officials; Contracts between funder government and agency drawn by HRC	County commission adopts plan and HSP oversees implementation	Review and acceptance by HRC; implementation by city and county; use of state funds to construct five facilities	Recognition of funding problem: joint funding of model	Agreement by federal-state officials to change support formula
Monitoring the decision	Informal oversight of process by parties	HRC monitor findings of agency reports and provides technical assistance where needed	Progress occasionally assessed, HSP becomes advocates as center development slowed	Verbal progress reports	Executives group formed to oversee and develop long-term solutions	Data program and policy teams review

the issue was discussed in detail by the decision-makers and agreement on the problem was forged. At this point, a specific issue became a formal part of the group's agenda with appropriate research tasks delegated to the staff. The staff usually presented its findings in the form of a staff report with a recommended course of action or a summary with conclusions, depending upon the particular style and operation of the locale.

Third, the decision body reviewed the reports submitted, discussed possible solutions, and ultimately developed or adopted a course of action. Because those adopting a course of action had authority to speak for their program or jurisdiction, securing the necessary support was less problemmatic than when actors not in authority attempt to coordinate. Through very different means, each of the six IGBs demonstrated repeatedly that once an issue passed the agenda and fact-finding thresholds, representative partners could usually deliver for their jurisdiction. The next step was "going back home," so to speak, to get ratification, or at least informal support, from that jurisdiction. The entire process of investigating, ratifying, and then deciding, proved to be an extremely long process, but necessary for any hope of implementation.

Fourth, the course of action was translated from policy agreement into practice. Actually, the genesis of the action steps was almost always contained in the research or fact-finding process, which was modified as decisions were made. Many discussions and negotiations with service delivery agencies, funding bodies, and governmental jurisdictions were undertaken during the early stages to determine the willingness and commitment to carry forth a proposed course of action. In every case, the process was complex and somewhat cumbersome, but respected the basic interjurisdictional nature of the enterprise, a necessary ingredient for joint decision making. Decisions were made by the IGB and ratified by the respective jurisdictions and service delivery agencies. IGBs have little direct power to implement their decisions. Furthermore, they rely on several jurisdictions taking simultaneous action and/or the primary or project staff laying out the steps to be followed, parties to be involved, and resources required.

Fifth, the IGB or its staff attempted to monitor the course of action to provide an information base to be fed back to the decision body for assessment and modification of the course of action. As Table IX.1 suggests, this last step was not as closely followed as the others. Systematic attempts to follow what actually happened by the use of reporting mechanisms or internal program evaluations were not regularly undertaken. Rather, information on the progress of joint decisions was informal and irregular, and evaluation tended to be post-mortem discussions or unstructured progress reports. Consequently, with few exceptions, feedback to the IGB for assessment and modification of courses of action, while it did occur, tended to be limited and disjointed.

Why this final step was not followed can only be speculated upon. Perhaps the IGBs and staff had expended so much effort in the earlier phases that they lacked sufficient fortitude to follow up. It could be that success in achieving decisions and a course of action led to further problem-solving demands, thus displacing efforts to monitor and evaluate. Of course, it is also possible that systematic monitoring for feedback did not occur to them as a necessary step, or it did and was not deemed important. Most plausibly, the interjurisdictional nature of the problem-solving framework made the confederal body reluctant to directly oversee the operation of an independent partner. The decision-makers primarily represent jurisdictions on a selective problem-solving body where the independence of those jurisdictions is to be maintained and preserved at all costs. All of the intergovernmental problem-solving steps test that independence, but none appears more sensitive and threatening than monitoring and evaluating the performance of one or more jurisdictions. Hence, it may be extremely difficult to require, or even expect, this step to be followed.

Although the research did not directly test these five steps as an hypothesis, respondents' open-ended descriptions of developmental and decisional processes, as well as the breakdown of practices leading to problem resolution, directly support most of the sequence. Because the six localities participated in four of the five steps in this process, it seems safe to conclude that, while this may not be the only successful sequence, it is a reasonable process to follow when contemplating intergovernmental problem solving. Each IGB followed a remarkably similar step-by-step process to arrive at agenda items, investigate solutions, and reach and carry out decisions.

Essential conditions

In the process of following this sequence the IGBs also appeared to be confronting common issues or contextual factors. These contextual factors— introduced in chapter 1 as legal-jurisdictional, political, technical, and task issues—appear to be necessary conditions for solving intergovernmental problems. Problem solving in IGM was introduced as the need for actors to confront these issues, developing a focused or issue-specific solution. These contextual factors will be illustrated from the research.[2]

Legal-jurisdictional issues

IGM means that the autonomy of the various parties must be respected. In bodies that bring together governmental units and private sector interests, the legal and political incentives to remain separate are much stronger than those to cooperate. Thus, both structure and process must ensure that the core "boundaries" of any given jurisdiction are not seriously threatened and are respected throughout the process.

Jurisdictional respect means accepting different definitions of service missions by different units of local government. In Dayton, for example, the city sees itself as an advocate for its citizens with other jurisdictions rather than as a direct-service provider. In Indianapolis, the city-county sees itself as the promoter and organizer of a basically private system. Pueblo city and county elected officials, by contrast, see themselves as the planners, coordinators, and providers of a nearly total public system, mixing their support with state and federal dollars. The other parties have to recognize, respect, and work within these self-definitions of jurisdictional roles.

Each partner jurisdiction also has its own governance structure, processes, and procedures. For example, there may be an elected chief executive, an elected legislative body, an elected commission, and governing body appointed by elected officials, a self-perpetuating private citizen board, an appointed executive staff, and civil service administrators, all needing to mesh their decision-processes. Decision-making and reporting procedures are quite different among, say a city council, a county department, a United Way board, or a large state bureaucracy. Important operations such as budget cycles, application formats, and reporting and monitoring procedures also differ by jurisdiction. United Way agencies normally operate on an annualized allocation process that begins after their fund drives. Local governments have budget cycles that often differ from each other as well as from the state and federal governments. Each of these bodies is likely to have a different, but established, application format. Foundations, on the other hand, tend to operate with less rigid time frames and have less structured application policies. Most of these units operate with their own reporting procedures; some monitor their funded programs and some do not; and some evaluate programs whereas others do not. The six IGBs did not attempt to integrate these various modes of operation into a single framework. To reach any solution, the differences have to be "worked around," with respect for, and willingness to work through, very different modes of operation. The IGBs make their processes work within different frameworks. The jurisdictional issue means recognizing and respecting differences.

Another jurisdictional component of the success of these IGBs is based on their ability to move forward slowly, respecting jurisdictional issues, finding common ground on which the specific problems at hand can be resolved. Clearly, super-pragmatism must abound when independent jurisdictions work together to solve problems. None of the IGBs became locked into a structure, nor did they test it in the abstract. They allowed the structure to be determined by the successive resolution of problems.

Each new problem-solving experience provided a test of the structure as well as feedback concerning its viability, thus providing an invaluable learning curve. Each group had to be prepared to accept a less-than-ideal solution to the problem, but a course of action nevertheless. In many cases, the groups evolved into a "two steps forward, one step backward" mode to strengthen the structure. As indicated, three of the six bodies shifted from a comprehensive to a problem-solving planning mode. As each IGB demonstrated its ability to work on and provide successful reports and solutions, credibility was enhanced, which gave them even more latitude to take on new issues and problems. Development of a structural framework for solving problems means adjustments must be sought by finding space to operate between jurisdictional questions.

Solution frameworks also need to be flexible enough to allow for changes that accommodate jurisdictional respect and ability to solve problems. Although a few examples will be offered, the developmental scenario of each IGB bears this out. In Dayton-Montgomery County, the partnership moved into its initial problem areas—multiservice centers and social service allocations—and the leadership began to understand the need to involve the top decision-makers more intermittently and the top administrators regularly. Thus, a two-tiered structure evolved into a three-tiered structure. In Indianapolis-Marion County, the major actors discovered that a large advisory group could not properly screen work and make recommendations on the common data base, so it was abolished. A working screening committee of top administrators was formed instead to advise the high-ranking members of a coalition steering committee. Although the Pueblo HRC was initially designed as a citizen planning commission it quickly moved into two issues of immediate concern brought to the group by elected officials—general revenue sharing allocations and fostering agency coordination. This set a pattern of close working relationships between the staff and elected officials, in effect bypassing commissioners. The relationship with local government officials was made more formal in early 1982. In other words, formal IGB structures evolved as the groups attempted to adjust jurisdictional questions while handling specific issues.

Political issues

There is no way to avoid politics when the issues and decisions involve mayors, councilpersons, county commissioners, special district boards, and representatives of significant private interests. Rather than make attempts to sublimate politics in IGB deliberations—as is often the case in coordinative bodies—politics was encouraged, to a point. The type of politics that was encouraged included partisan issues and differences, politics relating to fear of losing jurisdictional power or autonomy, and ideological questions. All were encouraged to be brought out in the open in order to see where the political (as well as the jurisdictional and technical) barriers were. Each political problem had to be met and overcome in order to attack the problem at hand.

If the political element became so obstructive that it impeded problem solving, eventually counteraction was taken. For example, a county commissioner who constantly bottled up procedures with personal objections was replaced on the IGB by the president of the commissioners. In another case, a city council IGB representative had to force an issue with a mayor who was blocking action by successful resolution of a city council vote. But these are extreme cases. In most cases, when political objections threatened to prevent action, attempts to persuade were undertaken. But persuasion was only possible because the parties involved were aware of the political concerns of their actors. IGM allows the politics to come out, as long as politicians are ultimately willing to focus on solutions.

Another concern is that actors bring different political process perspectives to the problem-solving experience. For example, private sector politics in human services in many communities is perceived by the public sector as behind-the-scenes control by a few who are influential over community foundations, and the protection of old-line social agencies by United Way boards. Public sector actors believe that programs are funded because of their informal political influence rather than demonstrated need. Private interests, which can generally act rapidly, become frustrated with the open and protracted decision processes that city councils and county boards necessarily follow. Private sector actors become impatient when city and county executives fight with their legislative bodies over issues they see as clearcut. In cases where state or federal government civil service administrators are involved in IGB decisions, they usually cannot take political positions or advocacy positions. Moreover, these bureaucratic actors are often at the political and administrative mercy of their appointive superiors in the capitals. The latter frequently do not know the local scene but often make the final decisions. These political differences are frustrating to local government actors who are used to deciding, but they are accepted as part of the IGM process. Any forged solutions must work within such political constraints.

A third political issue is that a key to success in IGM is to approach the public and private sectors as equals. Creative federalism in the 1960s brought the private sector into IGR[3], but the public sector has obviously possessed superior financial resources and has had considerable program influence on private agencies.[4] In the six IGBs, the two sectors evolved toward equal footing. In the process of researching, developing, and implementing particular solutions, each side was forced to develop a deeper understanding of how the other sector worked. IGM requires that private sector members be considered as partners in all respects and not be treated as dependents, agents, or actors outside the intergovernmental system.

A final political issue is that mutual ownership—the feeling on the part of most parties that they shared a stake in the solution—is critical. This proved to be one of the most important political characteristics. Ownership consists of several components, including establishing and maintaining the interest of all parties, ensuring their active involvement, and sharing the products.

Establishing and maintaining the active participation of major human service funders, elected officials, and administrators means the parties have a vested interest in the IGB structure's existence and success. For example, the IGBs use a wide base of funding to ensure that the parties have a vested interest in both the content of the problem-solving and the success of the project. The issues addressed were of recognized joint concern and provided benefits for the local community. Seattle's energy assistance project and Columbus' study of the effects of group homes on property values represent problems whose resolutions provided mutual benefits to the parties.

Ownership is also facilitated by involving those parties with control over the programs, namely human service administrators and service providers. Continuous efforts are made to include these actors' input and information into IGB problem-solving activities. For example, Dayton uses information from service providers' opinions as to an appropriate policy stance for the partnership. Columbus incorporates human service administrators into its structure with its cabinet of executives and uses input from service providers on special project committees. Successful problem solving requires the spectrum of actors to have a sense of a community-wide self-help effort.

Finally, ownership of IGB products is shared. With mutual projects, the information sought and gained is provided through several agencies, individuals, and jurisdictions. For example, Dayton's research information is incorporated into almost every human services plan in the area. Products developed together are often used by individual partners in their agencies. Columbus' study of Franklin County residents' nutritional needs was used to arrive at certain priorities for the county's department of welfare. IGM requires that all problem-solvers feel they have a stake in the solution and thus own a piece of the action.

Technical issues

At some point in the IGM process the technical questions have to be researched and developed. In this study, questions such as the following became preeminent: How can an information and referral system be built? What steps have to be taken to build and maintain small group homes for the mentally disabled? What steps need to be undertaken in order to follow a contingency planning process? What kind of definitions, taxonomy, entries, and forms need to be employed in order to have a common data base? What goals, objectives, and criteria need to be instituted in order to develop an information framework suitable for an allocation process? How can attendance and enrollment be tracked in order to satisfy AFDC requirements? In other words, every one of the problems dealt with by IGBs had a technical strand that had to be woven into the fiber of IGM.

Technical issues usually involved extensive staff level "gut work" in digging deep into the problem at hand. It often meant months of looking at the current state of the art, talking to consultants, examining experiences in other communities using similar technology, investigating the existing and potential role of various IGB partners and service delivery agencies in implementing the technology. While these specifics were primarily working staff activities, they were interactively filtered up through the administrative and political actors. No problem was resolved without unraveling the techniques of how it was to be done in order that all parties could see it in proposed form, react to and ultimately agree on a course of action.

The process and the technical product are intertwined in IGM. Recognition that only so much time could be spent in IGB structure and process made it possible to move quickly to the heart of the problems—such as development of a common information system, planning for energy assistance, allocating revenue sharing, or reducing school truancy—as a means of testing the viability of the structure in developing technical solutions. Each body's process evolved and was reformulated as concrete strategies were developed. In Pueblo, for example, requests by elected officials to match GRS requests against alternative sources of funding and community priorities led to the need to establish an allocation process and then a grants management process. This output led to subsequent work in coordination and consolidation. In contrast, a concrete technical product was delayed for more than two years in Indianapolis because so much effort was placed in a single project, a common information system. The system required a considerable start-up investment, and the technical group delayed use of the system until 1980 census data were available. The delay jeopardized the stability of the IGB, until it finally moved to other issues. Thus, the technical work products—studies, task force reports, proposed solutions, plans, new resources—are essential to the life of the process. Jurisdictional participants will only continue to contribute their time, energy, and resources if products containing technically-oriented solutions to problems are forthcoming, which, in turn, reinforces their involvement. The process is dependent on products.

Task issues

In IGM, decisions must be made at several levels. The potential for consensus among intergovernmental decision-makers, or in the case of IGBs their policy bodies, is directly related to the kinds of decisions made prior to formal consideration of a proposal or plan of action. Decisions concerning the problem's pervasiveness, significance, potential for resolution and relevance to the different partners are made at many different levels before a problem is presented for formal consideration.

Administrative staff are the primary force behind this sequential decision-making process. They negotiate agreements with many different actors during the problem identification and verification stages. For example, the Columbus MHSC staff initiates a project with a staff report to the board of trustees. The staff report is the product of dialogue and negotiations with the relevant service agencies and administrators, plus active informal contact with the trustees. All MHSC members are aware of the report, its purpose, and importance to their individual interests before it is submitted to the board. The stage is set for the board's initial decision to approve the report for more extensive study. Similar processes have been followed in the other five IGBs.

A second stage or set of decisions occurs during the formulation of a problem resolution. In all the cases, major project studies led to a plan of action for the policy bodies' approval and implementation. The staffs also were instrumental in negotiating these decisions with administrators and funders. The partners are informed of their roles in the plan for resolution and are encouraged to begin discussions with their respective jurisdictions and agencies to identify and resolve agency-specific problems with the plan. All these decisions determine the final plan of action and lend an air of legitimacy to it in addition to facilitating its successful implementation. This process represents a kind of pragmatic "feeling your way through" approach to intergovernmental decision making.

Another component of the IGM task is to build an inclusive set of participants who decide in an overlapping fashion. Each IGB found it necessary to involve a wide range of individuals in decisions. This included a mixed group of: elected legislative officials, appointed government executives, general and special purpose government agency staff, council on government and regional planning staffs, foundation executives, executives and staff of private funding bodies, and private citizens. These persons share in the decision-making process. The very nature of the organizations that comprise the structures throw these actors together. The focus is always on the resolution of particular problems, perhaps the only reason such a disparate group cooperates.

In most communities, participation by numerous decision-makers was facilitated by different working levels. No two structures were alike.

Dayton used three groups: planners, executives, and policy makers. Columbus operated with a broadly representative commission of citizens, executives and decision-makers; a staff; and a cabinet of lead-agency executives. Indianapolis used a two-tiered decision-makers/executive level and screening committee made up of top professional staff from several jurisdictions. Pueblo involved the COG, the citizen HRC, and the staff. Baltimore employed three levels: government signators, policy teams, and staff. Even Seattle, which is basically made up of top executive staff members, used another level by bringing shared staff into their task force structure.

Sometimes these groups overlap, suggesting that more than one level is required to reach decisions. Most of the technical research, fact-finding, and basic oversight was conducted at the task force, staff, and working levels. Results and agency policies, legal questions, rules, regulations, discovery of resources, and possible accommodations were processed at the middle executive level. A top decision or policy level then reacted to the work, added political issues, if they were not already present, and fine tuned a decision or position to be implemented by the respective jurisdictions.

Compounding the complexity in intergovernmental decisions is the fact that these subgroups usually have to act simultaneously. The investment in a solution that is researched, planned and then turned down is considered too costly. Moreover, solutions often amount to the kinds of accommodations that can be reached through the array of jurisdictions. Thus, it is almost always necessary at the first, staff investigator level for people to check their work periodically with the second, working executive level for feedback, directions, and, above all, feasibility. In turn, the feasibility of actions at the working level has to be field tested by regular consultation with politicians and top-level private funders. While perhaps cumbersome to those who are used to more rapid decision making within a single organization, simultaneous decision making by overlapping participants representing different jurisdictions is necessary to ensure that some solution results. Sequential decisions appear to provide so many veto points that nothing can be accomplished between jurisdictions unless the potential vetoes are tested.

Another task component of IGM is the emergence of special administrative tools. These are interjurisdictional management supports designed to address particular tasks identified during the investigation of a problem. They represent a compromise between creating "single management approaches," which merge all the jurisdictions' practices into one, and disjointed jurisdiction-by-jurisdiction arrangements.

The need for these tools usually arises as a by-product of work on specific problems. For example, the Columbus MHSC study of the fiscal and program requirements from common local funders identified several problems with conflicting demands on service agencies. The commission decided to try to eliminate some of these conflicting requirements and began the process with the Unified Audit Agreement involving the city, United Way, and the mental health board. MHSC is also developing a unified application process for program and fiscal proposal submission by service providers. If the process succeeds, the final segment of this effort to eliminate conflicting requirements is a crosswalk service classification system for compatible program and fiscal monitoring.

Another example of special administrative tools is the Dayton Partnership's minimum capacity effort. Minimum capacity requires a survey of service providers and an updating of demonstrated economic and social needs data to provide information to agencies and funders in planning and fund allocation. This information is then incorporated into a methodology for establishing minimum levels of service that could be provided to meet county residents' needs. The study information also has been used to help determine a human services levy for the county.

Administrative tools are the means used to bridge the technical differences that exist between jurisdictions and sectors and are necessary for problem-solving. In a fashion similar to the tools and approaches used to support the policy management process, these emergent tools facilitate local assumption and jurisdictional perspectives on administrative and program decision responsibilities, a factor likely to become more important in the future.[5]

Finally, the most central IGM task issue is that administration is ordinarily a set of management actions by separate organizations. In very few cases did the IGB itself assume a role equivalent to a single governmental unit by carrying out a decision through its structure. The GRS contract monitoring process in Pueblo, GRS allocations for the City of Columbus, and Title XX allocations for Montgomery County, all follow this pattern. Federal and state grants to the IGBs are also administered through the staff of the structure.

IGM more commonly involves a complex execution of decisions by "mutual carrying out of agreements," through the two or more independent units that have participated in the problem solution. Although contracting sometimes occurs, jurisdictions are normally unable or unwilling to delegate complete program authority or transfer it to another jurisdiction. Thus, pursuing a course of action often means that a city government may perform one function, a county government another, and a private sector funder yet another. For example, in Dayton the decentralization of services strategy was pursued in the following manner: The city developed the physical structures with support from its Community Development Block Grant funds; the county provided the basic staffing by locating its welfare offices on site; and private agencies, funded by the mental health board and the United Way, "outstationed" personnel there. In Columbus, the same pattern was followed in the negotiated investment strategy approach. A city-driven change in the local county property tax base for child welfare was predicated on the state's seeking a waiver to amend its AFDC plan and the federal government's accepting it. The decision implementation process thus involved a set of actions by two or more jurisdictions.

Another execution pattern involved encouraging the partners to follow IGB decisions simultaneously. This pattern was exemplified in the Columbus contingency planning process, the Indianapolis access services model, the Dayton impact analysis project, Pueblo's A-95 review, and the Seattle common data base. These involved, or at least had implications for, the actions of all partners because they had the potential to affect the timing of funding decisions, shifts in priorities, changes in mechanisms by which funds were allocated, the processing of information, reporting, monitoring, or other administrative authority. In other words, at this level, the combined processes attempt to influence the way all individual jurisdictions are administered.

In a similar fashion, financial administration is conducted through separate organizations. With the exception of the small amounts of money contributed for staffing the IGBs, legal and program mandates usually require the resources to remain with the jurisdictions. This often leads to difficulties in allocating program costs among jurisdictions. IGBs find it difficult to assess fair and equitable costs. Because decisions have a differential impact on, and benefit to, partner jurisdictions, costs are often shared differentially. The means of supporting the IGB structure also varies. While most partners make unrestricted contributions, some contract for specific services, others offer in-kind services, and others trade-off resources, such as by providing buildings in lieu of money. Financing provides yet another example of mutual IGM action.

Thus, in most cases, the primary administrative activity occurs within one or more of the jurisdictions rather than the IGB. The IGB staff is responsible for convening, researching, moving the parties toward a decision, and sometimes overseeing, but only rarely executes for a unit of government. It operates at the periphery and is at the mercy of the administrative leadership, skills, and procedures of the unit. Carrying out decisions, therefore, is a task element that requires another set of pragmatic adjustments. The administrative task is ordinarily discontinuous, involving a set of combined management actions because of its jurisdictional base and its political and technical nature.

The examination of the four contexts in the six cases suggests that, to the extent that the IGB processes examined are representative of intergovernmental affairs, legal/jurisdictional, political, and technical factors converge on a task orientation to solve problems. The research has revealed a scenario in which individual problems are solved by a process of accounting for and dealing with these relevant considerations and applying them to the situation at hand. An essential element in the formula for success in IGM appears to be a focus on such direct action for realistic goal achievement.

Coordination Lessons

The research also offered some modest suggestions for overcoming the barriers to coordination. The willingness on the part of key actors to make adjustments while focusing on the narrow task at hand appears to explain these IGBs' relatively high levels of coordination. This conclusion is similar to Seidman's. He observed that federal interagency committees can be effective when: (1) they are assigned appropriate tasks within their competence; (2) members have the authority and motivation to do what is necessary to solve the problem; (3) they are not called upon to revise basic government policies, but to obtain agreement on the work that needs to be done; and (4) they see that decisions are carried out on a phased time schedule. Coordinating bodies are often unsuccessful because they are expected to solve problems they are inherently incapable of solving and which are alien to the purpose for which they were organized.[6] The exhaustive sequence of actions undertaken by the IGBs is not a prescription for others to follow, but a signal of what is likely to be in store for them if they are serious about coordinating activity, like multijurisdictional problem solving. Specifically, the sequence suggests that a large time investment is needed for development and mutual understanding; that the real political and administrative decision-makers must be involved, but the details must be left to the operatives; that the focus must be on the specifics of the issues at hand; that the constant testing and negotiating of solutions is essential; and that eventually the decision-makers must reach an agreement, put it on paper, and carry it out through the relevant jurisdictions. This process promises success with hard work, but is subject to the same limits and problems identified with matrix structures within organizations, such as power confusion, power struggles, scapegoating, fear that high costs will be associated with the structure, and the mistaken belief that the structure itself constitutes group decision-making.[7]

The focus on specific problems, instead of contrived means of cooperation, appears to be a particular keynote of success in these metropolitan areas. The real products of intergovernmental negotiations have been the solution of problems considered important to the local actors. Concrete solutions, such as a group home-zoning ordinance, housing units for the mentally ill, the provision of emergency shelter for homeless persons, new types of classroom instruction, and increased access to services, have been forthcoming. In many cases, the local parties could see important financial results, such as the more equitable allocation of scarce and declining dollars or easing of the local tax burden. As Pressman concluded, intergovernmental actors need to focus on creating a framework for collaborative day-to-day actions upon which joint policy formulation and implementation can occur.[8] Thus, the research provides indicators of how to overcome problems in coordination, such as lack of legal or statutory authority, low levels of agency interdependence or resource dependency, an absence of mutual understanding, and difficulties in standardization of procedures.

The study now concludes with a general analysis of problem solving in intergovernmental management, as well as an assessment of research in intergovernmental processes.

Notes to Chapter Nine

1. Robert Agranoff, "Alternative Difference Resolution Approaches in Intergovernmental Management," Paper presented at Midwest Political Science Association, Chicago, Illinois, April 1984.

2. This section is edited from Robert Agranoff and Valerie A. Lindsay, "Intergovernmental Management: Perspectives from Human Services Problem Solving at the Local Level," *Public Administration Review* 43 (May/June 1983), 230-35.

3. David B. Walker, *Toward a Functioning Federalism*, (Cambridge: Winthrop, 1981), 102-103.

4. Ralph M. Kraemer, *Voluntary Agencies in the Welfare State* (Berkeley: University of California Press, 1981), 152-252.

5. Robert Agranoff and Alex Pattakos, *Dimensions of Services Integration* (Rockville: Project SHARE Monographs, 1979), 97.

6. Harold R. Seidman, *Politics, Position and Power: The Dynamics of Federal Organization*, 3d; ed. (New York: Oxford, 1980), 215.

7. Stanley M. Davis and Paul R. Lawrence, "Problems of Matrix Organizations," *Harvard Business Review*, 56 (May/June 1978), 242-247.

8. Jeffrey L. Pressman, *Federal Programs and City Politics*, (Berkeley and Los Angeles: University of California Press, 1975), 137-38.

CHAPTER TEN

Conclusion: Solving Intergovernmental Problems

The cases document the work of intergovernmental actors—elected officials, public and private managers, and private sector leaders—as they attempt to tackle the daily business of making federal and state programs work within their communities. Even though the IGB structures are somewhat different, their problem-solving orientation ties them together. Characterizations like public and private cooperation, building local capacity, policy management, service delivery reform, making coordination work, and joint problem resolution suggest the variety of activities that constitute the routines of IGM.

Greater attention to such routines is needed if there is to be a complete understanding of this intractable subject. Much of our intergovernmental attention is directed to the dramatic: a state declines to participate in a grant program, a local government refuses to comply with a regulation and declares a willingness to litigate, a $30 million audit exception is announced, and a group of United Ways protest the way a state is handling social service grant contracting. While these actions represent significant means of defining the workings of the intergovernmental system, they mask thousands of routine transactions. The need to redirect grant money from meals to transportation in Columbus, or the need to streamline the means of verification of welfare children attending school in Baltimore, or the need to provide energy assistance in Seattle represent transactions that do not normally make the newspapers or come to the attention of mayors, governors or presidents. They rarely involve confrontational contacts and decisions, threats of penalty, high level political pressure, or class action litigation. Rather, as depicted in the six cases, resolution is achieved through protracted processes, leading to agreements made on the basis of administrative interpretations, single party or multiple accommodations, and other coordinated courses of action. Such accommodations are based on what appears to be reasonable and within the general scope of statutory and regulatory intent.

The routines followed by the IGBs appear to be relatively typical of the everyday issues faced by intergovernmental managers. The seventeen projects that were investigated in detail reveal a variety of problems faced by persons who are called upon to make the intergovernmental system work. Table X.1 characterizes these problems in a summary fashion by presenting a generic descriptor of each of the projects. This descriptor is written to roughly correspond to similar work likely to be performed by all types of managers at federal, state, substate, and local levels, as well as the private sector.

When viewed generically, or outside of their human services and IGB contexts, it is clear that these routines are broadly applicable. Most managers who deal with intergovernmental issues are frequently called upon to adjust categorical grants, understand the complexities of the system, allocate discretionary funds, make state and federal programs and dollars serve local purposes, adjust regulatory provisions to program intent, apply state codes within local jurisdictions, and so on. While there is, of course, no basis for comparison of these routines with another universe, they do stand as empirical illustrations of the type of IGM routines managers are called upon to deal with every day and therefore deserve attention to improve understanding of and operation within the system.

IGBs working primarily at the local level then became the lens through which the routines of IGM were examined. The local scene was selected as a laboratory because services are delivered at that level, and unsolved policy questions, administrative solutions, or requirements can no longer be passed on. To be sure, it is federal and state statutory, administrative judicial, and regulatory actions that are most responsible for the intergovernmental problems, and those issues must also be addressed.[1] But as "the system" is reformed, the local delivery agents must continue to solve the everyday problems of getting services to people and that task increasingly requires intergovernmental management.

The need to systematically engage in IGM appears to have been implicitly recognized in Dayton, Indianapolis, Columbus, Baltimore, Pueblo, and Seattle. Their problems were considered significant enough to work out structures and processes unique to the local situation but devoted to similar aims. These intergovernmental management experiments will become increasingly significant. The sheer complexity of the system, or nonsystem, with its categorical grants, block grants, jurisdictional responsibilities, public, quasi-public, and private auspices is almost beyond comprehension. While the array has become more diverse, it has also become more interdependent, with coordination requirements, multiple fund sources, matching requirements, and, most important, the need for providers in one jurisdiction to secure services from another.

Table 10.1   IGM Routines Represented by IGB Projects

IGB Location	Project	Routine
Dayton	Decentralization	Using combined funding sources to meet felt community needs.
Dayton	Title XX Allocation	Creating a method for allocating dedicated block grant funds.
Dayton	Impact Analysis	Providing policy makers information on the local impact of federal funding patterns.
Indianapolis	Access Services	Developing a joint operations model.
Indianapolis	Human Services Information System	Creating relevant decision-making information for a highly intergovernment-alized local delivery system.
Columbus	Negotiated Invest-ment Strategy	Reaching two- or three-level agreement on adjustments to categorical grants.
Columbus	Deinstitutionalization/ Group Homes	Assisting local decision-makers apply a a state code.
Columbus	Allocation	Developing a criteria-based formula for distribution of relatively unrestricted financial assistance.
Pueblo	GRS	Allocating and managing relatively unrestricted financial assistance.
Pueblo	A-95	Reviewing federal grant applications within local concerns.
Pueblo	Sector Planning & Coordination	Establishing linkages between disparate service providers in the same functional areas.
Baltimore	Foster Care Reform	Changing administrative procedures and standards
Baltimore	Welfare/School Enrollment	Reforming intergovernmental administrative practices and securing regulatory changes to achieve a program result.
Baltimore	Adolescent Pregnancy	Developing a comprehensive strategy to meet a local concern with multi level government action.
Seattle	Housing for Mentally Ill	Redirecting a state program to fit changing state and local priorities.
Seattle	Common Data Base	Crafting new tools for joint planning.
Seattle	Energy Assistance	Implementing a complicated, multi recipient federal-state program on a metropolitan-wide basis.

Also, as resources to pay for services have leveled off, or as they come under the pressure of severe reductions, jurisdictions look to each other for opportunities to pick up the slack, share or trade-off resources and find places where cuts can be made with the least pain. Finally, elected officials and executive-level administrators who are particularly close to financial questions at the local level call for greater efficiency, effectiveness, and accountability. These demands mean that more communities will inevitably have to coalesce the primary jurisdictions to meet over local issues.

PROBLEM SOLVING AS AN IGM APPROACH

In chapter 1 problem-solving was identified as one of the major qualities of IGM. Following the principles of creative management and conflict management, PS was defined as a formal process, which in the case of jurisdictional representatives requires that officials recognize a discrepancy between a current state and desired end, openly and creatively explore options, and reach a solution that is beneficial to more than one interest. Using a standard interorganizational conflict distinction, PS is thus distinguished from bargaining in that the latter focuses on issues in which one organization's gain is perceived to be tied to another's loss, communication tends to be selective and guarded, with parties attempting to control other's options.[2] Problem solving, by contrast, brings together parties in circumstances dominated by issues in which common interests are perceived as more important than conflicting interests, there are perceptions of common concern, there is relatively open exchange of information, and a search for mutual gains is pursued.[3] PS is now assessed as an IGM process.

Initially, a few observations about the utility of PS appear necessary. First, the process obviously does not require a formal structure like an IGB. As the policy implementation studies cited in chapter 2 indicate, intergovernmental managers should be able to act on a more *ad hoc* basis when they agree a problem exists and choose to follow similar steps to convening, identifying, solving, implementing and monitoring.

Second, the observed sequence was occasionally modified in the light of actual circumstances. There had to be room for many decision "loops" throughout the process, and in some cases it had to return to earlier steps. The Seattle data base project illustrates the difficulty of standardizing financial reporting, and the problem had been redefined several times. Also, the IGBs sometimes found it necessary to formally bypass steps when they had been completed elsewhere, such as when a problem had already been researched. The Columbus group home-zoning effort was initiated by MHSC after one of its partners had identified the problem. The Indianapolis access services model was built on a study that had been conducted by the Community Service Council. Rather than stand on procedure, they accepted what had been done to achieve results.

Third, social and psychological considerations not systematically investigated—such as the willingness to make adjustments, the willingness to reach agreement, put it on paper, and carry it out through relevant jurisdictions—also appear important. These qualities were repeatedly mentioned by key actors when asked what advice they would offer other public officials who were faced with similar problems. These apparently necessary conditions, along with the sequence of PS steps, proved to be a blueprint for focused or issue-based coordination between parties representing governments.

Fourth, and finally, PS is obviously not an all-purpose IGM tool. As will be suggested, there are situations where bargaining, structural reform or some other IGM approach is more appropriate. IGB officials and staff identified a number of discrepancies—e.g., state mandates and allocation formulas, federal substate districting requirements, burdensome statutory grant provisions, and tax limitations—that they felt were beyond the ability of their structure to attack through normal means of operation. However, in settings where PS can contribute to the resolution of differences between governments, it can be an extremely parsimonious and effective tool for managers. PS is used more regularly than is recognized, contributing to system and process development as well as to immediate problems at hand.

In IGM, the parties must agree that there is a discrepancy between an actual situation and some desired state and be willing to face that situation together. In this study, parties attempted to solve "middle-level problems" they had the capacity to deal with. Problems such as insufficient community housing for the mentally ill in Seattle, inadequate verification of school attendance in Baltimore, and the need to develop a strategy to deal with federal funding reductions in Columbus are examples. These and other issues—such as those related to the allocation of discretionary funding, sector planning and coordination, or changing federal and state interpretations—involved issues where the IGB parties could get the relevant actors to agree that they would work on them. Similar situations arise in other communities: a city manager and the director of a transit district find that a planned bus rerouting will disrupt city plans for some limited traffic areas; state finance department officials and town or village clerks are dissatisfied with the number of audit exceptions local officials receive for not performing according to state code; a state education board adds a computer literacy requirement and a fiscally troubled school district has considered increasing its computer instruction but is hard pressed to find the funds to meet this mandate.

There are also many situations where agreement cannot be reached. Numerous grant regulations turn out to be detailed statutory prescriptions that administrators feel compelled to follow closely and can allow no exceptions. In this IGB study, issues where the state or federal government would not engage in resolution, or where local politicians wished to avoid major confrontations, or where there was fear that the independence of jurisdictions would be threatened were avoided. But in many other situations there was sufficient agreement that a problem existed and could be approached, usually involving some minimal level of conflict conducive to a productive solution[4] that could be handled by the involved parties without outside or third-party intervention.[5]

In addition, the interests of the parties need to be common but not necessarily identical. Local elected official pressure to have a city-county strategy to allocate GRS funds in Pueblo, the agreed-upon perception by chief administrators in Dayton that there was inaccessibility to services, and Baltimore agency officials' concern for an adolescent pregnancy prevention strategy all constitute areas where parties had enough interest to commit to doing something about the issue. Following the previously mentioned situations external to the IGB study: the city manager and the transit district manager want public transportation in the congested area of the city; state officials supervising local clerks' financial management prefer, along with the locals, that they do a competent job and not be subject to civil or criminal penalties; and, the school board agrees with the intent of a state-mandated computer literacy program, even though it contests many details of the regulations. In many other IGM situations, however, such commonality does not exist. The jurisdictional factor in intergovernmental relations, as well as the constitutional and legal arrangements surrounding federalism, encourages autonomy. Intergovernmental actors need to see their interests as distinct, and therefore protect their interests at all costs. But commonality of interests is also possible, as implied in the "picket fence" federalism concept. Despite the obvious centrifugal tendencies of this characterization, Wright suggests that implicit in the notion is "a sense of program purpose, or one or more strategies for coordination, and a locus of responsibility."[6] This orientation is perhaps what drives officials to work on the resolution of problems. In PS there is merely a need for parties to come together, convene in some sort of forum, and agree that there is a problem surrounding an area of mutual interest.

PS also requires that an open exchange of information, related to the problem and its potential solution, be revealed by the involved parties. IGB processes revealed such an open participative pattern. Budgets and funding sources were openly exchanged in order to study the impact of funding reductions in Columbus and Dayton. The availability of funds, per diem costs, and housing slots was revealed by all parties in Seattle.

Fee and wage scales, service case-load slack, and purchasing practices were shared in Pueblo. Federal, state and local teams for Columbus did not hold back—they revealed what they could and could not do—during the issue-synthesizing stage of the Negotiated Investment Strategy Process. Again, following our other examples, the city manager and transit manager need to share their plans, funding sources, and funding requirements; local clerks must show state officials how they manage their books so problems can be discovered and improvements can be made; the school district must reveal available resources to meet the computer literacy requirement, whereas the state must explain what might constitute acceptable compliance.

There are other intergovernmental situations where such open exchange is not in the best interests of the parties. For example, when proposing grant objectives, potential recipients do not like to state anything that appears too jurisdictionally self-serving and inconsistent with funder program aims. Recipient jurisdiction intents in requests for grant dollars and even figures are often covert. A former state department head once related that he had two budgets, "one for the feds and a real one." But in PS openness offers the benefits of bringing out differences, contributing to understanding, clarifying the issues, building on ultimate acceptance, and suggesting procedures and ground rules for resolution.[7] In other words, the emphasis is placed on spontaneity and a more open participation pattern.[8] At a minimum, IGM parties need to focus on the issue in an open fashion, look deeply into the parameters of the problem using the shared information, while exploring avenues of possible resolution.

Next, there is a need to look for and to develop the most creative solution possible. It begins with a search of the openly shared information, proceeds to clarification of issues, and then, most importantly, focuses on the actual working out of an alternative. Through this process, the nonroutine, nonbureaucratic solution finally emerges. The policy implementation studies mentioned in chapter 1 demonstrate how officials often have to go outside of normal bureaucratic routines to make things work: for example, by using a network of technical assistants, by allowing unconventional practices not in the regulations and guidelines but consistent with program aims, and by administratively approving practices that were thought to require formal approval. In the IGB study, solutions such as a joint management model for multiservice centers in Dayton, a jointly financed and shared information system in Indianapolis, a common grants management process in Pueblo, and numerous joint or mutual administrative actions in Baltimore represent such creativity. Similarly, as in our other examples: the city and the transit district agree to reroute to the immediate fringe of the limited traffic area; the state and local officials work out a plan for informal compliance review or a pre-audit; and the school board and state agency work out an interim agreement to contract with an area vocational school for computer training at school sites.

How are such creative solutions developed? Petrella and Block's diagnostic work on creative conflict resolution offers important clues. After initial stages similar to those described in this study, parties must move to confrontation and bonding, i.e., establishing a working contract.[9] The authors suggest that parties are ready to confront the issues when they can clearly identify: (1) the important substantive issues, (2) the existence of mutual positive motivation, (3) the existence of a reasonable balance of power, (4) psychological readiness to confront differences, and (5) a belief, grounded in fact, that there is sufficient control to make a solution work.[10] Readiness for bonding can be identified in one or more of the following ways: (1) pressure by the group to develop solutions; (2) recognition that critical issues have been explored, and (3) visible symmetry in the parties' perception of (a) injustices endured because of the problem, (b) competency and the kind of contributions parties have to offer, and (c) the interdependence or the need each has for the other.[11] While the IGB study did not empirically test each of these social-psychological resolution states, a similarity of process—identifying the problem, developing a course of action, implementing the decision—required similar states of mind in confrontation and bonding.

Finally, solutions not only should be creative but as mutually beneficial as possible. In the IGB study, many benefits accrued as a result of the process: new sources of funding for agencies and reduced county property taxes in Columbus; a data base for all agencies and governments to use in Indianapolis; planning information for the state, new housing units for mentally ill clients, and relief of the overcrowded county jail in Seattle; and decreased federal, state, and local AFDC payments in Baltimore. In the three examples external to the IGB study: the city and the transit district end up with routes that minimize disruption and maximize ridership; state finance officials get increased compliance and local clerks suffer fewer penalties, and both parties ultimately decrease their overall work load; the state education agency gains compliance while the local school district minimizes staff and equipment costs, and both parties launch a new program. Of course, maximizing the benefits to all parties is not always possible in IGM. For example, most regulatory requirements in grants put the cost burden on the grantee. Standards set in grants typically require many hours and dollars in compliance. The results of negotiations between a state and the federal government over a waiver may set standards at a level where the state is paying a far larger share of the costs than anticipated. In PS, however, intergovernmental actors need not assume that one party's gain is necessarily another one's loss. The pursuit of a creative solution often leads to mutual gains.

PS is an IGM approach that should be encouraged as a means of resolving many differences when the parties perceive there is not great divergence of aims. The circumstances surrounding many issues requiring daily management *are* those of problem agreement, mutual interest, openness and potential mutual benefit. They are situations where bargaining may also be appropriate but unnecessary. Long-term working relationships, which are so critical in IGM, can be enhanced through creative solution building that benefits more parties. The cementing of such relationships, in turn, contributes to understanding and additional congruence of aims.

PS focuses on the daily execution of tasks within a "fixed" federal structure. That is, it is not a means of changing the system, but a means of living with it "as is." As such, it is a mode that makes it possible to conduct a considerable amount of business in "the middle ground" between strict compliance and open defiance. As intergovernmental managers seek means to make adjustments in order to implement programs they have more than these two choices: (1) to insist on or to narrowly follow the statutes, regulations and guidelines, or (2) to openly ignore or resist such legal mandates. In practice there are vast gray areas of interpretation, priority, direction, substantial conformance, and the spirit of the law, that are acceptable. PS, along with the IGM approaches such as bargaining and policy management, are important means by which the real IGM work gets done.

IGBS AND THE INTERGOVERNMENTAL MANAGEMENT PROCESS

Since IGBs provided the focus for examination of managerial processes between governments, their study should yield some general findings about IGM. As an exploratory study investigating six cases and some seventeen specific problems, no firm generalizations can be offered. Nevertheless, the study provides some empirical evidence about this increasingly important process. Moreover, IGBs were identified in chapter 2 as relevant laboratories for studying IGM in as much as they stand between more extensive intergovernmental changes (e.g., special districts and consolidated governments) and less involved efforts (e.g., *ad hoc* cooperation and voluntary associations of governments). Therefore, some research-based conclusions about IGM can be suggested.

The need to invest in IGM process

Like any coordinating activity, IGM involves a considerable amount of investment in actors' learning about one another, their styles and approaches, needs and agendas, and modes of operation. People need to recognize that they are confronting problems that cut across jurisdictions, that there is a mutual dependence, and that somehow they can blend styles and operations into action. In other words, *convening* effort is a worthwhile investment because parties are so disparate, so long as this threshold is met and the parties move on to the real work.

IGM is cumulative activity

Few transactions between governments prove to be one-time activities. Interaction tends to be continuous, over numerous activities. As a result, the investment in processing and building understanding and trust pays off beyond the immediate problem to be solved. The cumulative nature of the activity also means that more confrontational approaches, such as bargaining, are not always conducive to building long-term relationships. Problem solving, or other open means of accommodation, builds relationships for the future.

Accommodation is central in IGM

Since a high level of mutual adjustment is required to solve problems, parties learn its importance. Intergovernmental managers spend much of their time developing consensus about the existence of a problem, its parameters, and possible solutions. Consensus means that parties must look for common denominators, or openings in relative positions, for they become the triggers for accommodation. It is the need for adjustment that conditions process and products in IGM.

Agendas need to be open but conditioned

Once intergovernmental actors agree to work on problems, or to form a body, virtually any issue is subject to their attention. Ideas for mutual action can come from anywhere and cover a wide range of topics; however, IGBs found it prudent to avoid: (1) issues or problems so comprehensive that they could not deliver solutions, and (2) those so jurisdictionally sensitive that it would tear their working relationships apart. Some issues were not ignored, but left for a later time when relationships were more secure and actors had achieved some success. In other cases, they were ignored or left for two-party IGM action between the most affected jurisdictions. However, once an issue passed the threshold and became part of the agenda, it was either carried through to resolution or the process revealed an impasse. This open, but bounded, agenda process contributed to long-run stability and success in IGM.

IGM decision making involves top level officials

No matter how routine the IGB's problems, jurisdictional accommodations required that at some point policy-makers had to be involved.

IGM is rarely a matter of administrative routine; it goes to the heart of what is important to the critical boundaries of a jurisdiction. As a result, at the point of solution or decision elected officials or appointive policy-making administrators (and in the case of the private sector, their elected and administrative counterparts) need to become involved as the representatives of their jurisdiction, agreeing to or modifying the necessary accommodations for the party.

IGM requires simultaneous formal and informal decision making

The problem-solving processes investigated involved complexes of jurisdictions, actors, and levels. In part this is a result of the combined legal, political, technical and task dimensions of problem solving, but it also is a function of the need to touch all bases in an overlapping fashion. To "get it all to work," decision makers at different levels have to be involved, addressing different but overlapping questions nearly simultaneously. Some of this complex processing is part of the formalized IGB process, and some is informal. Together, they must work toward a pragmatic solution.

Recognize and respect interjurisdictional differences

When one is attempting to manage at the interfaces between legally and politically separate jurisdictions, it is better to understand and confront important jurisdictional concerns. IGM requires that "sore points," "hardened positions," "turf insecurities," "pet peeves" and "bottom-line positions" be aired. Most of the IGBs proceeded by recognizing and respecting, not sublimating, these concerns. As they were brought out, they were confronted and built into the work of the IGBs. This jurisdictional recognition and respect was accommodated into IGB structural operation, agendas, problem-resolution processes, and in the content of decisions.

Confront IGM questions systematically

On most issues that IGBs agreed upon as problems, they found it useful to invest in a set of activities that would facilitate understanding and a course of action. This involved investigating the parameters of a given problem, researching and developing alternative courses of action, exploring options for jurisdictional accommodations, and then trying to carry out the most desired options. This particular pattern is not essential to IGM, but it is essential for intergovernmental managers to approach problems with a workable framework.

IGM reaches beyond technique into law and politics

In no case or problem did management prove to be a purely technical exercise in "making something work." Jurisdictional-legal and political concerns were heavily involved. Perhaps this is not unique to IGM; it appears to be generic to public management. However, to a high degree in IGM, technique is blended with the other concerns. Indeed, the legal elements, jurisdictional concerns, and politics of different stripes *are* part of the technique. Intergovernmental managers need to pay a great deal of attention to technical solutions that are not neat but that work, i.e., those that accommodate law, jurisdiction, and politics.

The technical details are part of the problem and the solution

Just as jurisdiction and politics must be confronted, and technical workings of the problems cannot be ignored. After all, the purpose of IGM is to do something with a program that is not presently being done. In order to do that the program must be examined, as well as changes that might be made. That involves looking at the specifics of a program and the state of its art. The better the detail work and the more it is made to fit with political and jurisdictional concerns, the smoother the IGM solution.

Implementation is by mutual or simultaneous action

IGBs carried out most of their decisions as an extension of the accommodation process. Rarely was a central, or even confederal, executive function at work. Rather, intergovernmental parties took reciprocal or mutual action or a number of jurisdictions took simultaneous action. Occasionally there was a need to develop new interjurisdictional tools to support certain solutions. Mutual action was required both to reach and to administer a decision. Although there may be exceptions to this rule, such as the case of consolidated governments and transfer of functions between governments, whenever mutual decisions are made, it is essential to preserve mutual execution.

Credibility and success can be based on routine problems

While perhaps not a universal principle, the IGBs found that their long-term viability was based on their willingness to tackle routine problems and solve them. Those that have survived met the important concerns of their member governments, placing their questions before them. Issues of less immediate concern to governmental officials, whether they are specific service delivery reforms or more comprehensive community-wide problems, were postponed.

Success is product-oriented

Successful resolution of intergovernmental problems proved to exist in a set of real issues and problems. All of the convening, investigating, testing, negotiating, accommodating, and implementing derived from something concrete—a problem. Results were forthcoming because they flowed from a process that was, above all, rooted in real world issues. Intergovernmental cooperation, coordination, and adjustment was not pursued in the abstract. It was focused, issue-based coordination. In the long run, IGM products proved to be more significant than process.

Based on the limited research here, the nature of IGM, or at least its problem-solving aspect, becomes clearer. It appears to be a process requiring: (1) large interactive investments, which can (2) cumulate by cementing relationships, with (3) heavy amounts of jurisdictional accommodation, (4) pursued through open, but conditioned, agendas (5) involving top-level and working officials, (6) engaged in formal and informal processes that (7) recognize and respect differences, while (8) confronting questions systematically, (9) considering and accommodating law, jurisdiction, politics and technical details, and (10) executing by mutual or simultaneous action with (11) a heavy emphasis on product solutions that focus on resolution of concrete issues. IGM is indeed a unique and complex managerial process.

CONCLUSIONS AND IMPLICATIONS FOR IGM RESEARCH

In chapter 1 we identified the growth of the human services system as primarily generated by state and federal funding programs and delivered on the local level by a host of governmental and nongovernmental agents. While growth has been greatest in human services, other domestic program areas have expanded through fiscal transfers and accompanying conditions and regulations. During this century, intergovernmental fiscal transfers and program requirements have altered American federalism from that which stresses divided functions and the independence of levels of government to intergovernmental relations in which all levels of government and their agents share in the performance of expanding functions.[12] The six cases examined in this study are prime examples of how today's communities have to manage their intergovernmental affairs.

The investigation illustrates the emerging need to develop new and workable means of seeking adjustments in the intergovernmental system. David Walker's statement about the character of management between sectors captures the essence of this study. He describes the essentially nonhierarchic, nonsystematic, nonsuperior-subordinate character of the managerial task, taking the administrative activities outside of the normal planning, organizing, and delivering or services when he writes that:

"to treat the process as a series of disciplined servicing endeavors within a number of separate governmental jurisdictions is to ignore the ever-increasing interjurisdictional character of contemporary management."[13]

Pragmatism appears to be the dominant mode in IGM today. Walter Williams's study of the implementation of two block grants—the Comprehensive Employment and Training Act and Community Development Block Grant—concludes that federal agencies must shift their management strategies from a compliance mentality to one oriented to increasing local commitment to performance and to local capacity. His five-point management strategy emphasizes: bargaining and making workable adjustments as the primary guide to agency decisions and actions; reduction in the complexity and confusion faced by federal field personnel; efforts to increase the competence of federal field personnel and local grantees; creation of internal and external pressure points aimed at moving toward better organizational and programmatic performance; and development of an information process that supports agency field efforts at increasing local commitment to performance of national objectives and is consistent with local capacities.[14] The Williams's study provides a detailed case for the need for these federal managerial changes, again recognizing IGM as an evolving attempt to work out solutions that result in modifications of the system.

This type of intergovernmental strategy will also depend on the increased political strength and capacity of political actors. In his study of *Federal Programs and City Politics*, Jeffrey Pressman writes that local officials must beware of "pseudo arenas" for intergovernmental affairs, such as joint boards and task forces that are set up to facilitate communications but that do not have authority to make program decisions, requirements for rapid and comprehensive planning exercises that have no impact on budget and personnel, and concentrate upon commitments to vague and general goals. What is required, he concludes, is a collaborative framework.[15] But his study also concludes that intergovernmental programs can be vitiated by the absence of strong political bodies at the local level, effective arenas where federal and local officials can bargain over political resources. "Neither planning, communication, nor revenue sharing are adequate to deal with what are essentially political problems; the creation of viable sites for the exchange of resources and the mobilization of public support for programs."[16] He prescribes increasing the capacities of the political systems at all governmental levels, similar to the "development" process in underdeveloped nations. In many ways, the six cases in this study constitute exercises in developing real arenas, involving those who can speak for, or possess delegated authority from, a jurisdiction, working day-to-day toward solutions that are implementable. They can be considered exercises in local political development.

Services integration as an intergovernmental process

The concept of services integration—with its service delivery, program linkages, policy management and organizational structure dimensions—was introduced in chapter 2. It was identified as an intergovernmental strategy and its progress assessed. It was suggested that while services integration is no longer operative, as an official intergovernmental strategy, integrating activities appear to be very much alive. This IGB study provides evidence of such activity, as do other intergovernmental trends.

The six cases suggest numerous integrating activities, attempts to create interorganizational linkages, to develop operating policies, and, to a certain extent, to alter services delivery. Approaches such as joint funding, access services approaches, common data bases, coordinated emergency services, multisector allocations, multiservice centers, a continuum of services for substance abusers, joint intake procedures, unified audit systems, joint funded mental treatment homes, a coordinated child care group, and so on, represent the various components of services integration. What the case evidence also suggests is that *comprehensive* services integration strategies are not at work. Rather, the locales appear to be most successful at pursuing integration by attacking problems or clusters of issues.

The immediate future of intergovernmental human services is continued services integration activity of a specialized or problem-oriented type. First, the advent of new block grants, clustering categorical programs with fewer requirements, should provide states (and in some cases locales) greater opportunity in "small sector" planning and may perhaps link planning to budgeting. It is even conceivable that jurisdictions will find it easier to link planning and budgeting to either target populations (children, youth, and elderly) or problem areas (deinstitutionalization, handicapped, long-term unemployed). Second, fiscal reductions undoubtedly will lead to reassessments by decision-makers, which will lead to consolidations, mergers, and assumptions, as well as reductions in affected areas. Third, likely intergovernmental devolution—i.e., increased state and local responsibility for programs as the federal government either loosens the strings or extricates itself from an arena—will provide the potential for greater coordination. At the state and local levels, officials can affect the system because they control the instruments of service delivery; what they feel they have lacked is essential policy (i.e., fiscal) control. Devolution enhances the choice-making capabilities of state and local officials, allowing them to engage in policy management and linked services, should they choose to exercise their new options. Fourth, as long as external pressures from interest groups, legislatures, and the courts demand that the administrative branch solve the problems of the exinstitutionalized, difficult children, impaired elderly, and long-term unemployed, the necessary and sufficient "service packages" will have to be responsive. Administrators rarely have the luxury to wait and design the ideal comprehensive system. Rather, integration occurs as these particular problems are being attacked. And fifth, the technology of human services delivery is expanding in many ways, including the concept of a "continuum of services" that now includes self care, family care, in-home special care, nonprofessional help, and cooperative living facilities, as well as the traditional in-agency and institutional services. If a true services "system," does become reality, human services integration will be immediately triggered.

It therefore appears that services integration is continuing by issues, if not by grand design. While harder to identify than the special initiatives of the 1970s, integration is alive as a midrange, focused, intersectoral activity at the national government level, in the state capitols, in substate areas, and, of course, in locales like those studied.

The Role of Federal Involvement

While not a central research question, the issue of the role of federal participation was raised in chapter 2. As the cases have illustrated, the IGBs were not part of a single, federal initiative or program. Most emerged locally, as bodies that shared concerns about lack of integration. However, IGBs directly or indirectly were supported by federal research and demonstration dollars.

The lasting value of local management of intergovernmental affairs seems to be more important than federal dollars. The role of federal funding for five of the six IGBs was rather insignificant in terms of total dollars. To be sure, the money no doubt helped the IGBs at critical times. But most funding was generated locally, an indication that something of value was being produced for the local partners. In Baltimore, the one case where federal support was central and critical, difficulties occurred in selling the value of the IGB to state and local actors. To be sure, difficulties have also been attributed to the problem-solving approach the Blueprint adopted. But the Baltimore case seems to demonstrate that massive federal dollars spent to solve intergovernmental problems at the local level are not effective unless there are degrees of local recognition of problems and willingness to commit resources to solving them. Therefore, direct federal dollar support appears to be a helpful, but indeterminant, factor.

Were other types of federal involvement essential? Only in the Seattle and Baltimore IGBs were federal officials direct partners and thus formal actors in setting agendas and making basic decisions. In the other four IGBs, federal officials—based locally, regionally or nationally—were called upon when they were needed for participation in some adjustment to a program the locals requested. Because so many adjustments had to be made, this became an important, if not visible, federal role. Thus, the federal role was not central in terms of IGB operations but was essential in terms of making programs work.

Federal officials' involvement as parties in the solving of particular problems is an extremely valuable role. Local officials found that they could not change a Community Development Block Grant plan, readjust the way day care funds were spent, redirect Older Americans Act funds from nutrition to transportation, or use Energy Assistance service funds for information and referral unless they worked the program back through the intergovernmental chain. In this process they had to work at two levels: first, up the federal program line of authority, dealing with specialists in day care, senior citizens, housing and development, and so on; second, local officials worked with intergovernmental generalists, particularly in the federal regional offices and in the office of the secretary of the departments of Health and Human Services, Housing and Community Development, and Labor. To the extent that these federal officials could see themselves as partners with local officials in solving problems, they were providing extremely valuable services.

Another, more indirect federal role was that of encouraging the development of local capacity. To the extent that federal officials could assist local IGBs in better understanding the human services system, in improving its ability to plan and use resources, and in managing the local system for purpose, they helped make intergovernmental transactions easier. IGB representatives learned that where open lines of communication to federal officials existed, they could more easily adapt to federal wishes while maintaining local concerns. This process worked best when federal officials were open about their concerns and expectations regarding programs. Consequently, local officials were able to learn more about how to operate within a dynamic system while they enhanced their managerial capabilities.

Now that federal problem solving and capacity roles have been explained the discussion can return to funding. For the IGBs, the most important federal funding concern came not through the grant of operating dollars but as opportunities for local leveraging of federal funds. Most of the problem solutions involved some form of program and funding adjustment that required federal agreement. The capacity of local officials, coupled with the atmosphere of cooperation for both federal and local purposes, directly contributes to this central federal role of adjusting spending patterns in categorical and block grants. While such dollar leveraging is a more indirect type of federal involvement than is the case of direct grants, it proved to be more significant.

The federal government role hinged less on grant availability to IGBs than on their ability to work within other funding streams. As intergovernmental actors worked on problems and exchanged information relating to improved understanding and management of the system, they discovered that the way federal officials could serve the process best was by doing their part in making programs work.

Research issues

The contextual literature for this study, as well as the study itself, provides a conceptual understanding for intergovernmental managerial modalities. The pragmatic, problem-oriented, redefinitional nature of federalism should be clear. What is missing from this, and most intergovernmental studies, is the "how to manage" dimension. Beyond a few case studies and suggestions, there is a very shallow intergovernmental management literature.[17] Walker's earlier statement is essentially correct, that IGM transcends planning, organizing, and deliverying services within a single administrative system. Future research should go beyond these definitional statements.

The present research provides direct evidence of Wright's three component qualities of IGM: problem solving, understanding and coping with the system as it is, and contact and communication.[18] These three qualities, particularly problem-orientation, characterize the IGBs. Other work, such as that of the Advisory Commission on Intergovernmental Relations focuses on understanding the federal system as it is.[19] Works in policy implementation, such as the Williams and Pressman studies, works by Radin,[20] Bardach,[21] Meltzner,[22] Elmore[23] and numerous others, document and generalize about how to work within the system. Wright's many works on intergovernmental contacts and communication networks,[24] as well as those of others[25] contribute to our knowledge of this aspect of IGM. Some have looked at specific causes of IGM, such as assessing or calculating benefits,[26] the role of fungibility in dollar resource transfer[27], and the cost of system overload.[28] All of these efforts increase our understanding of the IGM process, focusing on managerial activity and providing increased information about the real workings of the system.

This IGB study suggests additional and complimentary research. First, research on problem-solving needs to be conducted in other substantive areas and settings, such as public works, public transportation, criminal justice, public safety, and environmental protection. These areas involve their own complexes of special and general purpose governments, state and federal officials and private sector actors. The similarities and differences in process and product are important to understanding IGM.

Second, focus should continue on the routine. The popular literature is replete with dramatic examples of intergovernmental events, usually confrontational. This research not only identifies a routine aspect of IGM but underscores the presence of consensus, or the development of it, as well as conflict. Only continuous study of routine transactions between managers and officials representing jurisdictions will capture the entire character of the undertaking.

Third, research should begin hypothesis testing. This study has developed a number of hypotheses that are now worthy of empirical testing. For example, intergovernmental accommodation appears to be successful when actors are dealing on focused issues or concrete problems. Another example is that successful IGM problem solving confronts and make accommodations among jurisdictional-legal, political, and technical domains. Yet another example is that the process involves all three dimensions—jurisdictional, political, and technical—and converges on a fourth, task orientation. A final example is, IGM process investments build relationships, which in turn lead to feelings of interdependence, which are conducive to problem resolution.

Fourth, intergovernmental structure research, like that of the IGBs, can shed light on emergent management structures within and between organizations. The contemporary literature emphasizes the need to develop structures that enhance group, lateral and creative behavior. Temporary structures, work teams, task forces, project management, matrix designs and a series of *adhocracies* are considered central to meeting the challenges of government and business. IGBs and other inter-governmental processes represent other forms of interorganizational process designed to enhance lateral efforts. To the extent that they are creative endeavors, there is much that can be learned about these structures from the IGM process.

Fifth, the same principles appear true in regard to the study of shared authority models. There are many similarities between the IGM processes depicted here and forms of shared authority and participative management within organizations. Examining these mutual authority processes and the role of numerous actors in IGM can shed additional light on such management modes, and the converse.

Sixth, more needs to be discovered about the routines of work in IGM and what they mean. That is, we tend to focus a great deal of our managerial and research attention on the discovery and decision-making stages of management, less on the processes of implementation. At a policy-process level this has changed recently, with studies of what happens to programs after legislative enactment. In IGM, focus must also be placed on the post-decision stages, i.e., what governments do after they agree on a problem and how to solve it. Some light has been shed here on the types of tools that emerge and how disjointed decisions are carried out, but considerably more needs to be done.

Seventh, since legal and jurisdictional accommodation proved to be so important in IGM, more must be learned about the boundaries of such activity. All IGM is embedded in a constitutional (referring to reciprocal authority and powers) and legal (referring to extent of responsibility and action) web which unfolds as the specifics are applied. Experience suggests the constitutional and legal web is not iron clad. In many IGM situations, powers, laws and rules are liberally interpreted or they are not strictly adhered to. More must be learned about the dimensions of these accommodations, because they appear to be at the heart of IGM.

Eighth, and finally, since political strength and governmental capacity are also at the heart of IGM more needs to be understood about their roles. The importance of political capacity was mentioned, but more needs to be understood about how and when it is used to manage intergovernmentally. How, for example, does the ability of a local politician to move recalcitrant actors in a state capitol or in Washington contribute to IGM? How does a strong planning or budgeting capability make it easier to make the accommodations necessary to cooperate with other governments? Answers to these questions will also enhance our knowledge of IGM.

Working through the system

The problem-solving activities described here as IGM provide another set of tools for use by managers in expanding their "policy space." The complexity of the intergovernmental system has led managers to look for ways to expand their residual decision-making authority after legal and other external program demands are met.[29] Federal and state programs have restrictions, but there are also ways to make them serve local needs. Single jurisdictions have been following this pattern for years; grants are made to fit local needs and conditions within a general framework of funder compliance. IGBs sought similar aims on a joint basis. PS, with its combined process and product orientation, proved to be a pragmatic means of reaching agreements and forging accommodations. In these six metropolitan areas, actors chose to manage their way through issues and agreed-upon problems by expanding their "policy space."

The PS results depicted offer evidence that the system of intergovernmental relations as it is basically structured is perhaps more workable than the rhetoric generally suggests. Many complaints have been registered that the system of categorical grants fosters too much federal control or, in the case of state grants, state control. They are said to unnecessarily restrict recipients' initiatives to meet their own needs. The evidence presented from the six IGBs suggest that the grant system does leave room for local actors to meet needs by making adjustments in federal and state programs. It is assumed that on a less formal basis than that of the IGBs, thousands of such adjustments are made, under similar conditions, in order to smooth discrepancies between perceived needs and actual conditions.[30]

The PS mode may not constitute a dramatic approach to IGM, but it is inevitable given the implementation structure of many public policies. So long as governments that enact programs eschew direct operation and choose a series of intermediaries — states, local-general and special purpose governments, nonprofit organizations, or for-profit organizations — through categorical grants, block grants, GRS, procurement contracts and cooperative agreements, there will be substantial room and need for maneuvering. Funder goals and recipient aims are inevitably field-tested as programs are actually put into place.[31] As is well known, each side has its weapons: funders have legal intent and fiscal sanctions; recipients have daily program control and the power of execution. Both sides, moreover, have politics if they care to use it and the substantive technical know-how if they care to acquire and use it. It remains to apply these issues to specific tasks as programs are put into place.

IGM is a complex jurisdictional-legal, political-technical and task-oriented exercise, which requires a simultaneous development process to be effective. The six cases reveal the essential interactive nature of politicians and managers as they forge pragmatic solutions involving multijurisdictions, altering textbook notions about the separation of functions within governments and powers between them. It is reasonably safe to assume that despite federal and state reforms that attempt to streamline the intergovernmental system, communities will continue to be faced with degrees of confusion, complexity, and overlapping responsibilities requiring either ad hoc or structurally driven solutions. The learning process from places like Dayton, Indianapolis, Columbus, Pueblo, Baltimore, and Seattle has just begun.

Notes to Chapter Ten

1. David B. Walker, *Toward a Functioning Federalism* (Cambridge: Winthrop, 1981), 258-59.

2. L. David Brown, *Managing Conflict at Organizational Interfaces* (Reading: Addison-Wesley, 1983), 223.

3. *Ibid.*, 224.

4. Joe Kelley, "Make Conflict Work for You," *Harvard Business Review* 48 (July/August 1970), 104.

5. Kenneth W. Thomas and Louis R. Pondy, "Toward an 'Intent' Model of Conflict Management Among Principal Parties," *Human Relations* 30 (December 1977), 1090.

6. Deil Wright, *Understanding Intergovernmental Relations* 2d ed. (Monterey: Brooks/Cole, 1982), 65.

7. Warren H. Schmidt and Robert Tannenbaum, "Management of Differences," *Harvard Business Review* 38 (November/December 1960), 112-13.

8. Richard W. Walton and Robert B. McKersie, "Behavioral Dilemmas in Mixed Motive Decision-Making," *Behavioral Sciences* 11 (September 1966), 380.

9. Tony Petrella and Peter Block, "Diagnosing Conflict Between Groups in Organization," in *Organizational Diagnosis*, ed. Marvin R. Weisbrod (Reading: Addison-Wesley, 1978), 139.

10. *Ibid.*, 140.

11. *Ibid.*, 141.

12. Michael D. Reagan, *The New Federalism* (New York: Oxford, 1972), 11.

13. David B. Walker, "How Fares Federalism in the Mid-Seventies?" *Intergovernmental Relations in America Today*, Annals of the American Academy of Political and Social Science 416 (November 1974), 30.

14. Walter Williams and Betty Jane Narver, *Government by Agency: Lessons from the Social Program Grants-in-Aid Experience* (New York: Academic Press, 1980), 233-34.

15. Jeffrey L. Pressman, *Federal Programs and City Politics* (Berkeley and Los Angeles: University of California Press, 1975), 138.

16. *Ibid.*, 140.

17. See Anthony W. Mitchell, "Dare to Compare: A Call for Performance Comparisons Among States," *New England Journal of Human Services* 1, no. 1 (Winter 1981), 23-29.

18. Diel S. Wright, "Managing the Intergovernmental Scene: The Changing Dramas of Federalism, Intergovernmental Relations, and Intergovernmental Management," in *The Handbook of Organization Management* ed. William B. Eddy (New York: Marcel Dekker, 1983), 431.

19. cf., *State and Local Roles in the Federal System* A-88 (Washington: Advisory Commission on Intergovernmental Relations, 1982).

20. Beryl A. Radin, *Implementation Change and the Federal Bureaucracy* (New York: Teachers College Press, Columbia University, 1977).

21. Eugene Bardach, *The Implementation Game: What Happens After a Bill Becomes a Law* (Cambridge: MIT Press, 1977).

22. Arnold J. Meltsner and Christopher Bellavita, *The Policy Organization* (Beverly Hills: Sage, 1983).

23. Richard Elmore, "Organizational Models of Social Program Implementation," *Public Policy* 26 (Spring 1978).

24. Wright, "Managing the Intergovernmental Scene," 442-49.

25. Robert W. Gage, "Federal Regional Councils: Networking Organizations for Policy Management in the Intergovernmental System," *Public Administration Review* 44 (March/April, 1984).

26. James W. Fossett, *Federal Aid to Big Cities: The Politics of Dependence* (Washington: Brookings, 1983).

27. Martha Derthick, *Uncontrollable Spending for Social Services Grants* (Washington: Brookings, 1975).

28. Catherine Lovell, "The Effects of Regulatory Changes on States and Localities," in *The Consequences of the Cuts* ed. Richard P. Nathan, Fred C. Doolittle, et al. (Princeton: Princeton Urban and Regional Research Center, 1983).

29. Frederick M. Wirt, *Power in the City: Decision Making in San Francisco* (Berkeley: University of California Press, 1974), 344-45.

30. Beryl A. Radin, Robert Agranoff, C. Gregory Buntz and Edward Baumhaier, *Planning Reform Demonstration Project Evaluation* (Report prepared for the

Office of the Assistant Secretary for Planning and Evaluation, U.S Department of Health and Human Services, October 1981), Chapter 5.

31. Richard F. Elmore, "Backward Mapping: Implementation Research and Policy Decisions," *Studying Implementation: Methodological and Administrative Issues* ed. Walter Williams, et al. (Chatham: Chatham House, 1982), 28.

Index